Advance Praise for
Ultimate Questions: Thinking About Philosophy

"The text is very user friendly, and engages the students perfectly well through *Food for Thought* exercises. . . . the arrangement and organization of the text is outstanding. . . . the author has a very engaging style of writing. The fundamental strength is in the *Food for Thought* exercises it presents for students to think about, spaced appropriately throughout the text."

Robert Abele
Illinois Valley Community College

"This is an excellent introductory book. It is clearly written, comprehensive, and capable of engaging readers on several levels. . . . The *Food for Thought* exercises that pop up within the chapters, instead of at the beginning or the end, are very engrossing and entertaining."

Naomi Zack
University of Oregon

"I like the overall approach and rationale of Rauhut's text. The *Food for Thought* exercises are often intriguing and . . . useful in stirring student interest and getting discussions going in class—even outside of class!"

Houston Craighead
Winthrop University

"[The text] is clearly written, emphasizes interactive learning and divides its chapters by the major problems of philosophy. . . . The writing style . . . is very clear and accessible. The concepts are well explained and the use of interactive exercises and the graphic illustrations are a great asset, because they are the main tools for enhancing the students' comprehension."

Maria Adamos
Georgia Southern University

About the Author

Nils Ch. Rauhut studied philosophy and history at the University of Regensburg (Germany). He received an M.A. degree in philosophy from the University of Colorado at Boulder, and a Ph.D. in philosophy from the University of Washington in Seattle. He taught at Weber State University in Ogden, Utah, and he is currently teaching at Coastal Carolina University in Conway, South Carolina.

Ultimate Questions

Thinking About Philosophy

Nils Ch. Rauhut
Coastal Carolina University

PENGUIN ACADEMICS

PEARSON
Longman

New York   San Francisco   Boston
London   Toronto   Sydney   Tokyo   Singapore   Madrid
Mexico City   Munich   Paris   Cape Town   Hong Kong   Montreal

Meiner Mutter
Hanna Therese Wilhelmine Auguste Rauhut (geb. Dusi) gewidmet.

Vice President and Publisher: Priscilla McGeehon
Marketing Manager: Wendy Albert
Production Manager: Douglas Bell
Project Coordination and Electronic Page Makeup: Nesbitt Graphics, Inc.
Senior Cover Designer/Manager: Nancy Danahy
Cover Illustration: Woodcut depicting a man exploring the meeting of the Earth
  and sky from *Popular Astronomy* by Camille Flammarion/Corbis.
Photo Researcher: Sarah Evertson, Image Quest
Manufacturing Buyer: Alfred C. Dorsey
Printer and Binder: R.R. Donnelley and Sons Company, Harrisonburg
Cover Printer: Phoenix Color Corporation

Photos on page 112 courtesy Ronald Reagan Library.

CIP data is on file with the Library of Congress.

Please visit our website at http://www.ablongman.com

ISBN 0-321-10893-0

2 3 4 5 6 7 8 9 10—DOH—06 05 04 03

Contents

Preface

"Protagoras, . . . when anyone makes a long speech to me I never remember what he is talking about." Although most teachers of philosophy agree with Socrates that long speeches are not the best way to teach philosophy, it is hard to avoid giving such speeches in introductory philosophy classes. One of the main goals of this book is to offer opportunities for genuine conversations about philosophy and to involve students actively in the process of learning to philosophize. The book contains more than one hundred *Food for Thought* exercises. At first glance, these exercises might resemble ordinary review or discussion questions, but they are designed to play a different role. Ordinary review or discussion questions are listed at the end of chapters and are rarely read or used in the classroom. The *Food for Thought* exercises in this book are presented in the middle of the text and most of them can be used in the classroom. The exercises are designed to elicit the students' reactions to philosophical problems and to give students a chance to test whether they have grasped important philosophical concepts. These exercises have grown out of my own experience of teaching introductory philosophy classes. I hope that they will help other teachers to create a more interactive classroom atmosphere.

Many philosophy teachers complain that introductory students fail to read the assigned texts. I have tried to write a book that seduces students into reading about philosophy. I do not presuppose that students come to this text with a natural inclination to think about philosophical problems. I try to awaken the student's curiosity by showing that our everyday thinking leads directly to the questions and puzzles philosophers have tried to unravel for many centuries. It is my hope that especially those students who begin reading this book with a sense of dread and the desire to read as little as possible will discover that they enjoy reading every page. Doing philosophy is not only fun, but also highly addictive. I have tried to write a book that reflects both of these features of the philosophical enterprise.

The first chapter, titled "Philosophical Tools," begins with an imaginary story about a teenager who lived several thousand years ago. This opening story is designed to illustrate the relationship between philosophy, mythology, and religion. It should not be read as a historical account of how mythology, philosophy, and religion indeed came about. The chapter continues with an explanation of the relationship between philosophy and science, and then introduces important philosophical terms and concepts. The chapter covers not only standard logical terms such as *argument*, *validity*, and *soundness*, but it also explains terms such as *possible world*, *causal* and *logical possibility*, *thought experiments*, *necessary* and *sufficient conditions*, and *counterexample*. I hope that this extensive discussion of basic philosophical terminology and methodology will benefit students throughout the rest of book.

The following six chapters cover some of the more prominent philosophical problems in the history of Western philosophy: knowledge, free will, personal identity, the relationship between mind and body, God's existence, and ethics. Each chapter begins with a careful explanation of how these problems are connected to our day-to-day thinking about the universe. *Food for Thought* exercises give students the opportunity to reflect on their own initial reactions to these problems. It is only after the significance and scope of each problem has been clarified that I turn to introducing the reader to some prominent responses to these problems. I have focused on those theories that are shaping the way contemporary analytic philosophers are thinking about these problems. Each chapter ends with some final remarks on the status of the problem in light of the most recent philosophical developments. Although the chapters are presented in a certain narrative and logical order, instructors using this book can assign chapters in almost any order. It might be beneficial to assign supplementary readings of original works in coordination with the individual chapters.

Acknowledgments

Many people have helped me in writing this book. First of all, I would like to thank my wife Karin, who helped me throughout the writing process in more ways than I can say. Special thanks are also due to Priscilla Mcgeehon from Longman for her support and advice throughout the many months of writing. Without her help and encouragement the book would never have seen the light of day. Several reviewers have provided helpful suggestions. I would like to thank the following reviewers: Maria Adamos, Georgia Southern University; Houston Craighead, Winthrop University; Elmer H. Duncan, Baylor University; Steven M. Duncan, Bellevue Community College; Lanning M. Garrett III, Lambuth University; Larry D. Harwood, Viterbo University; Blake E. Hestir, Texas Christian University; Anne Parella, Tidewater Community College; Daniel Skubik, California Baptist University; Danny Ursery, St. Edward's University; and Naomi Zack, University of Oregon.

Of special importance was the advice of Robert Abele, Illinois Valley Community College, and Peter Bradley, Washington University. Robert Abele provided very helpful suggestions on how to incorporate Eastern philosophical ideas within the text, and Peter Bradley's suggestions improved many of the *Food for Thought* exercises.

I would like to thank Coastal Carolina University for a faculty development grant during the summer of 2002. This grant allowed me to work closely with some of my best students to refine the learning exercises. I would like to thank Mary Boyd, Jason Fishel, and Amanda Stepp, who helped me enormously with this work. Several of my colleagues read parts of the manuscript and saved me from many mistakes. Of special importance was the advice of Teresa Burns, Dennis Earl, Michael S. Ruse, and Renee Smith. I would like to express my deep appreciation to all of them. I also would like to thank Billy Kelly and Lisa Ivers, who read through several versions of the manuscript and whose advice led to many improvements along the way. Without their feedback, the book would be much less readable than it is now. Finally, I would like to thank my sister Anke who helped me enormously during the final weeks of writing.

Nils Ch. Rauhut

CHAPTER ONE

PHILOSOPHICAL TOOLS

What Is Philosophy?

Although not everyone has an interest in physics, psychology, geography, or economics, most people have a pretty clear idea what these academic disciplines are about. The same is not true for philosophy. It is quite common to meet educated people who have only a foggy idea what philosophy is and what philosophers do. Let us therefore begin with a brief explanation of the nature and scope of philosophy.

One way to clarify the nature of philosophy is to explore an imaginary scenario. Suppose that 4000 years ago, you were a member of a typical nomadic tribe. Life is tough for your tribe; most of your time is spent hunting for food and shelter. However, there are also good days, especially during the summers when food is plentiful and temperatures are comfortable. Suppose that during one summer evening your 15-year-old daughter sits down next to you, points at the star-filled sky, and asks, "I am amazed at the beauty of the sky. I have the feeling that this whole universe is an incredible place. But looking at these stars also makes me feel very small and insignificant. Tell me: Do these stars care about us? Do they take an interest in what we do down here?" At this point you probably wish that your daughter would be more like the other teenagers in your tribe, who only worry about with whom to dance at the next sacred hunting celebration. But since it is such a fine summer evening, you sit back and try to respond to her questions as well as you can.

In order to answer your daughter's questions, you need to provide what one might call a "big picture" view of the universe. A "big picture" view of the universe always involves some kind of story that makes sense of the world in which we live. There are several ways to tell such a story. A natural way is the use of mythology.[1] Every culture has developed powerful mythological stories to make sense of the world. In the Western world, one of the oldest surviving mythologies is Homer's *Iliad*. Homer's poem of the battle for Troy not only tells us something about history and cosmology, but it also explores the nature of the underworld and the world of the gods. Mythologies provide an effective way to understand the cosmos and the role we humans play within it. So, one thing you could do in the imaginary situation with your daughter is to tell her a mythological story similar to Homer's *Iliad* or Hesiod's *Theogony*. Aside from merely entertaining your daughter by the campfire, you will be instilling in her a sense of how the heavens came to be and what interests the gods take in our deeds and actions. It is, however, apparent that mythological stories leave something to be desired. Imagine that you have a critical-minded daughter. After listening politely to your mythological story, she might very well respond, "Wow, this was a great story, but how do you know that this story is actually true?"

FOOD FOR THOUGHT

It might seem as if mythology is a thing of the past. Who would base his understanding of the world on simple, powerful stories? Upon closer examination, however, it becomes clear that our understanding of the world is still shaped by invented stories. List some examples of how invented stories still influence and affect our understanding of the world.

At this point you have several options. You might either point to the long tradition of your tribe and try to convince your daughter that your tribe would not have survived for so long if these traditional stories were all bogus, or else you can try to provide additional support to show that the story you have told is actually true. There are several ways to offer such additional support. One way consists in the claim that one of your ancestors was very close to the gods (or God), and that God revealed the truth of this story to him. When mythological stories are combined with divine revelations, mythology has a tendency to turn into religion.[2]

Religion is the second widely established way through which we can provide a "big picture" view of the universe. Religion resembles mythology in that most religions contain stories that—at first glance—have the sound and look of mythological stories. However, religious stories, unlike mythologies, contain a reason why we should believe that they are true: divine revelation. Divine revelation can take very different forms. It might come as a dream as with the Bible's Abraham; or it might consist of the discovery of holy texts as with the founder of the Mormon religion, Joseph Smith; or else it might take the form of an enlightening religious experience as with Buddhism's Siddartha. No matter what form these divine revelations take, they offer a reason why religious stories are true.

Let us go back to our imaginary scenario. Suppose you defend your story with the claim that the gods revealed the story to some of your ancestors. It might be that your daughter will respond to this defense as follows: "Oh, I do not doubt that our great ancestors were closer to the gods than we are now, but what makes me curious is this: I recently met a wandering medicine man from a tribe far away. He was not only very handsome, but also very knowledgeable. He told me about the religious beliefs that have guided his tribe for centuries. Guess what? Their religious beliefs support completely different stories about the world and the gods. What reason do I have to believe our own religious stories, while I reject those of other tribes?"

What this response shows is that religion, as a method of understanding the world, is challenged by the fact that not all divine revelations are compatible. When different religious systems come in contact with one another, it becomes rather difficult to decide which revelation is more trustworthy. Although some individuals (especially if they have had religious experiences) may be convinced that a particular revelation is true while all others are misguided, not everybody can justify such strong convictions.

It is at this point that philosophy enters the picture. Philosophy, in addition to mythology and religion, is a third major way of providing a "big picture" view of reality. The word *philosophy* derives from the Greek words *philia* (love) and *sophia* (wisdom). Philosophy can therefore be understood as love of wisdom. But what does this mean? We can understand the nature of philosophy better if we clarify the relationship between philosophy, mythology, and religion. Philosophy is related to mythology insofar as philosophers also try to provide a comprehensive, "big picture" view of reality. Philosophy also resembles religion in that philosophers provide reasons why their picture of reality is true. However, philosophers never appeal to divine revelation or to tradition in order to show that their theories are true; instead, they appeal to the power of reason. In a broad sense, **philosophy can therefore be understood as the attempt to develop a "big picture" view of the universe with the help of reason.**

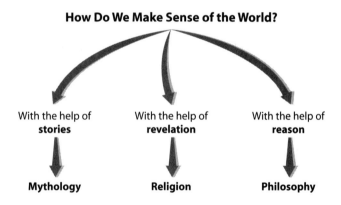

How Do We Make Sense of the World?

With the help of **stories**	With the help of **revelation**	With the help of **reason**
Mythology	**Religion**	**Philosophy**

FOOD FOR THOUGHT

We have seen that religion and philosophy are both powerful methods of understanding the world. Alas, they support their claims and explanations in different ways. Does this mean that philosophy and religion must necessarily produce different pictures of the world?

Let us go back to our imaginary situation. What would it mean to explain the cosmos to your daughter with the help of reason? Well, you might say something along the following lines: "You have asked me, among other things, whether stars take an interest in what we are doing. In order to answer this question we need to clarify the nature of stars. I believe that stars are balls of fire. You might not believe me, but here is a reason I think this is a plausible idea. Look at this campfire. It is a source of light. I have walked through many dark nights, and I can tell you that whenever I have seen light it had something to do with fire. Consider lightning, for example. It causes trees to burn and is also a kind of fire. So, it seems to me that wherever there is light, there must be fire. Since stars are a source for light, they too must be a kind of fire. Moreover, since fire does not seem to be able to perceive anything, I do not believe that stars are aware of what we are doing."

What you have just done is defend your belief that stars are not aware of our actions with the help of an argument. This is a key element in philosophy. Philosophers not only try to explain the world with the help of claims and stories, but they also try to defend their claims with the help of arguments. We start to philosophize when we present arguments in defense of our "big picture" view of reality.[3]

Although our understanding of philosophy is still incomplete, it is already possible to point to three key elements of philosophical reflections. First, in order to philosophize we need to know more about arguments. We need to know how to construct arguments and how to evaluate them. We will do this in a later section of this chapter. Second, the hypothetical situation that I described above illustrates that philosophy emerges as a response to persistent questioning. If your daughter had not been so reluctant to accept traditional stories, there would not have been any reason to present arguments in defense of your beliefs. Philosophy therefore comes most easily to us when we are in a critical state of mind and question whether our standard "picture of the universe" is really accurate. As long as we are absolutely convinced that our beliefs about the world are correct, we feel little need to justify our beliefs with the help of arguments. However, many humans encounter situations in their lives when they begin to question their beliefs and convictions. It is during these times when philosophy emerges most naturally.

FOOD FOR THOUGHT

Philosophy emerges most naturally in situations when we question whether our traditional beliefs about the world are true. The Russian writer Leo Tolstoy (1828–1910) describes in his *Confessions* how he started to question everything in his life. He writes: "Thus I proceeded to live, but five years ago something very strange began to happen with me: I was overcome by minutes at first of perplexity and then of an arrest of life, as though I did not know how to live or what to do. . . . " In normal everyday life we tend not to be as reflective and critical as Tolstoy was when he wrote his *Confessions*. However, it has been suggested that we all become self-doubting and perplexed at certain points in our lives. Is that true? If yes, what kinds of experiences or situations typically undermine our confidence that we understand the world correctly?

Finally, the hypothetical conversation with your 15-year-old daughter also shows that philosophy has a tendency to lead to a plurality of different answers. I can defend my claim that stars are balls of fire with the help of an argument, but there are also arguments in defense of the claim that stars are unchanging, perfect entities. For most complex questions there are different answers that appear—at least for awhile— equally reasonable. There are, of course, also some thoroughly misguided answers that one can show to be quite unreasonable. Although philosophy has the goal of producing one truthful picture of the universe, in practice it generates many different accounts of the world, which stand in opposition to each other. It often takes hundreds of years before some arguments are recognized to be mistaken. Progress in philosophy is a slow process. This is why those of us who like immediate results and absolute certainty tend to be annoyed by philosophical reflection. However, studying questions that lead to a plurality of opposing answers has the benefit of showing us new possibilities. The philosopher Bertrand Russell (1872–1970) wrote in this context:

> Philosophy, though unable to tell us with certainty what is the true answer to the doubts which it raises, is able to suggest many possibilities which enlarge our thoughts and free them from the tyranny of custom.

Thus, while diminishing our feeling of certainty as to what things are, it greatly increases our knowledge as to what they might be; it removes the somewhat arrogant dogmatism of those who have never traveled into the region of liberating doubt, and it keeps alive our sense of wonder by showing familiar things in an unfamiliar aspect.[4]

Whether or not you agree with Russell on this point can only become clear after you have investigated a couple of important philosophical questions. The remainder of this book gives you an opportunity to do just that.

The Relationship Between Science and Philosophy

In the last section, we defined philosophy as the attempt to explain the world with the help of reason. Some of you may find this definition puzzling. If philosophy is the attempt to explain the world with the help of reason, how then does philosophy differ from science? Scientists obviously also use reason when they explain the features of this world.

It is important to realize that what we call science was initially a part of philosophy. Aristotle (384–322 BCE), one of the greatest philosophers of antiquity, was a very influential physicist and biologist. Physics was historically described as natural philosophy. It is only during the last several hundred years that we tend to distinguish sharply between the various academic disciplines. Philosophy, the attempt to explain the world with the help of reason, has given birth to natural science, psychology, sociology, and linguistics. In today's world we seem to learn most of the things that we can reasonably claim about the universe not from philosophers, but from physicists, astronomers, biologists, or psychologists.

This raises a question: If philosophy has prepared the grounds for modern science, and if modern science currently is our best tool to explain the universe with the help of reason, what role does philosophy play in the world today? Can philosophy tell us something about the world above and beyond what the sciences tell us? Would we lose anything if we closed all philosophy departments and directed the money saved into the various science departments?

In order to answer this question we need to know a bit more about scientific disciplines such as physics or chemistry. Each scientific discipline deals with a specific subject matter. A physicist can tell you why you see lightning before you hear the thunder, but a physicist with his training and theories cannot explain to you whether going to law school will make you happy. Similarly, psychologists can explain to you why you begin to stutter when you talk to strangers, but they cannot explain to you why your cholesterol level is so high. What these two examples illustrate is that each scientific discipline only deals with a part of reality, but not with the whole. One might suspect that if we take all scientific disciplines collectively, this would account for all aspects of reality and would produce a comprehensive rational understanding of the universe. Fortunately (for philosophy), this is not the case. Even if we take all scientific disciplines together, we do not obtain a comprehensive rational analysis of the whole universe.

Let me illustrate this with an example. I have always been curious as to whether or not I have a soul. Souls, if they exist, are entities that we cannot see, measure, or weigh. Souls are not like rocks, fingernails, or other physical objects. Since science obtains information about the world predominately by measurements and experimentation, science can tell us a lot about rocks, clouds, and planets. However, science has a much harder time telling us about souls or a possible afterlife. Finding the answer to the question of whether or not we have souls requires not only observations and experiments but also a good deal of conceptual analysis; that is, we need to clarify what we mean by the concept "soul" before we can make any progress in determining whether souls exist. Analyzing and clarifying complex concepts is an integral part of philosophy. Such concept clarification often involves testing definitions and analyzing hypothetical situations. The question of whether or not we have souls is therefore a good example of a philosophical question. **We can define philosophical questions as questions that involve conceptual analysis and that require for their solution more than observations and experimentation. Philosophical questions are "open questions" in the sense that we cannot easily predict what would constitute a satisfactory solution to them. No scientific procedure can produce a quick answer to philosophical questions.**

FOOD FOR THOUGHT

The question of whether we have souls is a typical philosophical question, but there are many others. Make a list of questions that you take to be typical philosophical questions. Discuss the list with your neighbor and then with your class.

It is worthwhile to stress that the line between philosophy and science is not fixed. Some philosophical questions eventually turned into scientific questions once the appropriate scientific methodology was developed. For example, the question "Is there life on Mars?" is now clearly a scientific question, but it used to be a philosophical one. Similarly, the question "Are computers able to think?" is currently a philosophical question, but it might turn into a scientific question for cognitive scientists. However, most classical philosophical questions, like the question of whether God exists, appear to be such that it is difficult to imagine (in principle) that they can be answered with the help of any scientific procedure. This is the reason why some people find philosophy frustrating. They have the feeling that philosophers do not get anywhere, since they have been exploring some of the same open questions for thousands of years without arriving at final solutions. This is not a silly complaint, but before one concludes that philosophy is inherently a fruitless and frustrating activity, it is worthwhile to keep the following considerations in mind: Although it is probably impossible to answer open questions so that every "reasonable" person agrees with a given answer, it is very well possible to answer such questions satisfactorily in light of your experiences and observations of the world.

FOOD FOR THOUGHT

Take a look at the following questions and decide whether they are predominately scientific or philosophical questions. Keep in mind that some questions might have scientific as well as philosophical components.

Continued

1. How many chromosomes does a human being have?
2. Is it morally permissible to remove chromosomes from an embryo?
3. What caused the extinctions of the dinosaurs?
4. Is homosexual love unnatural?
5. Did extraterrestrials visit Earth in the past?
6. Are depressions chemical imbalances in the brain?
7. What caused the universe to exist?
8. Did life on Earth develop as a result of random natural processes?
9. Are quarks the smallest particles in the universe?
10. Are economic theories genuine scientific theories?

Philosophy, unlike science, has a personal component. The purpose of philosophical activity is to clarify in your own mind which solution to an open question seems most reasonable. This does not mean that you—insofar as you practice philosophy—can assert whatever strikes your fancy. Philosophy, as we have seen, is not mythological fantasy. Philosophers are committed to adopt the solution that appears most reasonable in light of the best arguments available to us. It is, however, quite possible that different rational persons answer the same open question differently because they have different experiences or because they make different background assumptions. One person, for example, might come to the conclusion that after-death experiences are all hogwash and the product of wishful thinking, whereas another person, who actually has had an after-death experience, is convinced that we will continue to exist after we die. Both positions might appear to be most reasonable in the light of the best arguments available to these two thinkers. The point of philosophical activity is, in part, to determine which solutions to open questions are most reasonable in the light of your experiences and thoughts about the world. It will, of course, not always be possible for you to select one solution to an open question as the most reasonable. You might conclude, for example, that you really do not know whether you are always responsible for your actions or whether you will survive your death. But this too can constitute progress. Many students who start a philosophy class with the firm conviction that they know the answers to most open questions later come to realize that their arguments weren't as convincing and reasonable as they initially thought. This awareness of the limits of our knowledge makes the world a more mysterious place. But mysteries are perhaps not only a key feature of good movies, but possibly also the key ingredients of a stimulating life.

FOOD FOR THOUGHT

What Is Your Philosophy?

Engaging in philosophical activity frequently causes us to change our attitudes toward fundamental questions. In order to see whether your attitudes will change during this class, it might be useful for you to record your positions at the beginning of this class. Answer the following questions with "Yes," "No," or "I don't know," and discuss them with the rest of the class.

1. On bodily death, a person continues to exist in a nonphysical form.
2. The ultimate goal in life is to live as pleasurably as possible.
3. Democracy is the best form of government.
4. God exists.
5. I am now the same person as I was when I was 5 years old.
6. I am always responsible for my actions.
7. To allow an innocent child to suffer needlessly when one could easily prevent it is morally reprehensible.
8. Ghosts exist.
9. One day there may be computers that understand Shakespeare better than I do right now.
10. It is wrong to impose the death penalty.
11. There are universal moral standards that apply to all human beings regardless of where they live.
12. The best way to treat depression is to inject chemicals into the brain.
13. If I had been born into a different environment, I might have become a professional killer.
14. It is impossible to know anything with absolute certainty.
15. The future is fixed; how one's life unfolds is a matter of destiny.

Continued

16. The life of a young child is more valuable than the life of a 22-year-old college student.
17. If God does not exist, then there are no moral obligations. In this case, no action would be right or wrong.
18. It is impossible to be truly happy if one is an immoral person.
19. The possession of drugs for personal use should be decriminalized.

The Main Branches of Philosophy

We have seen in the last section that philosophers try to find reasonable solutions to open questions. Traditionally, philosophical questions can be divided into five different fields of study: **Metaphysics, Epistemology, Ethics, Aesthetics,** and **Logic.** It is useful to be familiar with these different areas of inquiry so that one can obtain an overview of the major questions studied in philosophy.

Metaphysics is usually defined as the study of ultimate reality; however, this definition is not very illuminating. One way to get a better understanding of this field of study is to list all the things that we think exist in the universe. Most of us would probably start our lists with familiar things such as cars, trees, cats, and humans. However, after a while, some of us would perhaps also include items like angels, souls, and gods. If we compare our lists, certain questions will arise. For example, I might ask: "Do you really believe that there are angels in this world?" This question is a typical metaphysical question. Therefore, we can define metaphysical questions as questions that deal with the nature of existence.[5] "Can we still exist even after our physical body has ceased to function?" is another good example of a metaphysical question. As we will see later on, philosophers frequently wonder whether souls, gods, time, or colors really exist and how these entities are related to one another. Insofar as they study the existence and nature of these and other entities, philosophers are investigating questions that belong to the field of metaphysics.

Epistemology is the study of knowledge. Epistemology is important for philosophers because it sometimes happens that in the process of exploring a question, we come to the conclusion that we cannot possibly know what answer to the question is correct. Many people believe, for instance, that we can never know whether God exists or not. People who deny that we can know answers to certain questions are called **skeptics.** It is an important part of philosophy to determine under what conditions skepticism is a reasonable position to adopt. This project of determining the scope and limits of knowledge is the main part of epistemology.

The fields of **Ethics** and **Aesthetics** both deal with questions of value. **Ethics** is primarily concerned with discerning what values should govern our life. Are we, for example, always required to help people in need? If you answer this question affirmatively, you have given an ethical recommendation. Justifying ethical recommendations is a major element in the study of ethics. **Aesthetics,** on the other hand, deals with questions about art and beauty. Does a beautiful landscape have anything in common with a beautiful piece of music? Is beauty only in the eye of the beholder? These are examples of questions that are part of the study of Aesthetics.

The final—and in some sense most fundamental—area of philosophy is the field of **Logic.** We have seen that philosophy requires that we defend our claims about the world with arguments. However, it is obvious that not all arguments are equally good. Many arguments are actually quite misleading and weak. Logic is the field of study that clarifies how we can distinguish good arguments from bad ones. We will start our exploration of philosophy with a brief excursion into the field of logic.

The following chart should be useful for remembering the major fields of philosophy.

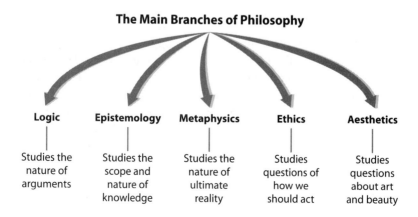

The Main Branches of Philosophy

Logic	Epistemology	Metaphysics	Ethics	Aesthetics
Studies the nature of arguments	Studies the scope and nature of knowledge	Studies the nature of ultimate reality	Studies questions of how we should act	Studies questions about art and beauty

Although some fundamental questions have metaphysical, epistemological, and ethical aspects, most philosophical questions belong in one of these categories. Practice your grasp of these fundamental disciplines by completing the following exercise.

FOOD FOR THOUGHT

Take a look at the following claims and decide whether they are predominately epistemological, metaphysical, logical, ethical, or aesthetic in nature.

1. It is better to suffer wrong than to inflict it on others.
2. Vampires exist only in movies or books.
3. Nobody can know whether a fetus is a person or simply a collection of cells.
4. A valid argument can have false premises.
5. Everything that exists is a physical object.
6. Paris is the most beautiful city of the world.
7. There are more irrational numbers than rational numbers.
8. Don't pursue a major that will not make you rich.
9. It is impossible to predict the future.
10. Your stories are, as so often, full of contradictions.
11. We will never understand why God lets innocent children suffer.

Philosophical Methodology

Philosophers as Detectives

We have seen that philosophy is the attempt to find reasonable solutions to open questions. But what exactly does it mean to be reasonable? Finding reasonable solutions to open questions is something philosophers and good detectives have in common.[6] Both use reason and logical analysis to make sense of a mysterious world. Since philosophical investigations follow a similar logical pattern as detective investigations, it is possible to explain the logical framework of philosophical investigations with respect to a murder case. Suppose the Duke of Forrestbrook has been shot in his castle. How would a good detective go about solving this crime?

The first step in a reasonable murder investigation is to **clarify** exactly what has happened. Where was the Duke of Forrestbrook shot? Was the murder weapon found? Are there any witnesses? We might call this step the clarification step. Philosophical investigations start in a similar manner. When we attempt to find reasonable answers to open philosophical questions, we need to begin our investigation by clarifying all relevant concepts. For instance, a philosopher who wants to investigate the question of whether every event has a cause needs to clarify what we mean by "event" and by "cause."

After we have clarified all the relevant facts (or concepts), we then proceed to **hypothesize** who could have committed the crime. Of course, it is not enough to consider the most conspicuous suspects. To do so would be unreasonable, since we cannot assume that the most likely suspect is always the culprit. A good detective keeps an open mind and investigates all possible hypotheses. A good philosopher does the same thing, and therefore considers all possible theories and hypotheses that might provide an answer to the open question under investigation. It would be unreasonable to restrict philosophical inquiry to those theories that are most compatible with so-called "common sense."

As a third step, we need to **test** whether we can eliminate any hypotheses. This is a classical element of any good detective work. Sherlock Holmes reminds Watson in the novel *The Adventure of the Beryl Coronet*: "It is an old maxim of mine that when you have excluded the impossible, whatever remains, however improbable, must be the truth." Philosophers proceed in a similar fashion. They test all possible theories and try to find counterexamples or hidden contradictions. If a philosophical theory has been shown to entail a contradiction, the theory is eliminated from the list of possible hypotheses.

The final step in solving a murder mystery is the most difficult one. After we have clarified the facts, identified all possible suspects, and eliminated those who could not have done it, we then need to **judge** who might have committed the murder. It is important to see that the available evidence might implicate more than one person, and that we cannot always tell beyond reasonable doubt that one person is the culprit. This is not something a good detective wishes for, but it certainly can happen. The same is true in philosophy. Although good philosophical investigations will narrow the list of possible theories, they will not always succeed in identifying one particular theory as the only plausible answer.

Reasonable philosophical inquiries therefore follow the same logical pattern as detective investigations. Both involve four logical steps. These four steps are illustrated in the following chart.

The Basic Logical Framework of Philosophical Investigations

1. Clarify the concepts that are used to formulate the question.

2. Hypothesize what theories provide a possible answer to the question.

3. Test whether there are hidden contradictions or counterexamples.

4. Judge what theory seems most plausible in light of all available evidence.

Although philosophers and detectives operate within a similar logical framework, philosophers make use of some unique logical and conceptual tools. These tools are introduced and explained in the following sections. Learning to use these conceptual and logical tools can at first be a bit challenging, but your effort in mastering these tools will pay off in later chapters when we discuss significant philosophical problems.

Conceptual Analysis: Necessary and Sufficient Conditions

In murder cases we start our investigation by gathering factual information. We want to know when the murder was committed and with what kind of weapon. In philosophy we start our investigation by clarifying concepts. Philosophical questions frequently contain abstract concepts. Consider the question of whether universals are more fundamental than particulars. This question only makes sense if we have a reasonably clear idea of what we mean by "universal" or "particular." Or consider the question of whether God exists. Before we can make any progress toward answering this question, it is obvious that we need to clarify what is meant by the concept "God." As you can see from these examples, concept clarifications can take a lot of time and effort. It is not a trivial affair.

Let us therefore look at what is involved when we try to clarify concepts. Consider—as an illustration—the familiar concept of being an animal. An intuitive way of visually illustrating this concept is to represent it as a set.

We can imagine that the set illustrated above contains all the things to which the concept "animal" applies. My favorite frog Esmeralda, for example, is a member of the set of animals, whereas my car and my soccer shoes are not members of that set.

One interesting thing to notice is that different concepts can be related to each other. Consider, for example, the relationship between the concept of being an animal and the concept of being a dog. To illustrate the relationship between these two concepts, we can draw the following picture.

If concepts are related, like the concept of being an animal and the concept of being a dog, we can say that being an animal is a **necessary condition** for being a dog, that is, something has to be an animal if it is to be a dog. Conversely, we can also say that being a dog is a **sufficient**

condition for being an animal. If you own a dog you must also own an animal. **In general we can say, a condition *q* is necessary for *p* if it is impossible for something to be *p* without being *q*. Moreover, we can say that a condition *q* is sufficient for *p* if it is impossible for something to be *q* and not *p*.** It takes awhile to grasp this distinction, but the following examples may be helpful. To be a freshman in college is a sufficient condition for being a college student, since it is impossible that a freshman at a college is not a college student. On the other hand being a freshman is not a necessary condition for being a college student, since many college students are juniors or seniors. Similarly, taking the final is (in most classes) a necessary condition for passing the class, since it is impossible to pass the class without taking the final. But taking the final is obviously not a sufficient condition for passing the class. Practice your grasp of necessary and sufficient conditions by completing the following exercises.

FOOD FOR THOUGHT

Answer the following with T/F:

1. Being stupid is a necessary condition for flunking out of college.
2. Getting only Fs is a sufficient condition for flunking out of college.
3. Acting against the law is neither necessary nor sufficient for being morally wrong.
4. Being able to make your own decisions is a necessary condition for being morally responsible.
5. Believing in God is a necessary condition for having faith.
6. Being able to communicate with others is a necessary condition for being a human being.
7. Being born in New York is a sufficient condition for being an American.
8. Being a mammal is a sufficient condition for being warm blooded.
9. Having a brain is a sufficient condition for being conscious.
10. Being omnipotent is a necessary condition for being God.
11. Being rich is a sufficient condition for being happy.

By specifying the necessary and sufficient conditions for falling under a concept, we can arrive at a precise definition of that concept. Suppose, for example, that you are not familiar with the concept of being a bachelor. In that case I can help you by telling you the following: To be an unmarried male is a necessary and sufficient condition for being a bachelor. Bachelors are by definition unmarried males. It is, however, not always possible to specify clear necessary and sufficient conditions for philosophical concepts. Take the concept of "freedom." As we will see in a later chapter, it is rather challenging to develop a satisfactory definition of freedom. Is it, for example, a necessary condition for being free to have the power to act otherwise than we did in fact act? Is it a sufficient condition for being free to be able to do what one wants? Philosophers disagree on these points. However, even if we deal with very complex concepts, the search for necessary and sufficient conditions helps us to understand the concepts more clearly than before. A good example of how the search for necessary and sufficient conditions can help us in clarifying a philosophical concept is provided by the Food for Thought exercise below.

FOOD FOR THOUGHT

In her article "On the Moral and Legal Status of Abortion," published in the journal *The Monist* in 1973, the philosopher Mary Anne Warren attempts to clarify the concept of being a person in the following way:

> I suggest that the traits which are most central to the concept of personhood, or humanity in the moral sense, are, very roughly the following:
>
> 1. consciousness (of objects and events external and/or internal to the being, and in particular the capacity to feel pain);
> 2. reasoning (the developed capacity to solve new and relatively complex problems);
> 3. self-motivated activity (activity which is relatively independent of either genetic or direct external control);
> 4. the capacity to communicate, by whatever means, messages of an indefinite variety of types, that is, not just with an indefinite

Continued

number of possible contents, but on indefinitely many possible topics;

5. the presence of self-concepts, and self awareness, either individual or racial, or both . . .

We needn't suppose that an entity must have all of these attributes to be properly considered a person. (1) and (2) alone may well be sufficient for personhood, and quite probably (1)–(3) are sufficient. Neither do we need to insist that any one of these criteria is necessary for personhood, although once again (1) and (2) look like fairly good candidates for necessary conditions, as does (3), if "activity" is construed so as to include the activity of reasoning.

Do you agree with Mary Anne Warren's suggestion that conditions 1 and 2 might be necessary and sufficient conditions for being a person?

Hypothesizing: Exploring Possible Worlds

While detectives are looking for possible suspects, philosophers search for possible hypotheses that provide answers to philosophical questions. The term "possible" has, however, two very different meanings. In a murder case investigation, we deal with **causal possibility;** in philosophy we deal—for the most part—with **logical possibility.** This important distinction can be clarified with the help of some examples. Consider the following two sentences.

1. It is not possible for Tiger Woods to run 80 miles per hour.

2. It is not possible that Tiger Woods wins all major men's professional golf tournaments in 2004, but loses the U.S. Open during that year.

Both of these sentences are true, but the meaning of the word "possible" differs between them. In the first sentence we are dealing with causal possibility. The reason Tiger Woods cannot run 80 miles per hour has to do with the laws of nature. A human body is constructed such that it is causally impossible to reach such a velocity. **In general, we can say that a state of affairs is causally possible if it does not violate the laws of nature.** It is, for example, causally possible that five different hurricanes hit Florida this year or that the Red Sox win the World Series.

However, it is causally impossible for an airplane to travel faster than the speed of light or for a human being to live without oxygen.

Consider sentence 1 again: It is causally impossible for Tiger Woods to run 80 miles per hour. Notice, however, that we can imagine that Tiger Woods runs that fast. It will never happen (on Earth), since the laws of nature do not permit such a thing. But one can conceive of it happening. It is therefore **logically** possible that Tiger Woods runs 80 miles per hour. A good test of whether something is logically possible is to ask yourself whether you could make a movie about it. If you have seen the movie *Forrest Gump*, you know that we can make movies about people who run very fast—faster in fact than is causally possible for humans. In the same fashion we can make movies about talking toasters, or flying horses. All of these states of affairs are logically possible. When students first get introduced to the concept of logical possibility, they tend to think that everything is logically possible. But this is not the case. Notice that we cannot make a movie that makes sentence 2 true. It is logically impossible that Tiger Woods wins all major men's professional golf tournaments in the year 2004 and also loses the U.S. Open during that year. The assertion that Tiger Woods wins all major men's professional golf tournaments in the year 2004 and the assertion that he loses the U.S. Open in 2004 cannot both be true at the same time. If we nevertheless assert both of them, we are involved in a contradiction. **We can say, therefore, that a state of affairs is logically possible when it does not entail a contradiction.** A contradiction is a sentence or a set of sentences that both assert and deny that something is the case. For example, it is logically impossible for there to be a triangle with four sides, or for there to be a soccer ball that is completely red and completely green at the same time.

<hr/>

FOOD FOR THOUGHT

It is important that you understand the distinction between logical and causal possibility very clearly. Answer the following questions with T/F:

1. It is causally possible for water to turn into gold.
2. It is causally possible that an earthquake will destroy all buildings in New York next week.

Continued

3. It is logically impossible that all faculty members at Yale are space aliens.
4. It is logically possible that a person is taller than herself.
5. It is logically possible for Britney Spears to turn into a frog.
6. It is causally possible for the sun to rotate around the earth.
7. It is logically impossible that a turtle is the creator of this universe.
8. It is causally impossible that one person robs all the banks in Boston during one day.
9. Being causally possible is a necessary condition for being logically possible.
10. Being causally possible is a sufficient condition for being logically possible.

In order to determine whether something is logically possible, we need to use our imagination and explore what philosophers call **"possible worlds."** This can be a bit confusing at first, but after awhile it should be a lot of fun to explore with your mind whether certain scenarios are indeed logically possible. When philosophers consider logically possible scenarios, they conduct **thought experiments.** Thought experiments often have the sound and feel of science fiction because they deal with remote, though still logically possible, scenarios.

The reason philosophers deal with these possibilities is the same reason why a good detective looks at all possible suspects. It is not always clear that the most plausible solution to a problem is the right solution. For example, there exists a strong causal connection between our brains and our minds. From this we might conclude that wherever there is no brain, there is no mind. However, it is certainly logically possible that somebody who has only silicon chips in his brain has a mind just like me (i.e., I could make a movie out of this scenario). What this thought experiment shows is that the link between brain and mind might be not as strong as we initially think it to be.

A good philosopher will take such possibilities into account and explore their significance within his mind. In the history of philosophy, it has often been the case that possibilities that seemed outlandish and bizarre turned out to be much closer to the truth than those ideas that were closer to so-called "common sense." Consider the following example from the history of science. It seems natural to suppose that heavy objects (like cannonballs), when dropped from a tower, move faster toward the earth than tennis balls. This is what common sense tells us. However, it is not only logically possible that both objects move at the same speed, but it turns out (as you might have learned in an introductory physics class) that this is the actual truth.

It is perfectly all right if you are a bit skeptical at this point of whether the notion of logical possibility can be of much use. That the ability to conceive of logically possible scenarios is useful will become more obvious in the following sections and in the context of studying concrete philosophical problems.

Testing Hypotheses: Thought Experiments and Counterexamples

Although good detectives as well as good philosophers have an open mind and consider all logically possible hypotheses, it is a hallmark of good philosophy as well as of good detective work to eliminate defective theories from further consideration. A theory is defective if it entails a contradiction or if it can be shown that the theory is open to **counterexamples.** We have already discussed what we mean by contradictions. Let us explore in more detail what we mean by "counterexample." A counterexample to a theory is a scenario that is incompatible with the truth of the theory. Suppose, for instance, that Antonio, a friend of yours, subscribes to the theory that those countries which practice the death penalty have lower crime rates than countries which do not practice the death penalty. You can challenge Antonio's hypothesis by pointing to the example of Canada and the United States. Although Canada does not practice the death penalty, Canadian society has a lower crime rate than the United States. This is a counterexample to Antonio's theory.

In order to find effective counterexamples, philosophers once more make use of their ability to conduct thought experiments. When philosophers test hypotheses, they imagine that a given hypothesis is actually true and then try to describe logically possible scenarios that are incompatible with the theory under investigation. Let us illustrate this important philosophical technique with the help of an example. Suppose somebody claims that being a human is a necessary condition for speaking

English. As of yet, we have not discovered a species other than humans that is capable of speaking English. This, however, does not establish the claim at issue. When we claim that being a human is a necessary condition for speaking English, we claim that there is a logical relationship between being human and being able to speak English. Whether this logical relationship really holds can be tested with the help of a thought experiment. Notice that we can easily conceive that nonhuman creatures on other planets can learn to speak English or that we can build a computer that can speak English. This shows that it is logically possible that nonhumans speak English. This logically possible state of affairs constitutes a counterexample to the claim that being human is a necessary condition for speaking English. The theory that being human is a necessary condition for speaking English is therefore flawed.

At first, many students find it surprising that logically possible scenarios can refute theories. Many people tend to think that theories can only be refuted by facts, that is, by events that really happen. But this overlooks the fact that philosophy is mostly concerned with clarifying the relationships that hold between concepts. Conceptual relationships are logical in nature, and this is the reason logically possible scenarios need to be taken into consideration.

The ability to test and refute conceptual claims with the help of thought experiments is an important philosophical technique. Practice your ability to find counterexamples to theories with the help of the next exercise.

FOOD FOR THOUGHT

Refute the following hypotheses by finding logically possible scenarios that constitute counterexamples to the claims:

1. In order to be completely happy it is necessary to have shelter and some clothing.
2. It is a necessary condition for being a person to be capable of self-motivated activities.
3. Every great nation must defend its interests with brute force.
4. If people lose their fear of hell, they will cease to go to church.
5. No rational person would choose to have an abortion if they knew that a fetus has a soul right from the time of conception.
6. We should always do what makes the majority of people happy.

7. Being honest is the best policy.
8. It is impossible to survive the death of one's physical body.
9. Every person pursues those things that bring her pleasure.
10. It is not possible to fool all people all of the time.
11. All people who commit suicide are unhappy and depressed.

The final step in philosophical investigations is to try to **judge** which possible theory provides the most reasonable solution in light of all the available evidence. This is the most controversial step since it requires that we construct and evaluate a wide range of **arguments** in defense of, or in opposition to, various possible solutions. To do this well, we need to know more about arguments. We will study the basic structure of arguments in the following sections.

The Basic Structure of Arguments

Most beginning students associate the word "argument" with a verbal disagreement. In ordinary language we frequently say things like the following: "I had a real bad argument with my roommate yesterday." However, this use of the word "argument" has nothing to do with how we use the word in philosophy. Philosophers use the term differently. Consider the following example:

> I believe that ghosts exist, because late at night I have heard strange noises in my room.

This is an example of an argument. It is—as we can easily see—not a particularly strong argument, but let us ignore that fact for the moment. Every argument has two components: a claim that the argument tries to establish, and reasons that are offered in support of that claim. The claim that an argument tries to establish is called the **conclusion** of the argument, and the reasons offered in support of the conclusion are called **premises.** In the example above, the claim that ghosts exist is the conclusion of the argument, and the fact that you have heard strange noises in your room is the premise of the argument. The presence of the words "because," "since," and "for" in a sentence is a good indicator that the sentence or some part of that sentence is used as a premise in an argument. When you see the words "therefore," "thus," and "it follows that" in a sentence, you are normally dealing with the conclusion of an argument. When you develop an argument yourself, it is always easy to know what the conclusion of your argument is going to be, because the conclusion is something you believe to be true and want others to believe as well. The claims "God exists," "All people are created equal," and "I know that I am not dreaming right now" all can function as the conclusion of an argument. It is, however, much more challenging to find good premises for these conclusions. The premises of an argument are the reasons you think your belief about the world is true. Good and reasonable premises for an important claim are hard to come by, since we very often know what we believe, but we often are not quite sure why we do so.

FOOD FOR THOUGHT

Construct some arguments that provide support for the following conclusions.

1. Some people can predict what will happen in the future.
2. Money, fame, and sex are what everybody desires in life.
3. It is wrong to torture animals.
4. It is wrong to eat animals.
5. All organized religions are corrupt organizations.
6. Handguns should be outlawed.
7. In some cases lying is morally permissible.
8. Women are superior to men.
9. Private property should be abolished.
10. Private property is the key to a successful society.
11. Marijuana should be legalized.
12. Beauty is in the eye of the beholder
13. Large corporations have too much political power.

Putting Arguments into Standard Form

The above exercise illustrates that arguments come in many forms and shapes, but not all arguments are worth our time. Many are fairly silly pieces of reasoning. In order to accurately assess the value of arguments, it is frequently useful to put them into so-called **"standard form."** An argument in standard form lists all the premises in numbered sequential order and then adds the conclusion at the end. Let us go back to our initial example: "I believe that ghosts exist, because late at night I have heard strange noises in my room." If we put this argument into standard form, we obtain the following:

1. I have heard strange noises late at night in my room.

Therefore: Ghosts exist.

The word "therefore" is sometimes also symbolized as "∴". Although arguments in ordinary discourse are rarely presented in standard form, it is useful to put them into this form since it becomes easier to determine whether the argument is reasonable or not. In philosophy, it is an important skill to put arguments, which are sometimes presented in convoluted ways, into standard form. The following exercise should help you acquire this skill.

FOOD FOR THOUGHT

Put the following arguments into standard form:

1. God exists. I know this since the Bible tells us that God exists and the Bible only contains the truth.
2. Yesterday, I met Billy for the first time after his brain surgery. He did not recognize me or any member of his family. Billy must have turned into a new person.
3. It is wrong to take the life of a human being. A fetus is a human being, and to conduct an abortion is to take the life of a fetus. I conclude therefore that it is wrong to conduct an abortion.
4. I have heard that you are planning to spend $2,000 on a wide-screen television set. I think that this is a morally wrong action. Don't you agree that we all have the moral obligation to perform those acts that make as many people happy as possible? And it is also obvious that giving $2,000 to a homeless shelter will make more people happy than spending it on a TV set.
5. Only those beings are free who can act in unpredictable ways. It is thus obvious that computers can never be free, for computers are programmed to act in predictable ways.

Continued

6. Only those who actually help to build the products should benefit from the sale of these products on the open market. I conclude therefore that the owners of factories should not receive any benefits, for the owners never help to build the products.

7. Either pacifism is crazy, or else we must dissolve our military. If pacifism were crazy, then Gandhi's philosophy should not be taken seriously. But Gandhi's philosophy is interesting and must be taken seriously. We must therefore dissolve our military.

As you can see from these exercises, it can be challenging to put an argument into standard form. Sometimes arguments in ordinary language contain surplus information that needs to be eliminated. Not every claim in an argument will function as a premise after we have put the argument into standard form. On the other hand, arguments in ordinary discourse sometimes imply premises that are not stated explicitly. In that case, we need to supply additional premises that are part of the original argument.

FOOD FOR THOUGHT

Put the following arguments into standard form and add the premise that is implied but not stated explicitly:

1. All free beings abuse their free will from time to time. Peter is therefore a sinner, since all people who abuse their free will from time to time are sinners.

2. Our proposals were not accepted, since all proposals in the green folder were rejected.

3. It is always irrational to believe a proposition on the basis of insufficient evidence. It follows therefore that belief in the existence of extraterrestrial beings is irrational.

4. Spending money on listening to boring lectures is a waste of resources. It follows therefore that spending money on college is a waste of resources.

5. You will not do well in the upper level English class, because the professor made it very clear that only students with strong writing skills have the chance to do well in that class.

6. Anybody who voluntarily decides to destroy one's own body is irrational. This shows that smokers are irrational people.

To put an argument into standard form is therefore not always a straightforward affair, and often involves some degree of interpretation. When arguments get very complex, philosophers sometimes disagree about how best to present the argument in standard form. In spite of these difficulties, it is nevertheless always a good idea to try to put an argument into standard form. An argument in this form is much easier to evaluate, since one can see its logical structure at one glance.

Deductive and Inductive Arguments

To evaluate an argument, we first need to classify it, since different types of arguments are evaluated according to different criteria. Arguments fall into two main classifications. Consider the following two examples:

Argument A:
1. If my brain stops functioning, then it will not be possible for me to have any thoughts.
2. When I die, my brain will stop functioning.

Therefore: When I die, it will not be possible for me to have any thoughts.

Argument B:
1. Every new freshman I have talked to has been enrolled in a freshman success seminar.

Therefore: All new freshmen are enrolled in a freshman success seminar.

It is easy to see that these two arguments belong in different categories. Argument A establishes its conclusion more firmly than argument B. We call arguments of this type **deductive arguments.** In deductive arguments, the truth of the premises guarantees that the conclusion must be true as well. On the other hand, arguments like argument B, which establishes its conclusions only to some degree of probability, are called **inductive arguments.** An inductive argument can be recognized as follows: even **if** one assumes that the premises of the argument are true, it is nevertheless logically possible that the conclusion turns out to be false. Let us illustrate this with respect to argument B. Even if it is true that every freshmen I have talked to was enrolled in a freshmen seminar, it is still possible that not all freshmen are enrolled in such a seminar. In order to recognize that an argument is inductive, we again have to make use of the concept of logical possibility and explore possible worlds. If we can imagine a world in which the premises of an argument are true, but in which the conclusion is nevertheless false, we know that we are dealing with an inductive argument. If, on the other hand, we are dealing with a deductive argument, it is impossible to imagine that the premises are true and the conclusion false. In order to practice your ability to distinguish these two types of argument, the following exercise will be useful.

FOOD FOR THOUGHT

Put the following arguments into standard form and determine whether they are inductive or deductive arguments:

1. A completely drunk person is not responsible for his actions. John behaves as if he is completely drunk. Therefore: John is not responsible for his actions.

2. I cannot know that a belief is true if there is a chance that it might be false. There is a chance that my belief that I have a soul is false. It follows therefore that I cannot know that I have a soul.

3. Every scientific theory that we have developed in the past has eventually been shown to be false. So, all scientific theories we develop in the future will eventually be shown to be false as well.

4. We have found a piece of hair on the victim which matches the sample of hair we took from Bob. Bob therefore is the killer.

5. If there are universal moral standards for all human beings then all human beings agree on what is right or wrong. But human beings disagree on what is right or wrong. It is thus obvious that there are no universal moral standards.

6. Either human cloning is immoral, or it will be a blessing for humanity. Human cloning is certainly not a blessing for humanity. I conclude therefore that human cloning is immoral.
7. Either the defendant refuses to take the stand or he confesses. If he refuses to take the stand, he must have something to hide. If he confesses then he is guilty. So, the defendant either has something to hide or he is guilty.

Evaluating Deductive Arguments: Validity and Soundness

Deductive and inductive arguments are evaluated according to different standards. Let us start by taking a closer look at deductive arguments. Good deductive arguments must be **valid.** A deductive argument is valid if it has the following characteristic: **If all the premises of the argument are true, then the conclusion *must* be true as well.** Please notice the "if"clause in this definition. Remember that an argument can be valid even if the premises are in fact false. Consider the following deductive argument:

1. All students have rich parents.
2. Peter is a student.

Therefore: Peter has rich parents.

This argument is a valid deductive argument, although premise 1 is obviously false. Notice that the argument has the necessary characteristic for validity. If the premises were true, then the conclusion must be true as well. It does not matter that premise 1 is actually false. Validity is a judgment about the logical relationship between the premises and the conclusion. If the relationship is *truth preserving*, that is, if the assumption that the premises are true guarantees that the conclusion would be true as well, the argument is valid. In order to practice your ability to recognize valid arguments, complete the following exercise.

FOOD FOR THOUGHT

Try to determine whether the following arguments are valid or not:

Continued

A. 1. Taking a human life is always morally wrong.
   2. Aborting a fetus is to take human life.

   Therefore: Aborting a fetus is morally wrong.

B. 1. No government has the right to force people to pay taxes.

   Therefore: The United States government has no right to force people to pay taxes.

C. 1. Many teenagers who watch violent movies act violently later on.

   Therefore: Watching violent movies causes violent behavior.

D. 1. All successful people are happy.
   2. Peter is happy.

   Therefore: Peter is successful.

Beginning students tend to be confused by the concept of validity. What is the point in determining whether an argument is valid, if that does not guarantee that the argument has true premises? The reason for this is the following. It is frequently not possible to establish beyond all reasonable doubt whether a premise is true or false. Since we can establish whether an argument is valid or not without having to know whether the premises of the argument are true or false, we can criticize an argument as invalid simply by virtue of its logical structure. Demonstrating that an argument is invalid is a powerful philosophical strategy to dismiss an argument. If I can show that an argument is invalid, I can say: "Well, I am not sure whether your premises are true or not, but even if they were true, it would not follow that the conclusion of your argument has to be true as well." Notice that in order to show that an argument is invalid, you again have to use the concept of logical possibility. For what you have to do is to show that it is logically possible that the premises are true and yet the conclusion is false. Moreover, valid arguments help us to clarify the logical relation between ideas. If we find a valid argument and dislike the conclusion (perhaps because it conflicts with what we want to believe about the world), we also know that we have to discard at least one of the premises. In order to illustrate this, consider the following example:

1. If all events are caused, then we are not free.
2. All events are caused.

Therefore: We are not free.

This argument is valid, but most of us will find the conclusion hard to accept. We tend to think that we are free beings who are responsible for our actions. However, since the argument is valid, it shows us that if we want to reject the conclusion we also have to reject at least one of its premises. For if both premises are accepted as true, the conclusion must be accepted as well. In this way valid arguments help us to clarify the logical relation between our ideas. If we want to reject one idea, we often have to reject other (much more innocent-looking) ideas as well.

Validity is, however, only a necessary condition for a deductive argument to be a good argument. When we explore the world with the help of arguments, we not only want our deductive arguments to be valid, but in addition we want our arguments to have true premises. **Valid deductive arguments with true premises are called** *sound arguments.* The ultimate goal in philosophy is always to produce and find sound arguments.

Evaluating Deductive Arguments: Logical Form

Deductive arguments can be identified and classified according to their logical form. Take a look at the argument below and compare it with the argument about free will in the previous section.

1. If Tony takes drugs, he is an irresponsible person.
2. Tony takes drugs.

Therefore: Tony is an irresponsible person.

It is easy to see that these two deductive arguments have the same form. The structure of the form can be expressed with the help of symbols. We therefore can obtain the general argument schema.

1. If p then q
2. p

Therefore: q

This deductive argument form is well known among philosophers and has its own name: **modus ponens.** It is easy to see that every argument which is an instance of modus ponens must be valid. It does not matter what words are substituted for the placeholders *p* and *q*, as long as the form modus ponens is preserved, the resulting argument must be valid. Being able to recognize the logical form of an argument is therefore an excellent and quick way to determine whether arguments are valid.

Closely related to the argument form called modus ponens is the deductive argument form called **modus tollens.** The following argument is an instance of modus tollens:

1. If the future is already determined, then I am not responsible for my actions.
2. I am responsible for my actions.

Therefore: The future is not already determined.

The logical form of modus tollens can be captured with the help of the following argument schema.

1. If *p* then *q*
2. not-*q*

Therefore: not-*p*

Another well-known deductive argument form is called **disjunctive syllogism.** The following is an example of a disjunctive syllogism.

1. Either Darwin's theory of evolution is wrong, or we humans are related to monkeys.
2. Humans are not related to monkeys.

Therefore: Darwin's theory of evolution is wrong.

The following argument schema expresses the general logical form of a disjunctive syllogism.

1. Either *p* or *q*
2. not-*q*

Therefore: *p*

A further famous argument form is called **hypothetical syllogism.** The following argument is an instance of this logical form.

1. If materialism is false, then Marxism is a faulty philosophical system.
2. If Marxism is a faulty philosophical system, then one should not believe everything Marx writes.

Therefore: If materialism is false, then one should not believe everything Marx writes.

It is relatively easy to see that the following argument schema expresses the logical form of hypothetical syllogisms.

1. If p then q
2. If q then r

Therefore: If p then r

There are many additional deductive argument forms, but to introduce all of them would go beyond the scope of an introductory textbook. Being familiar with modus ponens, modus tollens, and disjunctive syllogism should make you aware that many deductive arguments can quickly be identified and recognized because they are instances of well-known valid logical argument forms.

Before we turn our attention to inductive arguments, I would like to introduce one more important type of deductive argument, called **reductio ad absurdum.** "Reductio ad absurdum" is a Latin phrase meaning literally, "To reduce something into absurdity." Many of the most famous philosophical arguments have this type of logical structure. What all reductio ad absurdum arguments, or, to use the shorter expression, "reductio arguments," have in common is not their logical form but rather their argumentative/logical technique. Consider the following example.

1. Assume that God exists and that he is all good.
2. Every being that is all good will always help all those who are in need.
3. Some people who are in need receive no help from God.

Therefore: God either doesn't exist or he is not all good.

The basic idea of reductio arguments is to assume that something is true (although you are not convinced that it is), and then proceed to show that this assumption together with other plausible premises leads to a contradiction. In the above case the contradiction arises because premises 1 and 2 entail that all those in need will receive help from God, but this is logically incompatible with premise 3. We therefore confront the contradiction that all people who are in need receive help and that some people in need receive no help. Since it is a law of logic that any assumption which leads to a contradiction must be false, this reductio argument allows us to infer that premise 1 (God exists and is all good) must be false as long as we believe that premises 2 and 3 are true. As you can see from this example, reductio arguments are powerful intellectual tools. They force us to consider the relationship between all our beliefs. We are often not aware that there are logical tensions within our belief system because we do not examine all of our beliefs at the same time. Reductio arguments make us aware of these tensions and prompt us to reexamine our belief system. Reductio arguments have been famous since the time of Socrates, and you will encounter many of them in the later part of this book.

FOOD FOR THOUGHT

Put the following deductive arguments into standard form and determine whether the arguments are of the form modus ponens, modus tollens, disjunctive syllogism, hypothetical syllogism, or reductio ad absurdum.

1. Either Santa Claus exists or my parents have been lying to me. Santa Claus does not exist. I know therefore that my parents have been lying to me
2. If it is true that all people act always with only their own interest in mind, then no one can truly be moral. But if no one can truly be moral, then studying moral theory is pointless. It follows therefore that if all people act always with only their own interest in mind then studying moral theory is pointless.
3. In order to pass the class, I must score more than 90 percent on the final exam. I therefore did not pass the class, since I scored 85 percent on the final exam.
4. Either God is mad or the creation of the universe was simply a cosmic accident. God is certainly not mad. We must conclude

therefore that the creation of the world is simply a cosmic accident.

5. Assume God doesn't exist. In that case it is possible that we can think of a being just like God which actually exists. So, if God doesn't exist, we can think of a being greater than God, but this is impossible; for God is the greatest being we can think of. Therefore: God must exist.

6. If life on earth is simply the result of natural processes, then we should not be surprised to find other forms of life on other planets. Life is the result of natural processes. It follows thus that we should expect to find other forms of life on other planets.

7. If my senses are reliable, then whatever I see or hear is in fact true. My senses are therefore not reliable, because sometimes I see or hear things which are not true.

Evaluating Inductive Arguments: Probability

As we have seen already, an inductive argument is an argument whose premises support its conclusion only to some degree of probability. Take a look at the following example of an inductive argument:

1. All people I have ever met have lied whenever it was convenient for them.

Therefore: All humans lie whenever it is convenient for them.

Suppose premise 1 is true. This certainly gives us a reason for thinking that the conclusion is true as well. If everyone I come to know starts to lie whenever it is convenient for them, I certainly have reasons to believe that all humans do the same. Notice, however, that the conclusion does not have to be true. Given the truth of the premise it is still logically possible that there are some humans who never lie. This is the reason why inductive arguments, unlike deductive arguments, can never be valid. However, it would be silly to reject an inductive argument for this reason. In order to evaluate inductive arguments we do not check to see whether they are valid or invalid; instead, we try to determine whether they establish their conclusion with a high or low degree of probability.

Inductive arguments that establish their conclusion to a high degree of probability are called **strong inductive arguments.** Those inductive arguments that establish their conclusion only to a low degree of probability are called **weak inductive arguments**. It is relatively difficult to evaluate inductive arguments quickly. In philosophy, inductive arguments do not play as central a role as in other more empirical disciplines like psychology or sociology. However, three types of inductive arguments are worth mentioning.

Probably the most widely used type of inductive argument is called an **enumerative inductive argument**. The argument above is a good example of an enumerative inductive argument. The basic idea behind this type of inductive argument can be expressed with the help of the following argument schema:

1. All observed As have been Bs.

Therefore: Probably all As everywhere are Bs.

Although enumerative inductive arguments are frequently used, it is difficult to evaluate them. Recall that inductive arguments are strong if the truth of the premises make it very probable that the conclusion is true as well. An enumerative inductive argument is certainly stronger if we have observed a relationship between events of type A and events of type B to obtain frequently (i.e., if the sample size is large). But although a large sample size is a necessary condition for classifying an enumerative inductive argument as a strong inductive argument, it is not sufficient. Even if we have observed certain relationships frequently, the resulting enumerative inductive argument can still be weak. To illustrate this, consider the following example.

1. All cars that I have observed have been red.

Therefore: Probably all cars everywhere are red.

Notice that this argument remains weak even if I have seen thousands of red cars. The problem is that the relationship between being red and being a car is an accidental relationship. There is no underlying connection between being a car and being red. The fact that all cars I have observed are red is a pure accident. Enumerative inductive arguments are most successful when we are dealing with so-called "lawlike" relationships.

For example, if I have observed that several metal bars have expanded when they were exposed to heat, then I am justified to conclude that probably all metal bars expand when heated. In this case, there exists a lawlike relationship that explains why metal bars expand when heated. It is, however, far from clear how we can tell when we are dealing with lawlike relationships and when not. Fortunately, philosophers do not use enumerative inductive arguments as frequently as scientists, and it is therefore sufficient if we can recognize the logical form of the argument without yet knowing how to evaluate them properly. We will discuss the strength of these arguments in more detail when we discuss the classical epistemological problem of induction.

A second important type of inductive argument is called **analogical argument.** Consider the following example:

1. The human heart is like a motor pump.
2. Every motor pump can be repaired when it fails.

Therefore: The human heart can be repaired when it fails.

The crucial element of this argument is the idea of comparing human hearts to motor pumps. Analogical arguments can be very powerful and are frequently used in philosophical writings; however, it is easy to see that the strength of an analogical argument depends on the degree to which the two compared items are indeed similar to each other. In some respects human hearts are similar to motor pumps. Both function according to similar physical principles. But there are also some crucial differences between human hearts and motor pumps. A human heart is made of organic materials that limit the degree to which it can be repaired. This difference between human hearts and motor pumps undermines the strength of the analogical argument. There are no general rules according to which we can quickly tell whether an analogy is appropriate or not. Analogical arguments have to be analyzed on a case-by-case basis. If the analogy is a strong one, the resulting inductive argument is strong. If the analogy is weak, the resulting argument is weak. In this case the argument is rather weak, although it still might serve an important rhetorical purpose.

A final important type of inductive argument is called **inference to the best explanation,** or **abductive argument.** The key idea of this type of inductive argument can be explained with the help the following—by now somewhat familiar—example.

> 1. I have heard strange noises late at night in my room.
> Therefore: Ghosts exist.

As it stands right now, this inductive argument does not seem very strong. However, consider the following modification of the argument, which turns the argument into an inference to the best explanation.

> 1. I have heard strange noises late at night in my room.
> 2. The best explanation for these strange noises is that they are caused by ghosts.
> Therefore: Ghosts probably exist.

If premise 2 is indeed true, and the hypotheses that ghosts cause these strange noises is the best explanation available, then the argument is much stronger than before. This, however, raises a crucial question: How can we determine whether a given explanation of an event is better than all other explanations?

It is easy to see that any event can be explained in many different ways. Strange noises in the night might, for example, be caused by ghosts, or by mice in the attic, or by my roommate who is watching a horror movie. Our judgment of whether a given explanation is better than others depends on many factors. However, two factors frequently play a prominent role and are therefore worth mentioning:

1. An explanation A is better than explanation B if (all other things being equal) explanation A is simpler than explanation B.
2. An explanation A is better than explanation B if (all other things being equal) explanation A fits together better with the rest of my other beliefs about the world.

Principle 1 is often called **"Ockham's Razor"** in recognition of the medieval philosopher William of Ockham (1285–1347) who praised simplicity as a virtue in theory construction. Principle 2 can be called the **"principle of conservatism."** Both principles are somewhat controversial. The principle of Ockham's Razor requires a clear understanding of the term "simplicity." We normally think that an explanation is simpler if the explanation requires us to make fewer independent assumptions. But it is not always clear how many independent assumptions are involved in a given explanation. The principle of conservativism is rather subjective; that is, an explanation which is well compatible with the rest of my belief system might not fit well into your belief system. If I am a professional ghost hunter who has seen many ghosts in the past and who is spending a night in a haunted castle, the idea that strange noises are caused by ghosts might be the most conservative explanation available to me. On the other hand, if I am a person who has never seen ghosts and who is sleeping in a dorm room on campus, I will consider the idea that strange noises at night are caused by ghosts to be too outlandish (nonconservative) to be true. In this case it is easier to accept the idea that the noises are caused by a student next door who is watching a horror movie. This explanation is, in this situation, not only more conservative but also simpler, and thus probably the best explanation available.

As you can see from this example, "inferences to the best explanation" must be evaluated very carefully. It is often a contentious issue to decide which explanation is indeed the best, and reasonable people might come to different conclusions. However, this type of inductive argument plays an important role in philosophy and we will encounter it frequently during our exploration of well-known philosophical problems.

FOOD FOR THOUGHT

Discuss under what situations the following "best explanations" would seem unreasonable. Where possible, make use of the principle of Ockham's Razor and the principle of conservatism.

1. The best explanation for why I failed my mathematics exams is that I simply cannot do math.

Continued

2. The best explanation for why some people are rich and others are poor is that the rich people are hard working and the poor people are lazy.

3. The best explanation for why so many people call the psychic hotline is that these psychics can indeed predict the future.

4. The best explanation for why my friend's radiation therapy was successful, is that God created a miracle.

5. The best explanation for why I am fat is that my parents were fat as well.

Endnotes

1. I understand the term "mythology" in a very general sense as referring to any invented story that has been transmitted orally over many generations within a given culture. From an anthropological point of view, it might very well be false to think that mythological stories stand in any direct competition to philosophical, religious, or scientific claims. I am grateful to Steven Duncan for pointing this out to me. However, my imaginary scenario is not designed to make any anthropological or historical claims about how mythology, religion, and philosophy in fact developed. Instead, I simply use the imaginary scenario to stress that there are relevant logical and epistemological differences between mythological, religious, and philosophical explanations of reality. It is an additional empirical question, which I would like to leave unanswered, whether these logical and epistemological differences between mythology, religion, and science have had any actual historical significance.

2. I understand religion here predominately as an epistemological phenomenon, that is, as a method of shaping beliefs about the world. It should be quite clear that not all religions even have such an epistemological element, and that the term "religion" is typically used with a much broader meaning that includes a wide range of sociological and psychological phenomena as well. However, my goal here is not to say anything profound about religion, but I want to stress instead that religion tends to provide different types of explanations than philosophical inquiry.

3. It is worth noting that not all philosophical traditions make argumentation the center of philosophical activity. Robert Abele pointed out to me that in Eastern philosophy, it is traditionally not arguments and concepts that take first place. Rather, it is the experience of enlightenment that counts, through the use of various methods of meditation. However, even in the Eastern

philosophical tradition argumentation plays a significant role, and it is therefore not completely misleading to claim that arguments are an important ingredient of all philosophy.

4. Russell, Bertrand. *The Problems of Philosophy*. Oxford: Oxford University Press, 1912, p. 156.

5. It might be objected at this point that, according to this definition, there is no difference between ontological questions and metaphysical questions. But since ontology is normally considered to be only a part of metaphysics, it might be argued that it is misguided to equate metaphysics with ontology. I am, however, simply not sure whether we can draw a useful distinction between the term "metaphysics" and "ontology." For all practical purposes, there seems no big problem if we treat the two terms as synonymous.

6. Several others before me have suggested that one can compare the work of philosophers with the work of detectives. For a nice discussion of the similarities see Stewart, David: The Philosopher as Detective. In: Minton A. and Shipka, T (ed.). *Philosophy: Paradox and Discovery*. New York, McGraw-Hill, 1990, pp. 13–21.

For Further Reading

Bontempo, Charles J., and S. Jack Odell (eds.). *The Owl of Minerva: Philosophers on Philosophy*. New York: McGraw-Hill, 1975.

Giere, Ronald. *Understanding Scientific Reasoning*. Fort Worth: Holt, Rinehart and Winston, 1994

Grayling, A.C. (ed.). *Philosophy 1: A Guide Through the Subject*. Oxford: Oxford University Press, 1998.

Hacking, Ian. *An Introduction to Probability and Inductive Logic*. Cambridge: Cambridge University Press, 2001

Layman, C. Stephen. *The Power of Logic*. Boston: McGraw-Hill, 2002.

Rosenberg, Jay. *The Practice of Philosophy*. Englewood Cliffs: Prentice Hall, 1984.

CHAPTER TWO

WHAT DO WE KNOW?

What Is Knowledge?

Chapter 1 introduced a range of logical and conceptual tools. We are now in a better position to clarify abstract concepts, to test hypotheses, and to construct and evaluate different types of arguments. As we have seen, good deductive arguments have two important features: they must be *valid* and they must be *sound*. Logic can help us determine whether an argument is valid, but logic is not sufficient to establish whether an argument is sound. In order to do that we need to **know** whether the premises of an argument are true. This is where we enter the realm of epistemology—the theory of knowledge. This chapter will introduce some fundamental concepts and theories in the study of knowledge. By becoming familiar with these ideas, you may better recognize whether the premises of arguments can be known to be true or whether we can justifiably dismiss them as mere assumptions or unfounded speculations.

FOOD FOR THOUGHT

The word "know" can be used in a variety of ways. Consider the following three examples:

    A. I know that George Washington was the first American President.

    B. I know how to speak French.

    C. I know Woody Allen very well.

Example A we can call an instance of propositional knowledge because I know *that* something is the case. Example B we can call "knowledge-how" since it is concerned with how to do things like speaking French or fixing cars. Example C we might dub "knowledge by acquaintance" since it implies that we are directly acquainted with something or someone. *In philosophy we are nearly exclusively concerned with propositional knowledge.* In order to practice your understanding of these different ways to use the word "know" decide whether the following sentences are instances of propositional knowledge, knowledge-how, or knowledge by acquaintance.

1. I know exactly how you feel about her death.
2. "2 + 2 = 4," I know that for a fact.
3. I used to know Peter very well but in recent times we have grown apart.
4. I am not afraid to cheat on my exams because I know how to cheat without getting caught.
5. If only I knew more about the Second World War.
6. My father used to be the smartest man. Now, he has Alzheimer's and he doesn't know anything anymore.
7. You might know everything that is in your accounting book, but this does not mean that you know anything about how to run an accounting firm.

Initially, you might wonder why it is necessary to develop a theory of knowledge at all. Can we not simply be satisfied with an argument if we believe that its premises are true? The answer here is a clear "No." Simply, believing that the premises of an argument are true does not suffice to show that the argument is sound. Human beings believe many things, and unfortunately many of these beliefs turn out to be false. According to a 1997 *Washington Post* survey, a majority of the U.S. population believes that space aliens have visited Earth. But the fact that so many people believe this does not make it true. If you have ever browsed a popular tabloid newspaper such as *The National Enquirer*, you know that many people eagerly read and believe stories that have very little to do with the truth.

Believing something is easy. There are no rules for what you can believe. If you are so inclined, you might believe that you are the reincarnation of Genghis Khan or that Elvis lives in the house next door. There is, however, no necessary connection between what people believe and the truth. Clearly, simply believing something to be true in no way establishes that it is.

FOOD FOR THOUGHT

Although you can believe whatever you want, some beliefs seem unreasonable and irrational. Take a look at the following beliefs and decide whether you consider them reasonable or irrational. Explain your response.

1. I believe that cats are more intelligent than humans.
2. I believe that the average Asian student is better in math than the average Caucasian student.
3. I believe that space aliens assassinated President Kennedy.
4. I believe that President Kennedy was assassinated by the Mob.
5. I believe that anybody who works hard will eventually become a millionaire.
6. I believe that ghosts exist.
7. I believe that men never landed on the moon and that all of the pictures and television footage is an elaborate fraud by NASA.
8. I believe that it is warmer in the summer than in the winter because during the summer the earth is closer to the sun than during the winter.
9. I believe that Christianity is the most important religion on Earth.
10. I believe that poor people are all lazy.
11. I believe that the United States is the greatest country in the world.

FOOD FOR THOUGHT

Some thinkers have argued that people who are very gullible commit a moral wrong. The philosopher W. K. Clifford (1845–1879) claimed that it is wrong always, everywhere, and for anyone, to believe anything upon insufficient evidence. He wrote:

If a man, holding a belief which he was taught in childhood or persuaded of afterwards, keeps down and pushes away any doubts which arise about it in his mind . . . and regards as impious those questions which cannot easily be asked without disturbing it—the life of that man is one long sin against mankind . . . !

Do you agree with Clifford that those people who believe too easily are committing a moral wrong?

In order to establish a link between belief and truth, we need to be selective about what beliefs we accept. Although many beliefs are far removed from the truth, others seem to have an appropriate connection to the way the world is. I see lightning in the sky and, as a result of this observation, start to believe that I will hear thunder in the near future. In this situation, I have good reasons to assume that my belief is true. When a belief is appropriately linked to the truth, the belief counts as **knowledge.** The central task of epistemology is to clarify under what conditions our beliefs can be considered to be instances of knowledge.

But what exactly is knowledge? We have already seen that knowledge is a certain type of belief. For example, right now you can say "I believe that I am reading a philosophy book." But it seems plausible that you could have said equally well, "I *know* that I am reading a philosophy book." This shows that some beliefs are instances of knowledge. But how can we find out that a belief is actually a case of knowledge? What features must beliefs have in order to count as knowledge?

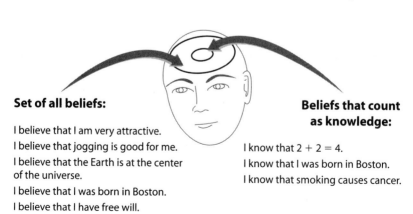

Set of all beliefs:

I believe that I am very attractive.
I believe that jogging is good for me.
I believe that the Earth is at the center of the universe.
I believe that I was born in Boston.
I believe that I have free will.

Beliefs that count as knowledge:

I know that $2 + 2 = 4$.
I know that I was born in Boston.
I know that smoking causes cancer.

It is apparent that we trust some of our beliefs more than others. My belief that I bought my car at the cheapest possible price is a relatively weak belief. Although the salesman guaranteed me that I received the deal of a lifetime and although I did some extensive price checking prior to buying it, I would not be surprised if the belief turns out to be false. If somebody were to ask me to bet on it, I would sensibly decline. There are, however, some beliefs I am willing to wager on. I believe, for example, that I am not going to be a millionaire by the end of this year. I believe this very strongly, and I am willing to bet on it. Since we hold some beliefs very dear to our hearts, we might suspect that the strength of a belief is the key to knowledge. If this were correct, we could say that we know something if we very strongly believe it to be true. Unfortunately, this is not a satisfactory definition of knowledge.

In order to illustrate the shortcomings of this definition, it is sufficient to consider the following example: Suppose you buy a lottery ticket and suppose that the chance of winning is 1:1,000,000. Given these odds, you probably believe very strongly that the ticket you bought is a dud. Nonetheless, would you feel justified in saying that you know that the ticket is a dud? Obviously not! It is only after the drawing, when you have compared the numbers on your ticket with the winning numbers, that you can claim to know that the ticket is a losing ticket. You did not know this all along, even if you believed it strongly all along; knowledge therefore is more than strong belief.

This lottery ticket example suggests a key insight: Truth is a fundamental component of knowledge. We can know something only if it is indeed true. Nobody can know, for instance, that $2 + 3 = 7$. You might believe it, if you happen to be very confused about numbers, but you cannot know it. Similarly, you can believe that Boston lies to the south of New York City, or that Los Angeles is located at the Atlantic Ocean, but you cannot know those things. Knowledge requires truth. We thus have found a necessary condition for knowledge: a belief that p can be an instance of knowledge only if p is true.

Still, it is apparent that the truth of a belief is not a sufficient condition for knowledge. Consider the fictional case of Mike, who participates in the quiz show *Who Wants to Be a Millionaire?* He is asked the name of the Greek city-state that defeated the Persians in the battle of Marathon. Mike has never studied Ancient Greek history, nor has he ever heard about the battle of Marathon. He nevertheless selects "Athens" as the right answer. In this situation, Mike had the belief that "Athens" is the right answer, and the belief actually turned out to be true, but it is clear that Mike did not know the answer. He was simply guessing. Correctly guessing is not the same thing as knowing.

Notice, however, how our impression of Mike would be different if he responded to the question as follows: "I'm certain that either Sparta or Athens defeated the Persians at the battle of Marathon, since these were the two dominant Greek military powers in the fifth century BCE. The Persians attacked from the East, but Sparta was located on the Peloponnese and hence a bit more in the West. It seems therefore more likely that the Athenians fought and defeated the Persians at the battle of Marathon, since Athens is located on the eastern shore." What Mike is doing here is providing a justification for his belief that Athens fought against the Persians at the battle of Marathon. If Mike can justify his belief, we naturally assume that he knows something about Ancient Greek history. This suggests that justification in addition to truth is the second crucial component of knowledge. Of course, at this point it is not quite clear how strong the justification must be before we can count a belief as knowledge. Mike's justification for his belief that Athens defeated the Persians at the battle of Marathon, for example, is not terribly impressive. We will see later on that different philosophers make different demands in this context. However, it is safe to say knowing that *p* requires some form of justification for why the belief that *p* is likely to be true.

Together, these three criteria put us in a position to formulate the classical, tripartite definition of knowledge. According to this definition, those who hold beliefs that are both true and justified can claim that they know. In short, **knowledge is true, justified belief.** This classical definition of knowledge has been around since Plato (ca. 428–ca. 347 BCE), who was the first philosopher to suggest it.

FOOD FOR THOUGHT

Practice your understanding of the classical definition of knowledge by deciding whether the following sentences, provided that they were uttered by you, are true or false. In order to determine

Continued

an answer, it is especially important to decide whether you could justify that the sentences are true.

1. I know that smoking causes cancer.
2. I know that I will get at least a B in this class.
3. I know that Santa Claus does not exist.
4. I know that God exists.
5. I know that water is H_2O.
6. I know that killing people is wrong.
7. I know that a triangle has three sides.
8. I know that dinosaurs have existed on Earth in the past.
9. I know that the earth moves around the sun.
10. I know that going to a classical concert is more enjoyable than eating a good meal.

FOOD FOR THOUGHT

Recently, some epistemologists have questioned whether the classical definition of knowledge is completely adequate; that is, whether the definition states indeed necessary and sufficient conditions for knowledge. There seem to exist situations, so-called Gettier Cases, in which true, justified beliefs do not amount to genuine knowledge. Can you think of such a situation?

Three Different Theories of Knowledge

The discussion in the last section has given us a better idea of what knowledge is, but we have yet to answer the most essential question in epistemology: What do we know? It would be ideal if we could answer this question once and for all, but the question is—as are all philosophical questions—an open one. That means there is more than one way in which we can answer it. The key objective is to develop a satisfactory theory of epistemic justification. We have seen that knowledge is true, justified belief. If we can clearly determine when and how our beliefs are justified, then we can also determine the scope and limit of our knowledge. Not surprisingly, different philosophers have developed different theories in response to this question. Our task is to explore what theory appears most reasonable. Roughly speaking, we can identify three major theories of knowledge: skepticism, empiricism, and rationalism. The three positions are illustrated in the following chart:

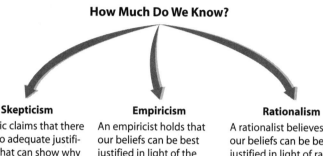

How Much Do We Know?

Skepticism	**Empiricism**	**Rationalism**
A skeptic claims that there exists no adequate justification that can show why our beliefs are true. We therefore know nothing. All we can have are beliefs but no knowledge.	An empiricist holds that our beliefs can be best justified in light of the evidence we receive from the senses. We therefore can know something if we can justify it with respect to what we see, hear, and feel about the world. According to empiricism, natural sciences like physics, chemistry, and biology produce the most reliable knowledge.	A rationalist believes that our beliefs can be best justified in light of rational evidence. We can know something if it appears true in the light of reason. According to rationalism, mathematics and logic provide the most reliable knowledge.

The chart is, of course, an oversimplification. In addition to skepticism, empiricism, and rationalism, alternate epistemological positions exist. It is nevertheless useful to start painting with a broad brush and discuss these three major epistemological theories first.

Skepticism

The Case for Skepticism

A skeptic is somebody who denies that we have genuine knowledge. According to the skeptic, we only have beliefs about the world, but none of these beliefs can count as knowledge. We can distinguish between two different forms of skepticism. On the one hand is "global skepticism." This is the position that no knowledge of any kind about any subject matter is possible. It is rare that somebody explicitly advocates global skepticism, since explicitly advocated global skepticism seems to undermine itself. Since a global skeptic claims that there is no knowledge whatsoever, we can conclude that he himself cannot know whether global skepticism is true or not. Later on, however, we will see how global skepticism can emerge in a more indirect and thus more threatening way.

FOOD FOR THOUGHT

A skillful global skeptic is difficult to defeat in conversation. The following conversation between Jack Gladney, a college professor, and his 14-year-old son Heinrich is described in the novel *White Noise* by Don DeLillo. Although Jack and Heinrich do not use the word "knowledge," it is clear that Jack wants to convince his son that he knows it is raining. Heinrich, on the other hand, wants to maintain a skeptical position. Do you think you could do better than Jack and convince Heinrich that it is indeed raining?

HEINRICH: "It is going to rain tonight."
JACK: "It's raining now."
HEINRICH: "The radio said tonight."
JACK: "Look at the windshield. Is that rain or isn't it?"
HEINRICH: "I am only telling you what they said."
JACK: "Just because it is on the radio doesn't mean we have to suspend belief in the evidence of our senses."
HEINRICH: "Our senses? Our senses are wrong a lot more often than they are right. This has been proved in the laboratory. Don't you know about all those theorems that say nothing is what it seems? There is no past, present, or future outside our mind. The so-called laws of motion are a big hoax. Even sound can trick the mind. Just because you don't hear a sound doesn't mean it's not out there. Dogs can hear it. Other animals. And I am sure there are sounds even dogs can't hear. But they exist in air, in waves. Maybe they never stop. High, high, high-pitched. Coming from somewhere."
JACK: "Is it raining or isn't it?"

HEINRICH: "I wouldn't want to have to say."

JACK: "What if someone held a gun to your head?"

Heinrich: "Who, you?"

JACK: "Someone. A man in a trench coat and smoky glasses. He holds a gun to your head and says, 'Is it raining or isn't it?, All you have to do is tell the truth and I'll put away my gun and take the next flight out of here.'"

Heinrich: "What truth does he want? Does he want the truth of someone traveling at almost the speed of light in another galaxy? Does he want the truth of someone in orbit around a neutron star? Maybe if these people could see us through a telescope we might look like we were two inches tall and it might be raining yesterday instead of today."

JACK: "He is holding the gun to your head. He wants your truth."

HEINRICH: "What good is my truth? My truth means nothing. What if this guy with the gun comes from a planet in a whole different solar system? What we call rain he calls soap. What we call apples he calls rain. So what am I supposed to tell him?"

JACK: "His name is Frank J. Smalley and he comes from St. Louis. He wants to know if it's raining now, at this very minute?"

HEINRICH: "Is there such a thing as now? 'Now' comes and goes as soon as you say it. How can I say it's raining now if your so-called 'now' becomes 'then' as soon as I say it?"

The more attractive form of skepticism we can dub "local skepticism." It is more limited in scope than global skepticism and focuses on particular fields of knowledge or particular methods of justification. A local skeptic will say that we cannot have knowledge about certain subjects (God, for example) or that certain ways of acquiring beliefs (such as reading fortune cookies) can never produce knowledge. Clearly, we are all local skeptics with respect to some ways of acquiring beliefs. I am, for example, a skeptic about psychic hotlines. If you were to tell me that you broke up with your partner because a psychic informed you that your partner was seeing someone else, I would think you extremely gullible. Your belief that your partner was unfaithful seems completely unjustified. You certainly would be wrong to claim that you knew it on the basis of that telephone call. Similarly, I am also a skeptic about astrology and alternative medicine, although a fair number of people put great faith in horoscopes and herbal treatments.

A local skeptic seeks to establish that a particular type of justification does not link our beliefs to the truth. For example, if you claim to know that you will spend a dream vacation with your partner because the moon is in Sagittarius, a skeptic about astrology would question the validity of your belief justification. How in the world, the skeptic would ask, is the position of the moon related to your vacation and your relationship? Unless there is some plausible connection, the skeptic seems in a strong position to reject all astrological belief justifications. You can, of course, hold on to your belief that the position of the moon has an effect on your vacation, but the skeptic has shown that this belief does not amount to knowledge. It seems epistemically irresponsible to modify one's beliefs about one's relationship in the light of one's beliefs about the position of the moon.

Although most people agree that astrology and psychic hotlines are not reliable ways to acquire true beliefs, the question arises whether we can trust any other methods of acquiring beliefs. I acquire, for example, a fair amount of my beliefs about politics from watching Peter Jennings on the evening news. But are the beliefs I acquire from listening to Peter Jennings so much more reliable than the beliefs I acquire from the psychic hotline? Sure, the psychic hotline is often wrong, but isn't Peter Jennings as well? This is actually the sneaky way in which global skepticism can make its stand. If it turns out that local skepticism is plausible with respect to all subject areas and all ways of acquiring and justifying beliefs, then local skepticism has suddenly turned into global skepticism. In the remaining part of this chapter, we will investigate whether such skepticism can and should be avoided.

FOOD FOR THOUGHT

How skeptical are you? Take a look at the following list of fields of "knowledge" and determine whether you are a local skeptic with respect to these fields. Justify your answer.

1. Tarot reading.
2. Psychotherapy (understood as a way to acquire beliefs about your present state of mind as a result of your experiences in early childhood).
3. Handwriting analysis as a means to analyze your personality and character.
4. Lie detectors.
5. Astrology.
6. Religious knowledge.
7. Alternative medicines.
8. Aesthetics.
9. Moral knowledge
10. Acupuncture.
11. Watching television news as a way to acquire beliefs about the world.

Descartes' Quest for Certainty

The French philosopher René Descartes (1596–1650) was the first modern philosopher who addressed the question whether we can prevent skepticism from undermining all and every claim to knowledge. Just as we do now, Descartes lived during confusing times. The 17th century was a period of change in Europe. The Reformation had weakened the credibility of religious authorities. New scientific thinking was challenging traditional ways of thinking about physics and the universe. In short, the 17th century produced a hodgepodge of competing beliefs about God and the universe. But which of these beliefs were worthy of being called knowledge, Descartes asked.

To find an answer to this question, Descartes followed an original strategy. According to him, we cannot trust any of our beliefs as long as there is any chance that they might be mistaken. He writes in this context: ". . . I ought no less carefully to withhold my assent from matters which are not entirely certain and indubitable than from those which appear to me manifestly to be false. . . ."[1] Through doubting and examining all of his beliefs, Descartes attempts to distill those beliefs that are certain and indubitable. These certain and indubitable beliefs truly deserve to be considered knowledge. This method of distinguishing mere belief from knowledge is often called **Descartes' method of doubt.**

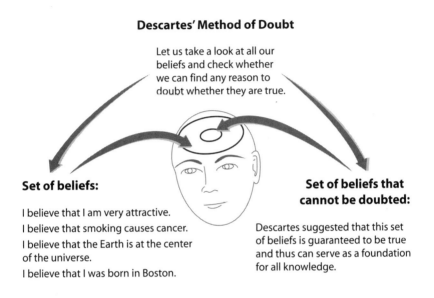

Descartes' Method of Doubt

Let us take a look at all our beliefs and check whether we can find any reason to doubt whether they are true.

Set of beliefs:

I believe that I am very attractive.
I believe that smoking causes cancer.
I believe that the Earth is at the center of the universe.
I believe that I was born in Boston.

Set of beliefs that cannot be doubted:

Descartes suggested that this set of beliefs is guaranteed to be true and thus can serve as a foundation for all knowledge.

FOOD FOR THOUGHT

Descartes suggests that a belief cannot be considered to be an instance of knowledge if it is possible to doubt that the belief is true. In order to develop an impression of how this method of doubt works, let us consider the following beliefs. Try to determine whether these beliefs can be doubted.

1. I will live at least until the year 2020.
2. I will pass this class.
3. The parents who raised me are indeed my biological parents.
4. I am more intelligent than the average American citizen.
5. Snow is white.
6. $2 + 2 = 4$
7. I am right now reading a philosophy book.

To respond to the threat of skepticism, let us follow this Cartesian method of doubt. Are there then beliefs that we cannot doubt to be true? In day-to-day life, most people do not doubt that what they see is true. When I walk across the street and see a truck approaching, I have little reason to doubt that the truck is really bearing down on me. I trust my senses and get out of the way of the truck. But are our perceptual beliefs, that is, those beliefs that are formed on the basis of perception, indubitable and certain? Descartes said no.

To show that it is possible to doubt what our senses tell us, Descartes presented a series of skeptical arguments. One of them is the famous dream argument. The argument can be presented in standard form as follows:

1. If it is possible that I am dreaming right now, then I have reasons to doubt whether my current perceptual beliefs are true.
2. It is possible that I am dreaming right now.

Therefore: I have reasons to doubt whether my current perceptual beliefs are true (i.e., my perceptual beliefs are not indubitable and certain).

Beginning students often misunderstand Descartes' dream argument. The point of the argument is not to show that one is dreaming or that life can be a dream. The point of the argument is simply to show that our current perceptual beliefs (the beliefs that are based on what I see, feel, and hear right now) are not indubitable and absolutely certain. The argument is an instance of the argument form *modus ponens*, which we discussed in Chapter 1. The argument is therefore valid. We thus need to turn our attention to the question whether the argument is sound. Are the premises of the argument true? The first premise appears very reasonable. For instance, at this very moment it seems to me that I am sitting in front of a computer. I am hearing the little humming noise of the ventilator and I see the cursor blinking. However, if it is possible that these experiences are part of a vivid dream, then I have reasons to doubt whether I am indeed sitting in front of a computer. For if it should be the case that I am really dreaming at this very moment, then I am probably lying in bed and there is no computer in front of me. So, premise 1 seems true. If it is possible that I am dreaming, then I have reasons to doubt whether my current perceptual beliefs are true. What about the second premise? Is it really possible that I am dreaming at this very moment? I feel very awake. I see my fingers moving across the keyboard. I remember waking up this morning and having breakfast. But does any of this make it certain that I am awake? Descartes denies this. He supports his claim with the following line of reasoning:

1. It is impossible to distinguish with certainty between dream experiences and waking experiences.
2. If it is impossible to distinguish with certainty between dream experiences and waking experiences, then I cannot know whether I am awake right now.
3. If I cannot know that I am awake right now, then it is possible that I am dreaming right now.

Therefore: It is possible that I am dreaming right now.

The argument is a combination of the valid argument forms *modus ponens* and *hypothetical syllogism*. The argument is therefore valid. Premises 2 and 3 are very plausible. The key premise is premise 1. Might this premise be false? Might it be possible to distinguish with certainty between waking experiences and dream experiences? Sure, sometimes when I am dreaming I am aware that my experiences are part of a dream. However, this is not always the case. Some dreams are so vivid that I am convinced that my dream experiences are real. How then can I tell with certainty that my current perceptual experiences are not dream experiences? Any experience that I have right now I can, at least in principle, also experience while I am dreaming. It follows therefore that I cannot eliminate the possibility that I am right now dreaming completely. Although my belief that I am right now awake is a strong one (i.e., I would be willing to bet a good deal of money on it), I have to acknowledge that the belief is not absolutely certain to be true. There remains the genuine possibility that my current experiences are actually part of an amazingly realistic dream.

FOOD FOR THOUGHT

Initially, most beginning students find the dream argument weak, for they are certain they can show they are awake. Take a look at some of the following attempts to defeat the dream argument and decide whether they are successful.

1. I always dream in black and white. I never dream in color. However, right now I am having color experiences (i.e., I see a red pen in front of me). This means that I must be awake and not dreaming.

2. Whenever I dream, I can tell that I am dreaming because I actively influence what happens in my dreams. I have learned this from a dream master in China. But I do not influence and shape what is happening right now. Therefore, I am not dreaming right now.

3. I have never been bored in any of my dreams. As a matter of fact my dreams are pretty exciting and are full of monsters and women who look like Angelina Jolie. Right now, however, I am experiencing incredible boredom while I appear to be sitting in this philosophy class. I must be awake.

It is easy to see that the essential idea behind the dream argument can be presented in a variety of ways. Descartes, for example, considered not only the possibility that we might be dreaming, but also the possibility that there might exist a devious and powerful demon who uses all his powers to deceive us. Descartes called such a being "evil genius" and argued that we couldn't be certain that such a being does not exist. In recent times, philosophers have presented Descartes' skeptical worries as the scenario that any of us might simply be a brain in a vat. Imagine a brain suspended in a liquid and wired to a computer. The computer feeds the brain all the current experiences you are having right now. If you were such a brain, nothing in your experience would reveal that you are actually a brain in a vat. You would believe, for example, "I am a six foot tall, brown-haired dude from California who is reading a philosophy book," but the belief, together with all your other perceptual beliefs, would be false. These skeptical arguments even find their way into popular movies. The movie *The Matrix*, for example, is constructed around the idea that we only appear to be living in a "normal" world. In reality, we are lying in bathtubs wired to the Matrix while machines harvest our energy.

FOOD FOR THOUGHT

We have seen that there are a variety of arguments in defense of Cartesian skepticism: the dream argument, the evil-genius argument, the brain-in-a-vat argument, the matrix argument. Although all these arguments are similar to each other, some of them establish a more fundamental form of skepticism than others. Compare the dream argument with the brain-in-a-vat argument. Which of the arguments presents a stronger version of skepticism?

It is important not to lose sight of the point of these skeptical arguments. Descartes tried to find beliefs that are indubitable and certain. These skeptical arguments are designed to show that there are no such beliefs. Every belief seems to be subject to doubt. How can we respond to this challenge? Three answers seem possible. First, we can simply accept global skepticism. If knowledge requires that we have to be certain that our beliefs are true, then we have to conclude in the light of these skeptical arguments that knowledge does not exist.

Second, we can follow Descartes and try to find certainty in spite of these arguments. This might seem impossible, but Descartes suggested an ingenious argument. Assume that the worst-case scenario is true and that we are brains in vats or deceived by an evil genius. Even in this situation, we can **know** that we doubt whether our beliefs are correct. Doubting is a form of thinking, and thinking requires a thinker. Thus Descartes concluded: ". . . after having reflected well and carefully examined all things, we must come to the definite conclusion that this proposition: I am, I exist, is necessarily true each time that I pronounce it."[2] This is Descartes' famous "I think, therefore I am" argument. It is an interesting argument. Even in the light of the most fundamental skepticism, I can know that I exist as long as I think.

FOOD FOR THOUGHT

Descartes' "cogito-argument" is much more complex than it appears at first glance. Descartes seems to assert that as long as he thinks he can know with absolute certainty that the sentence "I think" is true and that one can conclude from this that the sentence "I exist" must be true as well. Here is what Bertrand Russell (1872-1970) had to say about this argument in chapter two of his book *The Problems of Philosophy*.

> But some care is needed in using Descartes' argument. "I think, therefore I am" says rather more than is strictly certain. It might seem as though we were quite sure of being the same person today as we were yesterday, and this is no doubt true in some sense. But the real Self is as hard to arrive at the real table, and does not seem to have that absolute, convincing certainty that belongs to particular experiences. When I look at my table and see a certain brown color what is quite certain at once is not "I am seeing a brown color," but rather, "a brown color is being seen." This of course involves something (or somebody) which (or who) sees the brown color, but it does not of itself involve that more or less permanent person whom we call "I." So far as immediate certainty goes, it might be that the something which sees the brown color is quite momentary, and not the same as the something which has some different experience the next moment."

Decide whether you agree with Russell's criticism.

Even if we accept Descartes' claim that I can know that I exist as long as I think, the resulting view of what little we know is somewhat discouraging. Very few things are as certain as my belief that I exist. Ultimately, Descartes' project (although Descartes himself disagrees here) seems to lead to a philosophical position called "solipsism." Solipsism asserts that we can only know the contents of our own minds. This is a rather lonely view of the world. If solipsism is correct, it becomes very doubtful whether we can know that there is an external world, or whether there are other people with minds like us. But it surely seems as if we do know that there are trees, cars, and other people in the world besides us. It is therefore tempting to look for an alternative to Descartes' epistemic project.

The third, and by my lights, most attractive response to Cartesian skepticism, is to modify our demands for epistemic justification. As we have seen, Descartes insists that we can only know something if we can be *certain* that the belief in question is true. In short, Descartes requires epistemic justification to be infallible. That is perhaps too high a standard for justification. It might be quite reasonable to say that we are justified to believe that *p* even if there is a chance that the justification for why *p* is true is later on defeated by additional considerations. For example: Suppose that it is Saturday night and that you are watching *Saturday Night Live*. The actors on the show utter several times that the show is broadcast live from New York. In this situation it seems plausible to say that you are justified to believe that you are watching a live broadcast. Later, however, as you watch the credits for the show, you find out that the show was actually a recording. Although your reasons for thinking that the show is a live broadcast were later defeated, you had *prima facie* reasons for thinking that the show was a live broadcast. The term *prima facie* is Latin for "at first sight" and refers to evidence that is immediately available.

· It is tempting to construct a viable theory of epistemic justification on the basis of prima facie justification. To illustrate how such a theory might look, let us consider the *Saturday Night Live* example one more time. Suppose you are in the same situation as before. You watch *Saturday Night Live* on a Saturday evening and hear the actors announce that the show is a live broadcast. Suppose further that it is indeed a live broadcast. In this scenario you had prima facie reasons for thinking that the show is a live broadcast, and these prima facie reasons are not defeated by other evidence later. It is tempting to think that prima facie justification that goes undefeated might be sufficient for knowledge. Such undefeated, prima facie justification is obviously neither certain nor infallible, but it might nevertheless be the kind of justification we are looking for.

However, the danger we face is that such justification might permit too many weakly justified beliefs to count as knowledge. To determine whether there is room for a plausible, prima facie version of justification that is strong enough to lead to knowledge, we will have to take a closer look at two of the most attractive sources of prima facie justification for belief: experience and reason. We will start our discussion by investigating the most common theory of knowledge, empiricism.

Empiricism

Empiricism is a very plausible and intuitive theory of knowledge. It is closely associated with the British philosophers John Locke (1632–1704), George Berkeley (1685–1753), and David Hume (1711–1776). An empiricist maintains that we can know something if we can justify it with respect to what we see, hear, smell, touch, or taste. Let us call beliefs that are directly derived from our experiences basic empirical beliefs. For instance, my seeing a red telephone triggers in me the belief that there is a red telephone in front of me. This belief is a basic empirical belief since it is a direct result of having certain specific experiences. What an empiricist maintains is that basic empirical beliefs are justified beliefs and count as evidence.

The precise way in which basic empirical beliefs are justified is, however, a matter of philosophical controversy. We will see in a later section that an empiricist faces some tough questions in this context. Setting aside possible difficulties, let us agree with the empiricist that basic empirical beliefs are justified and count as evidence. The next step in the empiricist program is to insist that inferential beliefs, that is, beliefs that are about what is not directly observable, must be justified with the help of basic empirical beliefs. For example, the belief that dinosaurs once roamed the earth is not a basic empirical belief. I cannot see, touch, and feel any dinosaurs in my backyard or in a zoo. It is, however, possible to justify this belief in the light of what I can see right now, namely bones and other archeological remains (e.g., preserved footprints). It follows, therefore, that an empiricist would consider the inferential belief that there was a time when dinosaurs roamed the earth as justified in light of available empirical evidence.

An empiricist insists that all such inferential claims must (if they are to count as knowledge) be justified with respect to empirical evidence. Empiricists are therefore skeptical about any beliefs that cannot be confirmed or falsified with the help of empirical evidence. For example, the claim that "All men are created equal" is not linked in any obvious way to empirical observations. An empiricist will therefore conclude that we can believe this, but that we cannot know this to be so. Similarly, an empiricist will be skeptical about a claim like "God wrote the Bible," for it is hard to see how that belief can be justified in terms of basic empirical beliefs. In general, many empiricists are skeptical about claims of moral and religious knowledge.

FOOD FOR THOUGHT

Suppose that you are an empiricist. Which of the following beliefs would you consider to be part of our knowledge, and which of these beliefs would you dismiss as speculation? Explain your answers.

1. Smoking causes cancer.
2. If the United States had not used the atomic bomb, Japan would not have surrendered and many more people would have died in the subsequent fighting than died in the bombings of Hiroshima and Nagasaki.
3. Each year thousands of species go extinct.
4. The universe is more than five billion years old.
5. Something must have caused the Big Bang.
6. Taking Prozac has no harmful side effects.
7. There are many people who can predict the future.
8. O.J. Simpson killed Nichole Simpson.
9. There exists another universe parallel to our universe.

There is something sobering and appealing about empiricism. An empiricist will not quickly jump to grand conclusions. An empiricist will carefully consider the empirical evidence and see what conclusions are plausible in the light of that evidence. If the evidence is insufficient to support any final conclusions, an empiricist will withhold judgment.

The Case for Empiricism

Several arguments suggest that empiricism is the most promising epistemic theory. First, empiricists justify all knowledge in relation to basic empirical beliefs. This is attractive since basic empirical beliefs seem indeed more reliable than other beliefs. I might not know whether the stock market crash of 1929 was the main cause of the Great Depression, but I surely do seem to know how the world around me feels, sounds, and looks. There are, of course, situations in which my senses are off target and misleading, but overall they seem to paint a pretty accurate picture of how the world is. Keep in mind that we do not have to insist—as Descartes did—that justification is infallible.

Moreover, basic empirical beliefs seem directly linked to how the world around us really is. When I see a desk in front of me, something like the following seems to be happening: Light reflects off the desk into my eyes and causes cells in the retina of my eye to stimulate my optic nerves. The optic nerves in turn transmit information to my brain, where the visual information is processed. The details of this process are complicated, but it seems plausible to assume that we receive information through this process that produces reliable information *about* the desk. We do not "invent" what we see, feel, or hear. There is something objective about beliefs formed on the basis of empirical evidence. They are (for the most part) independent of other beliefs and directly related to how the world is.

Finally, empiricism is strongly supported by the success of the natural sciences. Physics, chemistry, and biology have made tremendous progress during the last 300 years and seem to have increased our knowledge of the world. Careful observations are an essential part of the scientific method. The success of natural science supports the conclusion that our knowledge ultimately rests on empirical evidence, and thus supports an empiricist perspective in epistemology.

Although empiricism is a very attractive theory of knowledge, it leads to a number of fundamental problems. Discussing some of these problems will help us determine whether empiricism is the most attractive theory of knowledge.

Problems with Perception

We have seen that an empiricist derives knowledge from basic empirical beliefs. It follows therefore that an empiricist needs to explain how we arrive at these basic empirical beliefs and why we are justified to believe that these basic empirical beliefs are likely to be true. In order to provide such an explanation, an empiricist has to say something about how we perceive the world. Roughly speaking, an empiricist wants to say that when we perceive a red car, then we are justified to believe that there is indeed a red car out there. So an empiricist needs to establish some version of the following principle:

> Whenever we perceive an object *P* (for instance a car) to have a property *A* (e.g., red) then we are justified to believe that object *P* (the car) has indeed property *A* (red).

Let us call this principle the principle of **perceptual realism.** Unfortunately, this principle is not obviously true. To understand why there is controversy about perceptual realism, it is helpful to distinguish between three different theories of perception: naive realism, indirect realism, and idealism.

Different Theories of Perception

Naive Realism

A naive realist believes that the world is *exactly* as we perceive it to be. So, when we see a square piece of wood, then there is indeed a square piece of wood out there. The naive realist believes that all the properties we perceive an object to have, the object indeed has.

Indirect Realism

An indirect realist holds that not all the properties we perceive an object to have are indeed in the object. For example, most indirect realists do not believe that physical objects truly have colors although we perceive them to have color properties. According to indirect realism, the world is ultimately a bit different than we perceive it to be, but it is nevertheless closely related to our perception.

Idealism

An idealist abandons the idea that there are "real" material objects "behind" our perceptions. An ordinary object like a table, for instance, is not a mind-independent thing but a collection of perceptions.

Among the three theories of perception, naive realism provides the best support for empiricism. If we can trust that the world outside our minds is exactly as we perceive it to be, then empiricism is by far the most promising way to gain knowledge about this world. On the other hand, naive realism is difficult to defend. First, we cannot deny that we sometimes make perceptual mistakes. It can appear to us that there is a lake in the desert, but in reality there is none. It is not easy to imagine what a naive realist is going to say about these mistakes if he is absolutely committed to the principle that the world is exactly how it appears to us.[3] Second—and more important—there are excellent reasons for thinking that certain properties like color, heat, smell, and taste are mind-dependent properties. Consider the following situation: a person stands in front of three buckets of water. The bucket to the left is full of hot water, the one to the right full of cold water, and the one in the middle full of tepid water. The person is now asked to put one arm in the bucket with cold water and the other one in the bucket of hot water. The situation is depicted in the following diagram:

After several minutes the person is asked to put both hands in the bucket with tepid water. What will happen? It seems plausible that the person will report the following: "To my right hand the water in the middle feels cold, to my left hand the water feels warm." But this spells trouble for the naive realist. If it is possible that we perceive the same body of water at the same time as being both warm and cold, then we cannot maintain any longer that the world is exactly as we perceive it to be. For one and the same body of water cannot be both hot and cold at the same time.

Empiricists like John Locke were very much aware of this difficulty. Locke thus rejected naive realism and suggested instead that we distinguish between two kinds of properties: primary properties and secondary properties. According to Locke, some properties that we perceive objects to possess are not really "in" the objects. A good example is color perception. If you ever looked at the ocean, you might recall that the color of the ocean changes constantly. At times the ocean looks blue, then gray, and on other days it looks emerald green. So what color does the water in the ocean really have? According to John Locke, the ocean has no color. Color is created when we look at the ocean. So color is a secondary property. It is a property that we perceive the ocean to have, but which the ocean in itself does not have. Locke suggested that taste, smell, and heat are further secondary properties that our minds "create" but which are not truly in the objects of the physical world.

But not all properties are secondary properties. Locke suggested that properties like size, shape, molecular texture, and motion are primary properties, that is, when I perceive an object to be 6 feet long then it is indeed 6 feet long. The size of a physical object is not created by my mind; its length is something the object really has.

FOOD FOR THOUGHT

In day-to-day life we define and identify salt probably in the following way: salt is the stuff that tastes salty. Now, this definition is problematic. For one, it seems circular, but secondly the definition attributes to salt something (namely a certain taste) that according to Locke is not *in* the salt at all. Remember that taste is a secondary quality. Locke would prefer a definition of salt that only makes reference to primary qualities of salt. What would such a definition look like?

The distinction between primary and secondary properties leads to the idea of **indirect realism**. According to this theory of perception, the world around us is not exactly as it appears to be. The world, as it exists independent of our perception, has neither color, nor smell, nor taste. It consists in extended, little, microscopic objects that possess only primary properties, namely size, shape, and motion. Since indirect realism can escape the objections that were raised against naive realism, it seems to be a more plausible theory. Moreover, it is also well compatible with the view that the universe ultimately exists of small physical particles and collections of these particles. This metaphysical view was held by John Locke, and is sometimes referred to as *corpuscularianism.* However, indirect realism makes empiricism a bit more complicated. For if indirect realism is true, we cannot simply know that the world is as we perceive it to be. Indirect realism thus requires that we distinguish between how the world appears and how the world really is. The world as it appears to our senses has both primary and secondary properties. But the real world supposedly only has primary properties. This distinction leads to epistemic difficulties. An empiricist holds that we can know something if we can perceive it. But indirect realism removes the real world from our direct perceptual reach. We cannot perceive a world without color, taste, and smell. An empiricist who accepts indirect realism must admit therefore that we cannot know the real world directly through our experiences. The best we can hope for is that we can infer that such a world exists. But such inferences cannot easily be justified in the light of our experiences. This opens the possibility that pure empiricism might lead to a form of skepticism.

George Berkeley pointed to a second, more serious, problem for indirect realism. The distinction between primary and secondary properties is not clear cut. We have seen that Locke argued that color is a secondary property since the color of an object depends on how one looks at the object, that is, the same table might look blue from one perspective and gray from another. Berkeley pointed out—correctly, as it seems—that the very same can be said about primary properties as well. For instance, shape is a primary property, but it is possible that a round tire looks round from one perspective and elliptical from another. What then is the real shape of the tire? An analogous thing can be said for motion, which supposedly is also a primary property of objects. Whether or not we perceive something to be in motion depends fundamentally on the perspective of the observer. The danger is that all properties of physical objects might turn out to be somewhat mind dependent. Berkeley concluded from this that we should abandon the distinction between primary and secondary qualities and instead admit that the world ultimately depends on our minds. But if we have to give up on the distinction between primary and secondary properties, then we have to abandon the theory of indirect realism as well.

Berkeley, a committed empiricist, was happy to draw this conclusion. He suggested instead that physical objects like cars, telephone poles, or toothbrushes are ultimately nothing but perceptions. The famous phrase here is "Esse est Percipi," which is Latin for "To be is to be perceived."

FOOD FOR THOUGHT

Most people have heard the question, "If a tree falls in the forest and there is nobody around to hear the fall, does it make a sound?" This question strikes us at first to be a bit silly. But this sort of question was raised by Berkeley, and we can now see why he thought it was an important question. Berkeley wants to show that things (in this case the sound of the falling tree) need a perceiver to exist. Do you agree with him on this point? Suppose you put on a CD and push the "play" button. You then leave the room before the CD starts playing. Suppose further that nobody else is in the room. Will there then be music in the room?

Berkeley's position is known as **idealism.** Berkeley's idealism is compatible with empiricism. For if we say that physical objects are ultimately perceptions, then we can be sure that we can know objects through perceptual experiences. However, idealism seems awfully counterintuitive. Who in the world would think that physical objects like tables and chairs are ultimately only perceptions? We have a strong inclination to think that physical objects are made out of matter that can exist independently of being perceived. Of course, the fact that a philosophical theory goes against the grain of common sense is not necessarily a serious flaw. However, all things being equal, it is always preferable to adopt a theory that squares well with our common-sense view of the world.

The more serious weakness in Berkeley's idealism is that it seems to make it very difficult to distinguish between true and false perceptual beliefs. In certain situations, we are prone to experience perceptual illusions. For example, when we walk through the desert we might experience a mirage and see water in the distance, although in reality there is only hot desert sand. If we believe in the existence of a mind-independent physical world, we can explain these situations as follows: Our perceptual belief that there is water in the distance is false, because our perception was not caused by water but by the hot air above the desert sand. This explanation requires us to think about the hot air above the desert sand as a mind-independent physical object, since only mind-independent physical objects can play the appropriate causal role. We have seen, however, that Berkeley's idealism denies that there are mind-independent physical objects. According to his analysis, physical objects are ultimately perceptions. So, Berkeley cannot explain the mirage in the same way we just did. At this point, an idealist has two options: either admit that perceptual beliefs can never be false, or else revise the ordinary account of how perceptual beliefs can be false. The first option does not seem very attractive, and the second option suggests that idealism is philosophically rather complex. According to Ockham's Razor, we have reasons to prefer a simpler explanation to a more complicated one. Berkeley's idealism is a logically possible scenario, but it does not offer the simplest explanation of how perceptual beliefs can be mistaken. We thus have reasons to be very hesitant before we embrace any form of idealism.

Let us quickly summarize the main conclusions of this discussion of perception. We have seen that empiricism stands in need of some theory of perception that supports the principle that if we perceive an object P to have a property A then we are indeed justified to believe that an object P has property A. This principle is best supported by naive realism. But naive realism seems, on closer scrutiny, to give way to indirect realism about perception. Indirect realism in turn seems to lead to skepticism or to collapse into idealism. And if we combine, as Berkley did, idealism with empiricism we seem to be in conflict with the principle of Ockham's Razor. None of this is fatal for empiricism, but it shows that an empiricist has to do serious philosophical work before he can confidently assert that our knowledge of the world goes hand in hand with our experiences of the world.

The Problem of Induction

The second major problem for empiricism stems from the fact that our experiences of the world can only confirm or disconfirm particular facts, but not general and universal claims. If we want to know, for example, whether a particular sunflower is yellow, we can simply look at that particular sunflower. However, if we want to know whether all sunflowers are yellow, we cannot directly determine that by looking at a couple of sunflowers. The empiricist needs a procedure to move from knowledge of a particular set of objects, to knowledge of universal and general relationships. Such a procedure that moves from our knowledge of particular instances to knowledge of universal claims is called *induction.* We encountered this term in Chapter 1, when we discussed enumerative inductive arguments. The difficulty for the empiricist is to explain how and why we can know on the basis of experience alone that enumerative inductive arguments (or inferences) are justified. The philosopher David Hume was the first to draw attention to this difficulty.

At first glance, you might wonder whether empiricists cannot simply give up on induction altogether, and resign themselves to the fact that we can only know particular facts but not universal claims. The difficulty with this move is that empiricism is supposed to underlie and explain the success of the empirical sciences. Scientific knowledge, however, is centered on general laws like Newton's three laws of motion, and laws are good examples of universal claims. So, if empiricism is supposed to explain how scientists can know that there exist lawlike relationships in the physical world, then empiricists need to explain how inductive inferences can expand our knowledge. This is, as we will see, far from trivial.

Let us consider a relatively straightforward example. Suppose that Peter is a biologist who has spent a good deal of his time observing the habits of loggerhead turtles. He observed, for instance, that the same loggerhead turtles come to the same beach to lay their eggs every 2 years. After observing this again and again at very different beaches and with respect to a large sample of different loggerhead turtles, Peter infers that loggerhead turtles lay eggs every 2 years. The enumerative inductive argument in defense of his claim looks as follows:

1. All loggerhead turtles that I have observed during the last 20 years have laid eggs every 2 years.

Therefore: All loggerhead turtles lay eggs every 2 years.

This enumerative inductive argument poses an epistemic problem for the empiricist. How can an empiricist *know* that all loggerhead turtles (past and future) lay eggs every 2 years based on his observation that many loggerhead turtles have done this in the past? Notice that it is certainly logically possible that loggerhead turtles will suddenly change their egg-laying habits. How can Peter *know* that this will not happen? If all of Peter's knowledge stems from his experiences, then he cannot know what loggerhead turtles will do in the future. However, if Peter is a well-trained scientist, he will probably appeal at this point to the principle of the *uniformity of nature*. The principle says that if we observe certain lawlike relationships in the past, then we can also know that they will occur in the future. According to this principle, nature is uniform; nature does not suddenly change its course.

If Peter could know that nature is uniform, then it is also clear how Peter can know that loggerhead turtles will not suddenly change their egg-laying habits. The problem, however, is that if Peter is an empiricist, he cannot directly know that the principle of the uniformity of nature is true. This is, after all, not something that he can observe directly. The only way an empiricist can know that the principle of the uniformity of nature is true is by some form of induction. But now we have come full circle. We tried to justify our confidence in inductive procedures by appealing to the uniformity of nature. But in order to show that the principle of the uniformity of nature is true, we need to presuppose that inductive procedures are reliable.

Again, this might not be a fatal problem for empiricism, but it shows one more time that committed empiricists have philosophical work to do before they can claim that we can know scientific laws solely on the basis of experiences. A potentially elegant solution to the problem of induction is to claim that we can know the uniformity of nature not on the basis of experience, but rather with the help of reason. This would show, however, that in addition to experience, human knowledge needs a second leg to stand on: namely, reason. Philosophers who claim that our knowledge depends predominantly on reason rather than experience are called **rationalists**. We explore this epistemic theory in the next section.

Rationalism

Rationalism, the third major epistemic theory, is not immediately as plausible as empiricism. But there are some crucial similarities between these two major theories of knowledge. An empiricist believes that our knowledge is ultimately based on basic empirical beliefs. Rationalism is similar in that rationalists also hold that our knowledge is based on basic beliefs. The difference is that rationalists do not justify basic beliefs with the help of experience, but rather with the help of pure reason. This might sound a bit strange. What in the world is "pure reason" supposed to be and how is it supposed to lead us to knowledge? An example might help to illustrate the basic thrust of rationalism.

Suppose David, a skeptical friend of yours, asks: "What do you think? Is 200763 the largest natural number?" You answer: "No, 200763 is not the largest natural number. As a matter of fact there is no largest natural number. For any natural number you can name, there is always a larger one." Suppose David is not impressed by your answer. He inquires: "How in the world can you know these kinds of things? Have you looked at all natural numbers? I have a feeling that you do not really know this, but that you simply make these claims up."

Two things seem fairly obvious at this point: First, we do indeed seem to know that there is no largest natural number, and second, we do not know this on the basis of experience. Consider how silly it would sound if one were to say, "I know that the number 3 is odd since I saw it yesterday on my way to work and it indeed looked as odd as usual." Numbers are not the kind of things we can see, feel, and touch. So if we have knowledge about them, that knowledge cannot be based on experience, but rather on our ability to think (i.e., reason).

What rationalists claim is that when we think about certain propositions, we can immediately understand and grasp that the propositions must be true. For example, we can immediately grasp that the number 3 is larger than the number 2, or that any two people either know each other or they do not, or that nothing can be green and red all over at the same time. A rationalist claims that these propositions have something self-evident about them. Simple reflection suffices to show that we are justified to believe that these propositions are likely to be true.

FOOD FOR THOUGHT

Take a look at the following propositions and decide whether you know that they are true or false simply by reflecting on what they assert.

1. If one multiplies any natural number by 2 then the resulting number is even.
2. The income of the average worker in the United States is higher than the income of the average worker in Europe.
3. Every state must have some form of government.
4. Every event has a cause.
5. If any nation should ever use nuclear weapons again, then millions of people will die.

6. Every recession in the economy is eventually followed by an economic recovery.
7. If a person freely performs an action, then the person can be held responsible for the action.
8. Sugar is sweet.
9. All human beings have the same fundamental rights.
10. All cats are animals.

It is useful to introduce some technical terminology that is frequently used when philosophers discuss rationalism. The kind of justification that is crucial for rationalists is called *a priori* justification. "A priori" is a Latin phrase that literally means "from the former." The words "a priori" are used to refer to a justification that can take place prior to consulting any empirical evidence. So I can know something a priori if I can know it without first seeing, touching, or hearing anything in particular. It is, for example, possible to know a priori that all red cars are colored cars since I do not have to look at any cars to determine that the claim is true. I can also know a priori that every triangle has three sides for I do not have to see or touch any *particular* triangle in order to know that the claim is true. Students are frequently confused at this point. They often say the following: "How can you know that all triangles have three sides without having experiences? In order to know something about triangles, one surely must have seen some triangles. So it seems false to say that I know a priori that all triangles have three sides." The difficulty here is to understand that a priori does not mean justification without reference to any experiences, but rather justification without reference to any particular experience. In order to know that tigers are animals, I might have to see some tigers or pictures of tigers to acquire the concept of what a tiger is. However, it is not necessary to see any particular tiger. It is therefore correct to say that I can know a priori that tigers are animals, since I do not need to refer to any particular and specific experience of tigers. Any experience that allows me to acquire the concept of a tiger is sufficient to allow me to know that tigers are animals. On the other hand, I cannot know a priori whether my neighbor has a ferocious tiger in her basement. For in order to know that I need to inspect the basement of my neighbor (i.e., I need to have a particular experience).

A priori justification is normally contrasted with *a posteriori* justification. "A posteriori" is a Latin phrase that literally means "from the latter." A posteriori justification is the kind of justification that is typical for empiricism. It requires that we refer to specific experiences of the world. For example, I can only know a posteriori that Jody Foster's son has red hair. For in order to know that I must have had the chance to see Jody Foster's son. I cannot know the hair color of Jody Foster's son a priori without reference to particular experiences. Similarly, I can only know a posteriori that there are nine planets in our solar system or that the average household income in New Jersey is higher than the average household income in Tennessee.

FOOD FOR THOUGHT

In order to test your understanding of the terms *a priori* and *a posteriori*, decide whether the following sentences are true or false.

1. I can know a priori that all bachelors are not married.
2. A fully committed empiricist holds that all our knowledge is justified a posteriori.
3. It is impossible to know a priori whether New York has more inhabitants than Mexico City.
4. I can know a priori that there is life on other planets.
5. All of mathematics is based on a priori reasoning.
6. Nobody can know on the basis of a priori reasoning that the Empire State Building is the tallest building in the world.
7. I can know a priori that if somebody is shot to death then somebody must have been the shooter.
8. I can know a priori that a cube must have 12 edges.
9. I can know a priori that all swans are white.

In addition to the terms "a priori" and "a posteriori" it is also useful to understand the terms **"necessary truth"** and **"contingent truth."** A proposition is contingently true if its truth depends on how the actual world is. For example, whether the sentence "Britney Spears has sold more records than Madonna" is true depends on whether Britney Spears has indeed sold more records than Madonna. So this proposition is contingently true. Similarly, the sentences "Abraham Lincoln was shot in a theater" and "The Broncos won two successive Super Bowl titles" express contingent truths as well. On the other hand, the sentence "If Britney Spears has a female sibling, then Britney Spears has a sister" is true whether Britney Spears actually has a sister or not. Similarly, the sentences "The number 9 is larger than the number 3" and "Every rose is a flower" express necessary truths as well. A good way to determine whether a sentence is contingently true or necessarily true is to ask yourself if it is logically possible that the sentence could be false. For example, it is logically possible that the sentence "Abraham Lincoln was shot in a theater" is false, for we can imagine a situation in which Abraham Lincoln was not shot at all. It follows therefore that this sentence expresses a contingent truth. On the other hand, it is not logically possible that the number 9 is smaller than the number 3 or that roses are not flowers.

FOOD FOR THOUGHT

In order to test your understanding of the differences between necessary and contingent truths, determine whether the following sentences are necessary truths or contingent truths.

1. The moon moves around the earth.
2. All bachelors are not married.
3. The United States withdrew from Vietnam in 1975.
4. If Frank has more than two sisters, the he has at least three siblings.
5. There are infinitely many prime numbers.
6. In order to graduate from Northwestern University, one has to take at least three English classes.

It is relatively easy to see that there exists a tight connection between necessary truths and a priori knowledge, and contingent truths and a posteriori knowledge. If we can know something a priori (i.e., prior to looking at the world), then the truth must be a necessary truth. On the other hand, if we know something a posteriori (with the help of experience), then the truth must be a contingent truth. What a rationalist maintains is that there are important necessary truths that we can only know on the basis of a priori reasoning and that these necessary truths form the foundation of all our knowledge.

The Case for Rationalism

A fair number of thinkers do not find rationalism all that plausible. They ask: "Where are these great necessary truths that we are supposed to know on the basis of reason alone?" At first glance, this seems like a reasonable complaint, but if we look more carefully we can see that rationalism is a more persuasive element in our knowledge than is initially apparent. To illustrate this, it is instructive to look at some examples. Consider, for instance, the text of the *Declaration of Independence*, written in 1776:

> . . . We hold these truths to be self-evident, that all men are created equal, that they are endowed by their Creator with certain unalienable Rights, that among these are Life, Liberty and the pursuit of Happiness.—That to secure these rights, Governments are instituted among Men, deriving their just powers from the consent of the governed,—That whenever any Form of Government becomes destructive of these ends, it is the Right of the People to alter or to abolish it, and to institute new Government.

What is striking here is the reference to self-evidence. The crucial claims of the *Declaration of Independence* are presented as self-evident truths, that is, truths that are justified in the light of reason alone. Moreover, the claims at issue, namely,

1. All men have equal rights, and

2. People have the right to revolt against their Government if it fails to protect them in their rights

are, if they are true, necessarily true. For it is not a contingent feature of humans to have rights. If humans have fundamental rights, then they have them necessarily. This suggests that moral knowledge is justified predominantly on the basis of a priori reasoning. The weakness with this line of reasoning is, of course, that not all people agree that moral claims are really true or false, that is, there are many people who are skeptics about moral claims. We will discuss this question more thoroughly in

Chapter 7. However, we can nevertheless suggest a conditional argument in defense of rationalism, which takes the logical form of *modus ponens:*

1. If we have moral and political knowledge, then rationalism plays an important role in justifying our beliefs.
2. We have moral and political knowledge.

Therefore: Rationalism plays an important role in justifying our beliefs.

FOOD FOR THOUGHT

The argument above depends on the claim that we actually have moral knowledge. What do you think—do we know that all humans have equal rights or do we only believe that all humans have equal rights?

A second argument in defense of rationalism is based on the claim that a priori knowledge does not seem to be as vulnerable to a certain type of skepticism as empirical knowledge. We have seen in the last section that empiricism goes hand in hand with the natural sciences. Notice, however, that the natural sciences are in a constant process of change. Physicists used to believe that matter was made out of indivisible, small, solid particles (atoms). Then, they discovered that atoms themselves consisted of parts, and that atoms were not solid pieces of matter but contained a good deal of empty space. Now they have even detected that electrons and neutrons have parts. An end to this process of new discoveries is not in sight. Empirical claims are always subject to revision. This has convinced some philosophers that the natural sciences do not produce genuine knowledge, but rather only beliefs. For genuine knowledge is supposed to be timeless and unchanging. The philosopher Plato first raised this objection against empirical knowledge. Plato was a rationalist, and he didn't think that empirical investigations of the physical world could lead to genuine knowledge, but only to beliefs. Plato, like all rationalists, was much more impressed by the knowledge of mathematics. He thought that a mathematical proof once discovered would not be revised later on. This seems plausible. When we learn classical geometry today, we learn the same proofs that the Greek mathematician Euclid discovered more than 2000 years ago. Unlike natural science, mathematics seems to lead to knowledge that is eternal and solidly justified in the light of reason. The gist of this argument then is to increase the importance of a priori knowledge by discrediting the status of empirical knowledge. The convinced rationalist might therefore say that if there is any knowledge, it must be a priori knowledge since empirical investigation only produces beliefs.

Problems for Rationalism

We have seen that there are some reasons supporting the idea that a priori justification plays a crucial role in justifying our beliefs. However, rationalism also faces some serious challenges. One of the more influential challenges to rationalism goes back to the writings of David Hume, but was most prominently advocated by a group of twentieth century philosophers called Logical Positivists. Rudolph Carnap (1891–1970), Moritz Schlick (1882–1936), and Carl Gustav Hempel (1905–1997) are some of the more prominent members of this group. Logical Positivists were committed empiricists and believed that a priori knowledge had only very limited value. To understand their attack on rationalism and a priori reasoning, one needs to understand the distinction between **analytic** and **synthetic truths**. Consider the following sentence: "All electrons are subatomic particles." The sentence is obviously true, but it is true for trivial reasons. An electron is by definition a certain type of subatomic particle. We can know that the sentence is true simply by analyzing the meaning of the word electron. No observations are necessary in order to determine whether the sentence is true. Sentences of this type express analytic truths. We can define analytically true sentences as sentences that are true simply in virtue of the meanings of the words involved. Other examples of analytic sentences are "All bachelors are not married" or "All birches are trees."

Of course, most sentences are not analytically true. For instance, the sentence "Electrons have less mass than neutrons" cannot be determined to be true by analyzing the meaning of the word "electron." In order to find out whether the sentence is true, we need to conduct experiments and observations. Sentences of this kind are called synthetic sentences. Further examples of synthetic sentences are "George Bush owns a Ford Focus" or "New York City has more inhabitants than Lincoln, Nebraska."

FOOD FOR THOUGHT

In order to sharpen your understanding of the distinction between analytic truths and synthetic truths, determine whether the following sentences are analytic or synthetic.

1. All pencils and pens are writing utensils.
2. Electrons are the smallest physical particles in the universe.
3. More than 20 million people died of AIDS last year.
4. There are more heterosexuals than there are homosexual humans.
5. Earthquakes are natural disasters.
6. Dogs and cats are both animals.
7. Texas is larger than Oklahoma.
8. The average lawyer makes more than $70,000 per year.
9. All cubes have 12 edges.

Once we have grasped the distinction between analytic and synthetic truths, it is easy to see that there is something trivial about analytic truths. If somebody tells me "All bachelors are unmarried men," I can immediately see that the he is telling me something true, but the truth is not very interesting. Analytic truths do not contain information about the world, but only information about how we use the words in our language. Once we understand this feature of analytic truths, we are in a position to appreciate the attack of logical positivism on rationalism.

Logical positivists claim that a priori reasoning only allows us to grasp analytic truths. If this is correct, then logical positivists have shown that a priori reasoning does not offer us any information about the world, but only information about the meaning of words. But that result is devastating for a rationalist, who claims that a priori reasoning is a key element in all our knowledge.

To resist this attack, a rationalist has to show that there are important necessary truths that we can know a priori and that are not analytic. One option here is to point to important moral claims like "All humans have equal rights." We have seen that these claims, if they are true, are necessarily true and the claims are synthetic and not analytic. However, this move is problematic. Logical positivists, for example, simply denied that we have moral knowledge. Arguments that appeal to moral knowledge are therefore not always effective.

A second defense for the rationalist is to claim that there are important synthetic and necessary truths that shape our understanding of the physical universe. Traditionally, rationalists claimed, for instance, that the sentences "Every event has a cause" or "The shortest distance between two points in space is a straight line" are synthetic and necessary truths about the universe.

The problem here is that progress in science suggests that these seemingly self-evident truths are not only contingent but probably even false. This seems to leave the rationalist with only one option to escape the attack of logical positivism: the rationalist's all-time favorite field of knowledge, namely mathematical truths. However, the problem here is that the status of mathematical truths is hotly debated. Many positivists, for instance, have been fond of the idea that mathematics ultimately reduces to analytic truths as well. Whether rationalists can escape the attack of logical positivism and deny the claim that all a priori truths are analytic truths is an open question and still debated among contemporary philosophers. No clear answer to the question has yet emerged.

Final Remarks on Epistemology

It is time to draw some conclusions from our introduction to epistemology. Although some of the arguments have been a bit complex, it is important not to lose sight of the big picture. We can answer the question of whether we have knowledge in three fundamental ways. First, we can be **skeptics** and claim that we know very little and that most of our so-called knowledge is in fact nothing more than a bunch of beliefs. A dose of skepticism is a necessary ingredient of all philosophy. If we are too confident that we know what the world is like, we will not ask the necessary questions that initiate philosophical reflection. However, the crucial epistemological question is whether we can prevent skepticism from turning into global skepticism and thus undermine all our philosophical and scientific knowledge. We have seen that Descartes' method of doubt did not produce an entirely satisfactory response to global skepticism. Fallible versions of either **empiricism** or **rationalism** seem more promising. An empiricist argues that we can know that *p* if we can justify *p* a posteriori with respect to our experiences of the world. A rationalist, on the other hand, maintains that we can know that *p* if we can show a priori that *p* is necessarily true. Both positions have their respective strengths and weaknesses. In actual philosophical conversation, most people appeal to a priori justification as well as a posteriori justification. It is, however, important to determine what kind of justification plays the more fundamental role. An answer to this question will not only influence our strategy for resisting skepticism, but it will also influence how we approach and evaluate arguments. An empiricist, for instance, will be very skeptical toward premises that cannot be justified in the light of our experiences. A rationalist, on the other hand, will try to solve philosophical questions predominately with the help of a priori considerations. Equipped with these basic epistemological and logical tools, we are ready to explore some classical philosophical problems.

Endnotes

1. Descartes, Rene. *Meditations on First Philosophy.* Trans. by Elisabeth Haldane and G. Ross. Cambridge: Cambridge University Press, 1931, p. 145.
2. Ibid., p. 146.
3. The most promising way of overcoming these difficulties is to advocate a version of *direct realism.* A direct realist about perception does not believe that the world of physical objects is exactly as it appears to us. However, the direct realist nevertheless maintains that we perceive material objects directly, without mediation of ideas or sensory representations. For a contemporary version of direct realism see: Huemer, Michael. *Skepticism and the Veil of Perception.* Boulder: Rowman and Littlefield. 2001.

For Further Reading

Audi, Robert. *Belief, Justification, and Knowledge.* Belmont: Wadsworth, 1988.

Audi, Robert. *Epistemology: A Contemporary Introduction to the Theory of Knowledge.* London: Routledge, 1998.

Chisholm, R. M. *Theory of Knowledge.* 3d ed. Englewood Cliffs: Prentice-Hall, 1989.

Lehrer, Keith. *Theory of Knowledge.* Boulder: Westview Press, 1990.

Pollock, John and Joseph Cruz. *Contemporary Theories of Knowledge.* Lanham: Rowman and Littlefield, 1999.

Plantiga, Alvin. *Warrant and Proper Function.* New York: Oxford University Press, 1993.

Plantiga, Alvin. *Warrant: The Current Debate.* New York: Oxford University Press, 1993.

CHAPTER THREE

THE PROBLEM OF FREE WILL

Why Is There a Problem with Free Will?

For many of us, few things are as certain as the claim that we have free will. When we go through our lives, it is obvious that we deliberate about what we are going to do in the future. Consider the example of John, who just graduated from high school and who is trying to decide what to do next in life. He has the chance to go to college, and an opportunity to work together with his friends for a year in Palm Beach, Florida. He can't do both and so John has to make a decision. It seems obvious that the choice he is going to make depends on his will. He seems free either to go to college or to go and work for a year, and if he can't make up his mind, then he can stay home with his parents for a year and watch TV. It is John's decision. This is one example of a person who makes use of his free will. In general, we can say that having free will means that we can make choices in our lives and that these choices are up to us. The basic idea behind having free will can be illustrated with the help of the following diagram:

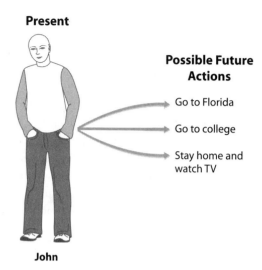

Present

Possible Future Actions

Go to Florida

Go to college

Stay home and watch TV

John

We all have a tendency to believe that we are like John and that we have the ability to make choices and shape our future. Why then do philosophers worry about free will? To understand why philosophers question whether we actually have free will, it is useful to expand the above picture and consider the past as well as the future. The picture then looks as follows.

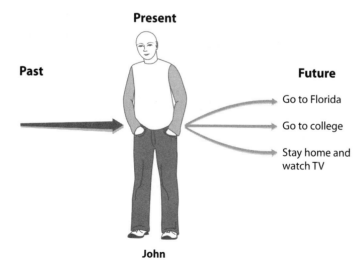

Present

Past

Future

Go to Florida

Go to college

Stay home and watch TV

John

What is interesting to notice here is that the past is quite different from the future. The future seems open. It seems to be up to us to shape the future. But the same cannot be said about the past. There is only one past, and it cannot be changed. John, for example, was born on October 17, 1982. His parents divorced when he was 12, and he drank his first beer on his 15th birthday. All of these events are part of John's past. It is not within John's power to change any of it. The past is set in stone.

The question that arises is the following: How much power does the past have over the future? If the link between the past and the future is very strong, and if there is only one past, then the possibility arises that there is also only one future. The theory that the future is fixed by the past is called **determinism.** The following illustration captures the basic idea behind determinism.

The Threat of Determinism

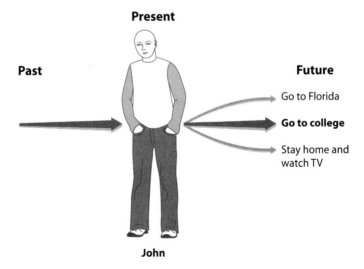

It is important not to misunderstand the effects of determinism. If our future is determined by our past, we may not feel forced to perform one particular action. On the contrary, we will still deliberate about what to do in the future. In a deterministic world, John still contemplates what he should do with his life after high school. He will try to find out what option looks most attractive to him. It's just that John, given his particular past experiences, is determined to make one particular choice, namely to go to college. The other choices are not really open to him.

The German philosopher Arthur Schopenhauer (1788–1860) illustrated the effects of determinism as follows: "Let us imagine a man who while standing on the street, would say to himself: 'It's six o'clock in the evening, the working day is over. Now I can go for a walk, or I can go to the club; I can also climb the tower to see the sun set, I can go to the theater; I can visit this friend or that one; indeed I can also run out of the gate, into the wide world, and never return. All of this is strictly up to me, in this I have complete freedom. But still I shall do none of these things now, but with just as free a will I shall go home to my wife.'"[1] What Schopenhauer nicely explains here is that we do not lose our sense of freedom even if our future is already determined. The man who stands in the street and contemplates what to do after work was determined to go home to his wife. He is nevertheless quite happy to think about all the things he might do instead. The point, however, is that, given his past, he is not going to do any of them.

We are now in a much better position to understand why the idea of free will leads to problems. The main philosophical issue is to explain how the past is connected with the future, and what impact this connection has on our ability to make free choices. In general, we can identify four main responses to this problem: hard determinism, indeterminism, soft determinism, and libertarianism. It will take awhile before the differences between these philosophical positions clearly emerge, but the following overview should help you to develop an initial grasp of the various positions.

Responses to the Problem of Free Will

Hard Determinism

A hard determinist believes that the past completely determines the future. Since all future events are caused by past events, the future is causally determined. It is not within our power to shape the future. Free will is an illusion.

Indeterminism

An indeterminist denies that the past has a strong effect on the future. According to indeterminism, at least some events in the future are not caused by events in the past. The future is somewhat random and unpredictable. This avoids the threat of determinism.

Soft Determinism

A soft determinist holds that we can have free will even if the future is determined. We are free and responsible for our actions as long as these actions are caused in the right way. We can distinguish two different forms of soft determinism.

Libertarianism

A libertarian insists that human beings are agents and that agents have special causal powers. They can initiate (cause) events on their own account and are therefore free to shape the future.

Traditional Compatibilism

A traditional compatibilist holds that actions are free if:
a. They are caused by the will of the agent.
b. They are not forced.

Deep Self-Compatibilism

A deep self-compatibilist holds that actions are free if they are caused by desires that are truly our own (authentic desires).

FOOD FOR THOUGHT

In order to determine which of these various positions on free will is most similar to your own thinking, it will be useful to answer the following questions with T/F. We will see later on that, depending on which philosophical position we adopt, we will answer these questions differently.

1. All events are caused.
2. We are responsible for all our actions.

3. In some situations people perform actions, but they are not responsible for what they do.
4. In each and every situation in my life, I could have acted otherwise than I in fact acted.
5. If we were to roll back time to the year 1950, history would unfold in the same way as it actually did (i.e., President Kennedy would be shot in 1963 in Dallas, Reagan would have been elected President in 1980, etc.).
6. God knows what will happen in the future. He knows especially what will happen in my life later on, that is, he knows when I will die and what I will have for dinner tomorrow evening, etc.
7. Nobody (not even God) can know what will happen in the future because the future has not yet happened.
8. If I had experienced a different childhood, then I would make different decisions right now.
9. Even if one has a terrible childhood, one still can pull oneself together and make free and responsible choices about one's life.
10. Some people have no choice when it comes to drinking alcohol. They are bound to become alcoholics.
11. We sometimes act on desires that are not our own, but which are implanted in us by advertising or peer pressure.

The Case for Hard Determinism

According to hard determinism, the past completely determines the future. To make this view plausible, we need to understand better how past and future are related to each other. In virtue of what is the past able to exercise such a powerful influence over the future? Hard determinists respond to this question by pointing to **causality.** The past **causes** the future, and this causal link determines what the future looks like.

To assess the plausibility of this claim that there is a tight causal link between the past and the future, we need to take a closer look at the idea of causality. What exactly happens when a particular event causes another event? Let us look at an example. Consider a set of domino pieces lined up in a row.

Now consider what will happen if at time t_1 the first domino piece is knocked over.

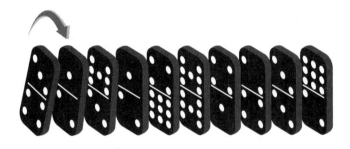

One does not have to be a physicist to predict what will happen. If the first domino falls at time t_1 then at some later time t_n the last domino will fall as well. The reason for this is obvious. The fall of the first domino *causes* the second domino to fall; the fall of the second one will *cause* the third one to fall, until the last one is knocked over. This is a good example of how causality works. Causality is a relationship between events. One event (called the cause) triggers a second event (called the effect) and this event in turn causes a new effect, and so on. What is interesting to notice are two things:

1. The cause of an event happens prior to the effect.
2. Once the cause has happened the effect has to happen as well (i.e., causes are sufficient conditions for bringing about their effects).

These two conditions explain how the past can shape the future. If the past contains the causes for a specific event E, then it is causally determined that E has to happen as well.

This insight by itself is not yet sufficient to establish determinism. We can admit that some events (e.g., the falling of the last domino) are bound to happen because they are caused by prior events (the falling of the first domino) without yet losing our sense of freedom. Who is to say that our actions are caused by prior events in the same manner as the falling of the last domino is caused by prior events? Can we be sure that all events (including our actions) are caused by past events?

Unfortunately, there are excellent reasons for thinking that all events (including our actions) have causes. Consider the following example. Suppose you are sleeping for the first time at your friend's house. Late at night you hear a strange noise. It sounds as if someone is scratching with fingernails at your door. You are so frightened that you pull the blanket over your head and pray that you survive the night. In the morning, you ask your friend about the noise. Suppose that she answers as follows: "Oh, this is a very old house. It is full of strange noises. But do not worry; nothing causes these noises. The noises simply happen." It is obvious that you will not accept that as an answer. If there are noises, then there must be a cause for these noises. Noises do not just happen out of the blue. But what is true for noises is true for all other events as well. Consider an airplane crash. We might not know exactly why an airplane has crashed, but we do seem to know that something must have caused this crash. The same is true for rainstorms, earthquakes, anger tantrums, or asthma attacks. Wherever and whenever anything happens, it is caused by something. If we accept this plausible principle, then free will is in trouble. For now, we are in a position to advance the following argument in defense of hard determinism.

1. All events have causes.
2. Our actions are events.
3. All caused events are determined by the past.

Therefore:

4. Our actions are determined by the past.
5. If our actions are determined by the past, then we have no power to act other than we do indeed act.

6. If we have no power to act other than we in fact do act, then we have no free will.

Therefore:

7. We have no free will.

This argument for hard determinism is pretty persuasive. It is certainly valid, and none of the premises appears to be clearly false.

FOOD FOR THOUGHT

The convicted rapist Matias Reye had a horrible childhood. When he was 2 years old, his mother sold him to his father for $400. At age 7, two older boys sexually abused him and threw him in a river. By age 17, he was living alone on the streets of New York, scratching for money as an East Harlem delicatessen clerk and sleeping in a van outside of the store. Do you think Matias Reye freely chose to become a rapist or do you think that his childhood caused him to become a dangerous sexual predator? In general, do you think that it is possible that certain people, in certain situations, are condemned by their childhood experiences to perform certain actions?

Although we have discovered a plausible argument in defense of hard determinism, most people find this argument impossible to accept. In our day-to-day lives, we hold each other responsible for our actions. Suppose that I have promised to pick you up from the airport late at night. I fail to show up and you have to take a $60 cab ride. You are mad at me, and the next day when I call, you end our relationship. In this situation, it is clear that you think that I could have acted otherwise. The reason you are mad is because you think that I could have been at the airport if only I truly cared for you. However, if hard determinism is true and if I have no free will, then I was determined by my past to miss our appointment at the airport. There is nothing I could have done differently, and I deserve neither praise nor blame for my failure to be at the airport. But this conclusion does not sit well with what we do in our daily lives. We do blame each other, and find fault with our actions. And we also praise each other if we do something well, or when we cease to engage in destructive habits like smoking or drinking. Given that we hold each other responsible for our actions, we are in a position to advance a powerful argument against hard determinism. The argument goes as follows:

1. If hard determinism is true, then we have no free will.
2. If we have no free will, then we are not responsible for our actions.
3. We are responsible for our actions.

Therefore: Hard determinism is false.

This argument too is very persuasive. The logical structure is valid, and the premises appear likely to be true. We are now in a difficult situation. We have found two plausible arguments, one for hard determinism and one against it.

FOOD FOR THOUGHT

The argument in defense of free will is based on the claim that we are responsible for our actions. Are we, however, always responsible for what we do? Take a look at the following situations and decide whether the people in these situations are responsible for what they do.

1. A very drunk person decides that he can still drive his car home.
2. An illiterate person signs a loan with a 300% interest rate.
3. A 10-year-old child whose parents are professional thieves takes $5 from his parents without permission.
4. A student who has been told by everybody that he is bad at math fails another math exam.
5. A person who had a very bad and painful back injury is told to take strong pain medication. He takes the medication and becomes addicted to painkillers.
6. A 15-year-old girl who has been told all her life by her mother that she is too fat becomes anorexic.

Continued

7. A 15-year-old boy who grows up in a violent slum neighborhood drops out of high school and starts selling drugs.
8. A person who is chronically depressed and without health insurance, and therefore without medical treatment for the depression, commits suicide.
9. A 40-year-old man takes his first Viagra pill. The pill has a very strong effect. He subsequently decides to spend $1000 on a sex hotline.

A majority of philosophers are defenders of free will and personal responsibility and prefer to reject the argument for hard determinism. If we want to follow this road, we need to explore whether any of the principles on which the argument for hard determinism relies can be rejected. We will explore this possibility in the next sections. However, it is important to keep in mind that if it turns out that none of these alternative views is plausible or coherent, we might have to admit that hard determinism is the most successful position on free will.

Can Indeterminism Save Free Will?

The main argument for hard determinism is based on the idea that all events have causes. Since this principle gives us so much trouble, it is tempting to give it up. This is the crucial idea behind **indeterminism.** An indeterminist maintains that at least some events (especially our actions) are not caused by anything. For if our actions are not caused, then they also cannot be determined by the past. Indeterminism weakens the link between past and future, and thus seems to create space for free will.

Indeterminism is supported by recent advances in physics. Small particles like neutrinos or quarks behave differently than medium-sized physical objects like chairs and tables. A table, for instance, has at each moment in time a certain set of determinate properties. It either stands in the middle of the room or it does not. It would be silly to think that the table exists in two different positions at the same time. The same is not true for small particles like electrons. Although these small particles obey a fixed set of rules, the world of small particles is not a deterministic world. We cannot say that a small particle is at each given moment in a clearly determinate state. All we can say is that if we measure the particle then there is a certain probability that we will find the particle in a certain position with certain properties. Take the example of an electron in a magnetic field. The electron's spin may be either in alignment with the field, which is known as a spin-up state, or opposite to the field, which is known as a spin-down state. Prior to conducting any measurements, the electron is in a so-called superposition, meaning that it is simultaneously in a spin-up and spin-down position. Electrons and other small particles are therefore not like chairs and tables. They do not possess at each given moment a set of clearly determined properties. Thus, small particles do not live in a fully determined world.

We can take this indeterminism and apply it to what happens in our brains when we make a decision. When we deliberate whether we should go to a party or not, something like the following might be happening in our brains. Suppose a particular small particle is in a superposition of spin-up and spin-down. As we decide whether we should go to the party or not, we conduct in our brains what amounts to a measurement of the particle. If we find it in a spin-up position, we will go to the party; if we find the particle in spin-down position, we will stay at home. Whether we will find the particle in one or the other position is not causally determined by prior events. Both outcomes are physically possible and can happen. In this way, indeterminism liberates us from the curse that the decision whether we will go to the party is determined by past events. If our decisions are ultimately dependent on indeterministic physical processes, then we do not have to be afraid that our future is fixed and predictable on the basis of our past.

Although indeterminism can explain nicely why the past has no power over our decisions, it runs into serious difficulties of its own. The contemporary philosopher Richard Taylor describes well why indeterminism is as hostile to personal responsibility as hard determinism. He writes:

> Suppose that my arm is free, according to [indeterminism]; that is that its motions are uncaused. It moves this way and that from time to time, but nothing causes these motions. Sometimes it moves forth vigorously, sometimes up, sometimes down, sometimes it just drifts vaguely about— these motions all being wholly free and uncaused. Manifestly I have

nothing to do with them at all; they just happen, and neither I nor anyone can ever tell what this arm will be doing next. It might seize a club and lay it on the head of the nearest bystander, no less to my astonishment than his. There will never be any point in asking why these motions occur, or in seeking any explanation of them, for under the conditions assumed there is no explanation. They just happen, from no causes at all.[2]

What Taylor shows nicely is that according to indeterminism, my actions become random events. But nobody can hold me responsible for something that happens at random. A good illustration for this is Tourette's syndrome. A person with Tourette's syndrome experiences recurrent, involuntary, rapid, purposeless motor movements like blinking, nose puckering, grimacing, or squinting. People with this syndrome are often embarrassed about their involuntary body movements, but it would be ridiculous to hold them responsible for them. These bodily movements are, after all, not under their control. They simply happen. If indeterminism is correct, then our actions and decisions are as random as the body movements of people with Tourette's syndrome. This is hardly a satisfactory account of human freedom. Indeterminism, therefore, is a dead end. Although it promises to create space for free will, it ultimately eliminates it. To escape the threat of hard determinism, it is not enough to simply deny that our actions are caused. If we want to explain how we can be responsible for our actions, we need to look for other alternatives.

FOOD FOR THOUGHT

Some people are trying on purpose to act randomly. Take the example of Claude, who is well known for his erratic behavior. One day you see Claude at a party as he drinks heavily. You ask him why he drinks the tenth shot in a row and he responds: "I have no idea, man. I simply do things. I never ask why." Everybody around Claude laughs at this answer. They say: "That is a typical Claude answer. He does crazy stuff for no reason at all." Do you think that Claude has genuine free will?

Soft Determinism

What our analysis of indeterminism shows is that we should be careful before we abandon the idea of causality altogether. Only if our actions are caused, can we have any control over them. Genuine freedom seems to require that our actions be caused appropriately. The attempt to combine causality and free will is the central idea behind **soft determinism.** Soft determinism is sometimes also called **compatibilism,** since it holds that freedom and causality are compatible with each other. The philosophers Thomas Hobbes (1588–1679) and David Hume (1711–1776) defended early versions of soft determinism.

Although soft determinism offers the hope that we can combine the idea that all events are caused with our conviction that we are free, the theory is not easy to understand. The best way to approach the central idea behind soft determinism is to compare two situations. First, suppose that you are walking down the street late at night and that a menacing-looking guy comes up to you and yells: "Your money or your life!" Feeling intimated and scared for your life, you decide to hand over your money. The second situation is different. You are again walking down the same street late at night, but this time a skinny, forlorn looking teenager asks you whether you could help him to stay alive. Overcome by pity, you give the teenager all the money you have.

What is interesting to notice here is that in both situations, your decision to hand over the money was caused. In the first case it was caused by the threat of the menacing-looking guy, and in the second case it was caused by your feeling of pity for the teenager. A soft determinist maintains that our freedom and responsibility are not threatened by the fact that our actions are caused. Our actions can still be free as long as they are caused in the right way. In the first situation, the decision to hand over the money was forced upon you. The action is therefore not a free action. In the second situation, however, the decision was caused by our own will. It seems therefore appropriate that I take responsibility for the action, in spite of the fact that the action was caused. Soft determinism is built around the idea that our actions are free as long as they are caused in the right fashion. There are different versions of soft determinism since different philosophers have had different ideas about what kinds of causes are best compatible with free will. We will discuss two major versions in the following sections.

Traditional Compatibilism

A traditional compatibilist takes responsibility as a guide to freedom. He maintains that a caused action should be considered to be a free action as long as it is plausible to say that we are responsible for the action. This leads the traditional compatibilist to suggest two conditions for freedom and responsibility. According to traditional compatibilism, an action is free if

1. The action is caused by the will of the agent, and
2. The action is not forced.

Let us explain these two positions in more detail. The first condition is, at least at first glance, easy to understand. One can be responsible for an action only if the action is caused by some internal state of the agent. If I shoot somebody out of jealousy, or if I hug somebody because I love them, then these actions are truly my actions and I am responsible for them. On the other hand, if I have been put under a hypnotic spell that I should hug everyone in the room and then proceed to embrace every person in the room, then I am not responsible for the action, and it would be false to classify the action as a free action. In this case, my decision to hug everyone is not caused by my will but rather by the actions of the hypnotist. We thus can say in general that only those actions that are caused by my internal states (like desires, hopes, beliefs, or wishes) are actions for which I can be responsible and are thus free actions.

The second condition of traditional compatibilism is a bit more complex. It seems obvious that we are not responsible for an action when we are forced to perform it. However, it is not trivial to say precisely what this condition amounts to. When somebody grabs my hand and puts it into a jar of peanut butter (although I do everything in my power to prevent this from happening), then I am clearly forced to do this. But what should we say about blackmail? Suppose I am working for a corporation with an evil computer network analyst. The analyst (with the help of spy software that he has installed on my computer) finds out that I work very little on my office projects but spend most of my time in the office playing computer games. He threatens to tell my supervisor unless I pay him $300 per month. Am I forced to pay him $300? Traditional compatibilists tend to clarify this question by introducing a hypothetical analysis. We are free (and therefore not forced) with respect to an action if, had we chosen differently, we would have been able to act otherwise. Let us clarify this rather complex criterion with respect to the evil network analyst example. Suppose that I decide to pay the analyst $300 per month. In this situation, it would have been possible for me to choose a different course of action. For instance, I could have chosen to quit my job altogether. If I had chosen this, I could also have done it. The evil analyst did not have it in his power to stop me from quitting my job. So in this situation I was not forced. If I had chosen otherwise I could have done something else. So, if I end up paying $300 per month, the action is still a free action and it is an action I am responsible for. Let us now consider the mugging example one more time. Suppose a menacing-looking guy who shouts "Your money or your life" threatens me in a dark alley. I decide to hand over my money. Was I forced to so? It depends on the guy who is mugging me. If the guy is determined to shoot me if I make any attempt to run away, then a traditional compatibilist would say that I am forced to hand over my money. For if I had decided to keep my money and run, I would not have been able to do so. Notice, however, that the situation would be different if the mugger had no bullets in his gun. If that had been the case, I would have been able to run away if I had chosen to do so. A traditional compatibilist would therefore say in the latter situation that I had some freedom in that situation. As you can see from these examples, traditional compatibilism requires us to analyze situations very carefully before we can assert that the agent was forced. The crucial question to ask in these contexts is whether the agent could have acted differently if he had chosen differently.

FOOD FOR THOUGHT

Test your understanding of traditional compatibilism by deciding whether a traditional compatibilist would think that the following decisions are free decisions. Explain your answers.

1. You decide to loan $400 to your roommate after he says: "You are my last hope. If you do not loan me $400, I will have to kill myself."
2. After drinking heavily, you decide to dance naked on the table.

Continued

3. After your friend drives you home, you decide to remain in the car with him and listen to his CDs. Only afterwards you find out that your friend had locked the door to his car and would not have opened them unless you first listened to all his CDs.

4. After your best friend commits suicide, you decide to make plans to kill yourself as well.

5. After the college you attend raises tuition by 40 percent, you realize that you cannot afford to pay for it anymore and decide to quit college altogether.

6. You decide to quit your job. As you tell your boss, she tells you (truthfully) that she would have fired you today anyway.

7. While you are sleepwalking, you go to the refrigerator and make yourself a sandwich.

Traditional compatibilism leads to a very commonsensical theory of freedom and responsibility that is similar to the conception of freedom that we find in courts of law. If one is accused of a crime, and the prosecution can establish that the crime was premeditated and that one could have avoided the crime if one had wanted to do so, then one normally gets awarded the highest possible punishment for this type of crime. For in this case, people tend to think that we are fully responsible for this deed. On the other hand, if I am accused of a crime and I can show that I could not have avoided committing the crime even if I had chosen differently, then I am normally awarded a more lenient punishment. A good example in this context might be a car accident. Suppose that I have been negligent about the tires on my car. They are run down, and although my mechanic has warned me about this, I continue to drive my car with the old tires. The inevitable happens, and I crash into the back of another car. Suppose now that it is winter, and that the road was extremely icy. If I can show that I would have crashed into the other car, even if I had completely new tires on my car, then my responsibility for the accident is greatly diminished. For in this case, even if I had chosen a different course of action and bought the new tires prior to the crash, the accident would have happened anyway.

Deep Self-Compatibilism

Although traditional compatibilism squares well with what happens in law courts, it also leads to a number of philosophical difficulties. Deep self-compatibilism is a refined version of soft determinism that can avoid these difficulties. The contemporary philosopher Harry G. Frankfurt developed this position in his writings. The best way to understand deep self-compatibilism is to come to a clear understanding of why traditional compatibilism faces some problems.

A traditional compatibilist holds that we act with free will whenever an action is caused by our desires, and if the action was not forced upon us. The possibility arises, however, that some of our desires (although they prompt us to act) are not identical with our will. This might sound strange, but the following example should help to illustrate the issue.

Consider the case of 15-year-old Hanna whose junkie boyfriend tricks her into trying heroin. He tells her that the white powdery stuff he bought is cocaine and not heroin. Hanna, who is an occasional cocaine user, agrees to use the powder. After Hanna realizes that she was tricked into snorting something she never would have snorted if she had known what it was, she runs out of the house and ends her relationship with her so-called boyfriend. Alas, she also finds to her surprise that she now has a strong urge to use heroin again. She struggles with all her might against this urge. She goes to support groups, talks to counselors, and undergoes therapy, but the urge is still there and grows stronger by the day. Finally, she succumbs and uses heroin again.

What should we say about Hanna's decision to use heroin for the second time? According to traditional compatibilism, Hanna's action was free and she is fully responsible for performing it. Her decision to use heroin for the second time fulfills the two crucial conditions that a traditional compatibilist has specified for responsibility and freedom. Hanna's action was caused by an internal desire, and she was not forced to perform the action. However, it seems strange to say that Hanna's will was completely free when she decided to use heroin for the second time. Hanna, after all, hates her desire for heroin. She does not want to act on it and does everything in her power to prevent her desire for heroin from becoming effective. It thus seems plausible to say that Hanna was unable to do what she really wanted to do—that is, to avoid taking heroin again.

FOOD FOR THOUGHT

Has it ever happened to you that you acted on desires that you did not identify with and thus were not truly your own desires? If yes, give a description of some of the situations in which you have acted on inauthentic desires. If not, describe how you can be sure that the desires on which you act are actually your own authentic desires.

We can agree with the traditional compatibilist that Hanna is responsible for using heroin, but still maintain that her will is not completely free. What the traditional compatibilist overlooks is the possibility that there might be situations in which we are unable to act on those desires we truly identify with. A satisfactory account of free will seems to require that we take into account whether the desires which we act on are truly our own. For our will is truly free, only if it is strong enough to guarantee that we act on our own desires.

At this point, deep self-compatibilism enters the picture. Deep self-compatibilism is also a form of soft determinism and thus subscribes to the idea that a caused action can be free. However, it differs from traditional compatibilism in that it holds that our will is genuinely free only if we act on desires that we have chosen and that we identify with. According to deep self-compatibilism, free will is dependent on what happens deep inside of us. Nobody can tell from the outside whether one truly acts on desires that one genuinely wants to have.

Let us consider an example to illustrate the basic idea behind deep self-compatibilism. Suppose Henry, a 22-year-old college sophomore, is still undeclared. His advisor and his parents urge him to declare a major. Henry is interested in biology, sociology, and computer science. In this situation, Henry has conflicting desires. He has a desire to study biology, a desire to study sociology, and a desire to study computer science. On which desire should he act? Suppose that Henry, after careful reflection, realizes that he only desires to study computer science because his father wants him to study something "practical." And suppose further that Henry only desires to study sociology because his mother is a sociologist. Henry realizes that his desire to study biology is something that he is truly comfortable with. In this situation, Henry is not neutral with respect to his desires. He wants his desire to study biology to be the desire on which he acts. If he manages to do so, then Henry has free will. If, on the other hand, Henry is not able to act on his desires (perhaps because he is afraid of his father), then his will is not genuinely free. For a deep self-compatibilist, free will is the ability to act on those desires we truly want to have. Let us call these desires authentic desires. Desires that are imposed upon us by other sources (parents, peer pressure, advertising) we can dub inauthentic desires.

FOOD FOR THOUGHT

Deep self-compatibilism argues that our will is free if we act on authentic desires. It is not easy to see how we can identify our authentic desires. The philosopher Friedrich Nietzsche (1844–1900) describes (in the following excerpt from his essay *Schopenhauer as Educator*) a methodology that might help to identify one's authentic desires. Read through his suggestions and determine whether you can apply Nietzsche's methodology to your own life. Does this help you to find your authentic desires?

When the great thinker despises human beings, he despises their laziness: for it is on account of their laziness that men seem like manufactured goods, unimportant, and unworthy to be associated with or instructed. Human beings who do not want to belong to the mass need only to stop being comfortable; follow their conscience, which cries out: "Be yourself! All that you are now doing, thinking, and desiring is not really yourself. . . . But how can we find ourselves again? How can man know himself? He is a dark and veiled thing; and if the hare has seven skins, man can shed seventy times seven and still not be able to say: "this is really you, this is no longer slough." In addition, it is a painful and dangerous mission to tunnel into oneself and make a forced descent into the shaft of one's being by the nearest path. Doing so can easily cause damage that no physician can heal. And besides: what need should there be for it, when given all the evidence of our nature, our friendships and enmities, our glance and the clasp of our hand, our memory and that which we forget, our books and our handwriting. This, however, is the means to plan the most important inquiry. Let the youthful soul

Continued

look back on life with the question: what have you truly loved up to now, what has elevated your soul, what has mastered it and at the same time delighted it? Place these venerated objects before you in a row, and perhaps they will yield for you, through their nature and their sequence, a law, the fundamental law of your true self. Compare these objects, see how one complements, expands, surpasses, transfigures another, how they form a stepladder upon which you have climbed up to yourself as you are now; for your true nature lies, not hidden deep within you, but immeasurably high above you, or at least above that which you normally take to be yourself . . .

A good way to illustrate the difference between traditional compatibilism and deep self-compatibilism is to consider the case of animals. Do animals have free will? According to traditional compatibilism, a dog that barks at night performs a free action. The action, after all, is caused by his desire to bark and the dog is not forced to bark. But a deep self-compatibilist would disagree with this analysis. Although the barking is caused by the dog's desire's to bark, the desire is not something the dog has actually chosen to have. According to deep self-compatibilism, animals should not be considered to have genuine free will, for they lack the ability to choose and identify with their desires. Human beings, on the other hand, have this capacity. Deep self-compatibilism maintains, therefore, that we act freely only if we act on those desires which we have chosen and which we identify with.

Food for Thought

In order to determine whether you find traditional compatibilism more plausible than deep self-compatibilism, it should be helpful to consider the following situations. Determine first whether a traditional compatibilist or a deep self-compatibilist would say that these people have free will. Decide then whether you agree with one or the other position.

1. Helmut S. sits in a high-security prison for killing a policeman. Helmut has come to the realization that he is a danger to society and he needs to be locked up. He thus decides that he

wants to stay in prison and that he would not leave even if they would let him go. Does Helmut have free will?

2. Andrea K. has a strong desire to undergo plastic surgery. She thinks that her breasts are too small. She spends her savings on a breast enlargement operation. A year later she breaks up with her boyfriend, and suddenly realizes that her desire to have larger breasts was caused by her boyfriend. She herself prefers to have smaller breasts. Did Andrea have free will when she decided to undergo her breast operation?

3. Nick decides to go to medical school. His father and his grandfather have all been physicians and he is expected to be one as well. However, what he really wants to do is play professional baseball. Does Nick have free will?

A Fundamental Problem for Soft Determinism

Traditional compatibilism and deep self-compatibilism are both forms of soft determinism. Although both philosophical positions have different ideas about what kind of causal history of our actions leads us to have genuine free will, they share the assumption that our actions can be free even if they are caused. It is this insistence that causality and freedom are compatible with each other that leads to the central weakness of soft determinism. To illustrate the central difficulty of soft determinism, let us consider the case of John P.

John P. decides at 11:00 AM to buy a hot dog for lunch. Let us suppose that John's decision is caused by his awareness that he has a desire for a hot dog. This awareness manifests itself in John's mind prior to his 11:00 AM decision at 10:59 AM. Since John's desire for a hot dog is the cause of his decision to buy a hot dog, the following conclusion seems inevitable: John's 11:00 AM decision to buy a hot dog was already determined to happen when he became aware at 10:59 AM that he had a desire for a hot dog. This means that at 11:00 AM when John actually makes the decision to buy the hot dog, it was not in his power to do anything else. Given how the world was at 10:59 AM, John was causally determined to buy a hot dog at 11:00 AM.

What this analysis shows is that soft determinism cannot explain how it can be in John's power to act in other ways than he in fact acted. Given that his decision (and the resulting action) is caused by his prior awareness that he has a desire for a hot dog, it was determined to take place. John could not have acted otherwise. However, this realization does not sit well with our sense of freedom. Many philosophers think that it is a necessary condition for freedom and responsibility to have the power to act other than we in fact have acted. If we agree with this demand, then we embrace the philosophical position of **incompatibilism.** Incompatibilists hold that a world in which every event (including our actions) is caused by prior events is incompatible with freedom. We have already seen that hard determinists are incompatibilists. There is, however, an additional philosophical position available that accepts incompatibilism and that also avoids hard determinism. This position is called **libertarianism.** Whether this position is more plausible than either hard determinism or soft determinism will be the topic of our next section.

Libertarianism

The Case for Libertarianism

Libertarianism is perhaps the most intuitive theory of free will. The central idea behind this philosophical theory is to draw a sharp distinction between different forms of causation. Consider the domino example one more time.

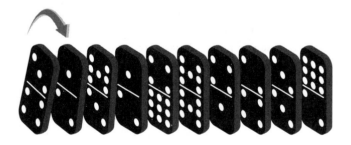

The falling dominos are a classical example of what a libertarian calls **event causation.** We have seen that the first event (the falling of the first domino) causes the second event (the falling of the second domino), and so on. What a libertarian maintains is that ordinary physical events like falling dominos or rainstorms are caused by other physical events and completely determined to take place. However, a libertarian insists that things are different when we deal with human beings (i.e., agents). When agents act, they cause something to take place. The actions of agents are not caused to take place by prior events, however. This means that agents are fundamentally different entities than domino pieces or vending machines. They have the power to cause something without themselves being subject to causal determination. A libertarian calls this kind of causation **agent causation.**

We can illustrate the difference between agent causation and event causation with the help of the following picture.

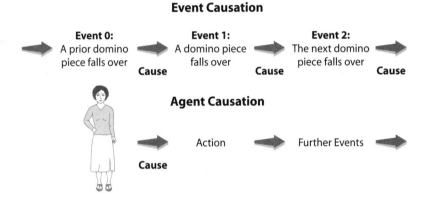

The key differences between event causation and agent causation are as follows: for any event that takes place, there is always at least one (or more) prior event that has caused it to happen. This means that when it comes to pure event causation, the causal chain goes back infinitely (or to the beginning of time). The same is not true for agent causation. When an agent causes an action to take place, there are no prior causes that trigger this decision. According to libertarianism, agents are substances and have *special causal powers* to cause actions without there being any prior causes that determine the agent to do so.

One way to make libertarianism intuitively clear is to think about a godlike being prior to the creation of the physical universe. Suppose that this being, let us call it Fred the World Maker, decides to create the physical universe. Two things are clear in this situation. First, the creation of the physical universe is caused by Fred's action. Second, Fred's action is not causally determined to take place by prior physical events. There is, after all, no physical universe prior to this action. The deed of Fred the World Maker is therefore a self-caused action that originates completely from within Fred. According to libertarianism, all of us are a bit like Fred when it comes to performing actions. Although we are the cause of our actions, we are not causally determined by prior events to perform the action. We therefore have genuine free will. American philosopher Roderick Chisholm (1916–1999) writes in this context: "If we are responsible . . . [and if libertarianism is true] then we have a prerogative which some would attribute only to God: each of us, when we act, is a prime mover unmoved. In doing what we do, we cause certain events to happen, and nothing—or no one—causes us to cause those events to happen."[3]

In some ways, libertarianism is a mixture of determinism and indeterminism. A libertarian agrees with the determinist that actions are caused by agents, but also agrees with the inderderminist that the agents themselves are not caused to act. Through this move, the libertarian gains two crucial advantages. First, by admitting that our actions are caused, the libertarian has avoided the conclusion that we have no control over our actions. We have seen in our prior discussion that this was the main difficulty for pure indeterminism. However, by claiming that agents themselves are not caused to act in certain ways by prior events, a libertarian makes room for the idea that it is within the agent's power to act other than the agent in fact did act. We saw in the last section that this is the key difficulty for soft determinism. Moreover, libertarianism is well supported by common sense. In our day-to-day lives, we do deliberate about what future actions we should perform. We also have the strong feeling that it is up to us what we will do. No matter whether we have had a bad childhood, or whether we attended a horrible public high school, we still feel that we have it within us to make good choices and break away from what our past makes us inclined to do. Libertarianism validates these feelings since it is based on the idea that agents have special causal powers to perform actions that are not causally determined to take place. In spite of these advantages, however, libertarianism also leads to some difficulties, which we will discuss in the next section.

Problems for Libertarianism

We have seen that philosophers tend to be careful when it comes to introducing new fundamental entities into our thinking. If it is possible to explain the world without referring to ghosts, vampires, witches, or black magic, then the principle of Ockham's Razor suggests that we should eliminate these entities from our understanding of the world. Simplicity is an intellectual virtue. Libertarianism, however, is quite a loaded philosophical theory. It introduces two fundamentally new entities into our understanding of the world: agent causation and agents. The question is whether it might not be better to avoid commitment to these entities.

Let us first consider the case of agent causation. According to libertarianism, something very special happens when agents cause actions. An agent can cause an action to take place without there being prior causes that prompt the agent to perform the action. A critic of this idea can point to two issues. First, there seems to be something mysterious when we say that agents cause actions without there being any prior events that cause the agents to do this. The philosopher Harry Frankfurt, for instance, observed that according to a libertarian account of freedom, any free action has the status of a miracle since it interrupts the natural order of causes.[4] But to give free actions the status of miracles is basically equivalent to admitting that there are no explanations how free actions are possible. Miracles are, after all, events that do not fit within our standard explanatory frameworks. Having free will turns, therefore, into something mysterious and inexplicable. This does not seem to be a very satisfactory result.

Second, it is far from clear why we are justified in distinguishing so sharply between agent causation and event causation. At first glance it seems that both of these processes are very similar and should be treated as instances of the *same* kind of process. The libertarian insistence that they are radically different processes seems implausible as long as there are no compelling reasons that establish that these processes are different. It is hard to see what these reasons could be.

Let us now turn our attention to the role of agents in the libertarian theory of free will. According to libertarianism, agents have special causal powers. A libertarian, therefore, needs an explanation why this should be so. Traditionally, libertarians have adopted a dualistic position about agents, that is, they maintained that agents consist not only of a physical substance but also of a mental substance. It can be argued that it is the mental substance in us that gives us the special causal power to bring about actions that are not caused by prior events. However, as we will see in Chapter 5, this kind of dualism is a philosophical position that leads to significant difficulties. Most contemporary philosophers would be extremely reluctant to base their defense of free will on the assumption that dualism is true. Moreover, even if dualism were true, it is not quite clear how it offers a satisfactory defense of why agents have special causal powers that escape the threat of determinism. If it is true that I can freely decide to lift my arm because my nonphysical mind causes me to make that decision, it is still not clear whether there are not prior mental events that have caused my nonphysical mind to cause this decision. A dualistic account of an agent does not necessarily explain how an agent could have acted otherwise.

Some libertarians have tried to avoid any commitment to dualism. According to them, agents have special causal powers not because agents have a nonphysical component, but rather simply because agents are special entities, namely **substances.** The term "substance" has a long and convoluted history in philosophical discussions. It is far from clear what exactly is asserted when we say that something is a substance. At minimum I suppose one means by this that agents are fundamental entities that cannot be reduced and explained in terms of anything else. A substance is something that through its actions can explain and cause other events, but nothing in the universe can cause or explain the behavior of substances. What this view then amounts to, it seems, is that it is a primitive fact that agents have the causal power to make choices, but that there is no explanation available why this should be so. This is hardly a satisfactory solution to the problem of free will.

Final Remarks on the Problem of Free Will

Among all philosophical problems, the problem of free will is perhaps furthest from any comprehensive solution. The contemporary philosopher Peter van Inwagen (1952–) writes in this context: "I conclude that there is no position that one can take on the matter of free will that does not confront its adherents with mystery."[5] Although there are good arguments in defense of hard determinism, indeterminism, soft determinism, and libertarianism, each position seems to run into serious difficulties. A beginning student might take this as evidence that philosophy is not going anywhere and is a waste of time. But this conclusion seems a bit hasty. Although we were not able to solve the problem of free will quickly and conclusively, our discussion shows that our own selves present one of the most mysterious and puzzling elements in the universe. Are we free agents with special causal powers? Or are we natural entities that are fully integrated within the causal network of the physical world? Both positions are plausible, but only one can be true. This is mysterious. Although we encounter our selves every day, the nature of our own selves stands in need of clarification. It is far from clear who or what we actually are. Thinking about the problem of free will has alerted us to the need to look at our own being more closely than we normally do in our day-to-day life. If we avoid this reflection, we run the risk, as the poet Rainer Maria Rilke observed, of treating our life like an envelope that we never open. Let us try to open this envelope, and continue our exploration of the self. We will do this is the next chapter when we discuss the next classical problem about the nature of the self: the problem of personal identity.

Endnotes

1. Schopenhauer, Arthur. *On the Freedom of the Will*. Oxford: Blackwell, 1985, p. 47.
2. Taylor, Richard. *Metaphysics*. Englewood Cliff: Prentice-Hall, 1974, pp. 51–52.
3. Chisholm, Roderick. "Human Freedom and the Self." In Pereboom, Derk (ed.): *Free Will*. Indianapolis: Hackett, 1997, pp. 143–155.
4. Franfurt, Harry. "Freedom of the Will and the Concept of a Person." In Pereboom, Derk (ed.): *Free Will*. Indianapolis: Hackett, 1997, pp. 167–183.
5. van Inwagen, Peter. *Metaphysics*. Boulder: Westview Press, 1993, p. 197.

For Further Reading

Fischer, John. *The Metaphysics of Free Will*. Cambridge: Blackwell, 1994.

Honderich, Ted. *How Free are You? The Determinism Problem*. New York: Oxford University Press, 2003.

Kane, Robert. *The Significance of Free Will*. New York: Oxford University Press, 1996.

Pereboom, Derek (ed.). *Free Will*. Indianapolis: Hackett, 1997.

Taylor, Richard. *Metaphysics*. Englewood Cliffs: Prentice Hall, 1992.

van Inwagen, Peter. *An Essay on Free Will*. Oxford: Clarendon Press, 1983.

CHAPTER FOUR

THE PROBLEM OF PERSONAL IDENTITY

Do We Always Remain the Same?

Our discussion of free will has made us aware that it is far from clear what kind of beings we truly are. Are we simply advanced animals, complicated machines, or godlike agents who shape the future? In this chapter, we will continue our exploration of the nature of the self by turning our attention to the problem of personal identity. A good way to introduce the issue of personal identity is to reflect on the various stages of one's life. Consider the following pictures that represent different stages in the life of Ronald Reagan:

THE LIFE OF RONALD REAGAN

Reagan
the Baby

Reagan the
Life Guard

Reagan
the Actor

Reagan the
President

The remarkable feature of Reagan's life is that he managed to do so many different things in one lifetime. He was a lifeguard in Illinois, an actor in Hollywood, and later in life a two-time president of the United States. Although most of us do not live such an eventful and varied life as Reagan, it is nevertheless true that all of us change a good deal during life. As time goes by, we grow from being a baby into an adult, and then change into an older person. Once we are aware that we change so much, an obvious worry seems to arise: Do we always remain one and the same person, or does it sometimes happen that we change so much that we actually become somebody new?

In day-to-day conversation, we often say that somebody is not "the same" anymore. For example, we can imagine a married woman who files for divorce because she thinks that her husband is no longer the same person she married 10 years ago. In religious contexts it is frequently said that people are "reborn." The boxer Cassius Clay, for example, changed his name to "Mohamed Ali" when he converted to Islam. Are we to take these transformations at face value? Is it really possible that we change who we are and become somebody else? This question is at the heart of the problem of personal identity, and we will try to find out what answer to this question seems most promising.

FOOD FOR THOUGHT

Look back at your life and list the ways in which you have changed. Do you still have the same hobbies? Do you like the same food? Do you listen to the same music? Is there actually anything you can point to that has not changed about you? If yes, is this something sufficient to make you the same person as you were in the past, or is it not more correct to say that you have become a new person?

Before we explore the various answers that have been developed in response to the problem of personal identity, we need to draw an important philosophical distinction. The use of the word "same" is ambiguous. When we speak of identical twins, we often say that they are the same. We mean by this that identical twins look alike and exhibit no visual differences. In similar fashion we might say that my neighbor has the same car as I have. By this we normally do not mean to assert that my neighbor and I own one and the same vehicle, but rather that my neighbor and I own two versions of the same type of vehicle. For example, we both might own a Ford Mustang. When we use the word "same" in this way, we refer to **qualitative identity.** Two things are qualitatively identical with each other if they look the same. Two brand-new copies of the book *Death of a Salesman*, for instance, are qualitatively identical with each other.

At times we use the word "same" with a different meaning. For instance, when I say that the guy across the street rides the same bicycle that was stolen from my garage last week, I do not want to assert that the guy across the street simply rides a bicycle that looks like my bicycle. I rather want to say that the bicycle of the guy across the street is the *very same* bicycle that was stolen from my garage. This sense of the word "same" is called **numerical identity.** Something is numerically identical with something else if and only if both are one and the same thing. The person who wrote the *Critique of Pure Reason* is numerically identical to the person who wrote *The Critique of Practical Reason*. One and the same man, Immanuel Kant, wrote both books.

FOOD FOR THOUGHT

Practice your sensitivity toward the ambiguity in the word "same" by determining whether the word is used in the following sentences as referring to qualitative identity or numerical identity.

1. Jane is the same age as Roberto.
2. The evening star and the morning star are the same.
3. I think this is the same policeman who pulled over my sister yesterday.
4. Why do I always get the same grade in all my classes?
5. You have the same haircut as Dick Cheney.
6. Peter is not the same any more.

It is clear that our attempt to solve the problem of personal identity is nearly exclusively focused on the question whether we remain numerically the same person. Although many people spend a great deal of time and money on trying to remain qualitatively the same as they were in their twenties, that is, to look identical, they are obviously fighting a lost cause. It is (causally) impossible that a person remains qualitatively the same throughout their life. Our thoughts change every minute, our hair grows every hour, and our skin ages by the day. Qualitative change is a manifest and inevitable part of our existence. The philosophically more interesting question is whether behind this qualitative change we can discover something that remains numerically the same throughout our lives.

FOOD FOR THOUGHT

To clarify your initial reactions to the problem of personal identity, it should be useful to answer the following questions with T/F:

1. If, after a serious accident, a person suffers from complete amnesia, then they have lost their sense of self and they effectively start a new life.
2. Even if we can't remember doing something, we are still responsible for what we have done.
3. If someone undergoes a successful sex-change operation and changes from having a male body to having a female body, then they do not remain the same person.
4. It is logically possible to survive one's death and continue one's life in a new spiritual body in heaven.
5. We change from moment to moment and become a new person every day.
6. It is logically possible that a conversion to a new religion turns us into a new person.
7. If a person has a severe case of Alzheimer's, then they are not the same person as they used to be.
8. What really makes us a person is not our body but rather our soul.
9. If after a serious car accident that destroyed my body a surgeon were to transplant my brain (and hence my consciousness) into a new body, then I would survive the accident although my body did not.

Let us look at the different theories that have been developed in response to the problem of personal identity. The following chart should provide a useful first impression of the various responses.

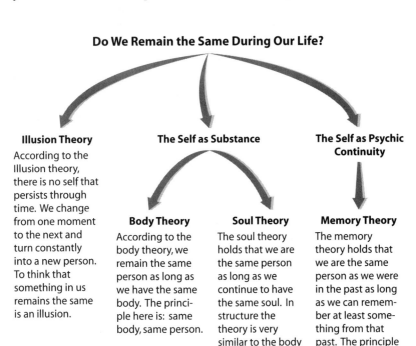

Do We Remain the Same During Our Life?

Illusion Theory

According to the Illusion theory, there is no self that persists through time. We change from one moment to the next and turn constantly into a new person. To think that something in us remains the same is an illusion.

The Self as Substance

Body Theory

According to the body theory, we remain the same person as long as we have the same body. The principle here is: same body, same person.

Soul Theory

The soul theory holds that we are the same person as long as we continue to have the same soul. In structure the theory is very similar to the body theory. The principle is: same soul, same person.

The Self as Psychic Continuity

Memory Theory

The memory theory holds that we are the same person as we were in the past as long as we can remember at least something from that past. The principle here is: as long as we have overlapping memories, we are the same person.

The Illusion Theory of Personal Identity

The Case for the Illusion Theory

The illusion theory takes its starting point from the observation that we undergo continuous qualitative change. From minute to minute our bodies are constantly gaining and losing physical material. According to recent biological studies, a human organism changes its entire physical make up every seven years. This means that seven years from now, no atom or molecule currently in your body will still be there. All of the current molecules and atoms in your body will have been replaced by new ones. We have already seen that many thinkers want to insist that there must be something permanent behind this process, but why do we have to make this assumption? If we are good empiricists and trust our senses we can only observe change, but no permanent self. The empirical evidence points to the possibility that there is no permanent and unchanging self. If we adopt this position, then we embrace the illusion theory of personal identity, which claims that all talk about a permanent self is merely an illusion.

FOOD FOR THOUGHT

The philosopher David Hume (1711–1776) was the first empiricist to draw attention to the fact that we cannot observe any permanent self. He writes in his *Treatise on Human Nature:*

> For my part, when I enter most intimately into what I call myself, I always stumble on some particular perception or other, of heat or cold, light or shade, love or hatred, pain or pleasure. I can never catch myself at any time without perception, and can never observe any thing but the perception. . . . The mind is a kind of theatre, where several perceptions successively make their appearance; pass, re-pass, glide away, and mingle in an infinite variety of postures and situations. There is properly no simplicity in it at any one time, nor identity in different; whatever natural propensity we may have to imagine that simplicity and identity.

Do you agree with Hume's observations that it is not possible to discover a permanent self when we analyze and reflect on what is happening in our minds?

The idea that everything in the universe (including ourselves) undergoes permanent change has been around for a long time. The ancient Greek philosopher Heraclitus (ca. 535–475 BCE) was the first to embrace it unconditionally. He wrote in a well-known fragment: "It is not possible to step twice into the same river . . . it scatters and again comes together, and approaches and recedes." If Heraclitus is right and every-thing changes, then it is indeed tempting to think about our selves in terms of a river. Although we call one river at different points by the same name, it is not possible to point to anything permanent that actu-ally is the river. The water in the river changes constantly and even the riverbanks undergo a constant transformation. If the illusion theory is correct, then we should think about our selves as something that under-goes constant change as well. The American philosopher William James (1842–1910) agrees with the view that we experience our personal selves as a constantly changing river. He writes:

> Thoughts connected as we feel them to be connected are what we mean by personal selves . . . [Our] consciousness is in constant change. I do not mean by this to say that no one state of mind has any duration—even if true, that would be hard to establish. What I wish to lay stress on is this, that no state once gone can recur and be identical with what it was before. . . . Often we are ourselves struck at the strange differences in our successive view of the same thing. We wonder how we ever could have opined as we did last month about a certain matter. We have out-grown the possibility of that state of mind, we know not how. From one year to another we see things in new lights. What was unreal has grown real, and what was exciting is insipid. The friends we used to care the world for are shrunken to shadows; the women once so divine, the stars, the woods, and the waters, how now so dull and common! . . . Con-sciousness . . . flows. A "river" or stream is the metaphor by which it is most naturally described.[1]

William James' observation that our consciousness undergoes perma-nent change appears credible. It follows then that not only our bodies undergo continuous change, but our minds as well. In light of this, it seems plausible to conclude that the idea of a permanent self that per-sists through time is indeed only a convenient illusion.

Many Eastern religions also support the view that there is no perma-nent self. Buddhists, for example, argue that the belief in a permanent self is the main source for suffering. If we believe that we exist in the present as well as in the future, then it is easy to be afraid that things will turn out badly for us. We consequently make preparations for the future and direct our attention away from the present. In doing this we spend all our energy planning and plotting for future success, and we forget that we need to pay attention to what is happening right now. This quickly leads to greed, regret, and ultimately suffering. According to Buddhism, it is a first step toward enlightenment to abandon the belief in a permanent self.

FOOD FOR THOUGHT

Christmas Humphreys, the former president of the Buddhist Society, summarized the central teaching of Buddhism and the self as follows.

> All that exists, from a mole to a mountain, from a thought to an empire, passes through the same cycle of existence—i.e., birth, growth, decay and death. Life alone is continuous, ever seeking self-expression in new forms. "Life is a bridge; therefore build no house on it." Life is a process of flow, and he who clings to any form, however splendid, will suffer by resisting the flow. The law of change applies equally to the "soul." There is no principle in an individual which is immortal and unchanging. Only the "Namelessness," the ultimate Reality, is beyond change; and all forms of life, including man, are manifestations of this Reality.

Do you agree with this perspective on personal identity? If yes, explain why; if not, explain why not.

There exist, then, a number of reasons that make the illusion theory of personal identity attractive. However, as always in philosophy, the illusion theory also seems to lead to some obvious difficulties. We will discuss them in the next section.

Problems for the Illusion Theory

Unlike other theories, the illusion theory does not lead to logical difficulties. There is no contradiction involved in assuming that there is no permanent self. It is also inaccurate to say that the illusion theory is not compatible with our evidence. We have already seen that empirical observations seem to support the key elements of the theory. In spite of this, the illusion theory does lead to certain uncomfortable practical implications. Whether these practical implications are sufficient to make us abandon the theory cannot be settled in a completely objective way. It depends in part on how we live (and want to live) our lives.

If we agree that there is no permanent self, then, strictly speaking, we will not be around tomorrow or ten years from now. From a pragmatic point of view, this is, obviously significant. A good deal of the things I do today, I do because I firmly believe that I will enjoy the benefits of these actions later on. For example, a good portion of my monthly paycheck flows into a retirement account. If the illusion theory of personal identity is correct, I should seriously rethink the wisdom of that practice. If there is no permanent self, then the person who will live comfortably from my retirement savings is not identical to the person I am today! So, the illusion theory of personal identity makes it look rational to spend most (if not all) of my money in the present, but this does not fit well with my natural inclinations. I do care about what happens in the future. I strongly believe (and hope) that the person who will live from my retirement savings is identical to the person I am today.

The illusion theory also has a hard time explaining why we punish people for crimes they have committed in the distant past. Suppose that Karl robbed a bank ten years ago. He managed to elude the authorities, but last Monday he was finally captured. It seems fair and just to punish Karl for what he did ten years ago, and few people would object to this practice. However, it is obvious that inflicting a punishment on Karl now is incompatible with the illusion theory of personal identity. If that theory is correct, we should conclude that we are punishing an innocent person. For the Karl who robbed the bank ten years ago is not around anymore, and he is certainly not identical to the Karl we captured last Monday.

These objections to the identity theory rest on pragmatic concerns. They show that we live our lives in the firm belief that we are going to be around in the future and that it is just to punish people for what they did in the past. The objections do not show that the illusion theory is defective. If we believe in the illusion theory strongly enough, we can even start to change our lives accordingly and thus eliminate the pragmatic concerns. We might start living more in the moment and stop worrying about the future. We can also stop blaming people for what they did in the past and thus eliminate a good deal of resentment and hate. However, if you are like me and you have a strong attachment to the belief that we persist through time and that there is good hope that the person who I am today is going to be around tomorrow, then it becomes interesting to look for alternatives to the illusion theory of personal identity. In the following sections, we will investigate how credible these alternatives theories of personal identity are.

The Body Theory of Personal Identity

The Case for the Body Theory

Among all theories of personal identity, the body theory is probably the most intuitive and the one that is most compatible with commonsense assumption. When we look at the pictures of Ronald Reagan at the beginning of this chapter, most of us are convinced that these pictures represent different moments in the life of one particular person. The reason for this conviction is easy to see: all of these pictures seem to show the same body. This supports the central philosophical principle of the body theory of personal identity: As long as we deal with the same body, we deal with the same person! It is important not to misunderstand this principle. By sameness we do not mean qualitative sameness, but numerical sameness. It is obvious that Reagan's body changed considerably throughout his life, but it is nevertheless correct to say that we are numerically dealing with the same physical body.

In day-to-day life most of us subscribe to the body theory of personal identity. Suppose you are a detective and you are supposed to determine whether the person you have caught is the famous serial killer Hannibal Lecter. In order to find an answer to this question, you might compare whether the DNA or fingerprints of Hannibal Lecter are identical to the DNA or the fingerprints of the person in jail. If they are, you know that the person in the cell has the same body as Hannibal Lecter. Most of us would then also feel justified to conclude that we are dealing with the same person. The principle, same body same person, is not only a cornerstone of criminal investigations but also a fundamental principle of our day-to-day life.

FOOD FOR THOUGHT

Although the principle that our personal identity is preserved as long as we inhabit the numerically same body is plausible and well established, it seems questionable at times. Consider the situation of Robert A. Robert used to be a very athletic person who spent all of his free time playing basketball and riding motorcycles. In August 2002 Robert crashed his motorcycle and is now paraplegic. Although Robert still has the same (numerical) body as before, he feels that he is not the same person since he cannot do the things he loves most. Do you agree with him? If yes, what consequences does this have for the body theory of personal identity?

Overall, there is a good deal to be said in defense of the body theory of personal identity. Let us investigate in the next section whether the body theory runs into any serious problems.

Problems for the Body Theory

A major reason why some thinkers object to the body theory of personal identity is connected with the prospect of life after death. Even if one does not believe that life after death is plausible (i.e., that it is causally possible), it seems that it should at least be logically possible that we continue to exist after our physical bodies stop functioning. It is, however, pretty easy to see that the body theory runs into fundamental difficulties when it comes to explaining how it is logically possible to survive one's death. First, according to most religions that speak of life after death, we will not have the same kind of body in the afterlife that we have had on Earth. Many religions introduce the idea of a spiritual body. But according to the body theory, this entails that I cannot persist through the change from my physical body to a spiritual body. For if I exist only as long as I have the numerically same body as I have on Earth, and if my new spiritual body is numerically distinct from my physical body, then I do not remain the same person. We can avoid this difficulty by insisting that God will recreate the very same physical body I had on Earth. However, in this case it is not quite clear whether my physical body will be in the same state as it was right before I died or not. If it is in the same physical state as it was when I died, then for most of us life in heaven is not very pleasurable since our old bodies are the sources of major discomforts. On the other hand, if God recreates our physical bodies in the state in which they were when we were 20 (or some other young age), then the question arises whether the body will start to age again. If my resurrected body is physically identical with my body on Earth, it is a matter of causal necessity that it will age again. But that conclusion is incompatible with the idea that we enjoy an eternal life in heaven. No matter how we twist the story, it seems as if the body theory of personal identity is not compatible with the idea that life after death is logically possible. Now, some people might take this as a reason to claim that the mere idea of life after death is logically incoherent, but most people will probably want to resist this conclusion and search for a different theory of personal identity.

In addition to the issue of life after death, there is a further closely related problem for the body theory. The philosopher John Locke (1632–1704) pointed out that it seems logically possible for two different persons to switch their bodies. Such body switches have been the subject of stories and fairy tales, and have also provided the theme for Hollywood movies. The movie *Freaky Friday*, for instance, deals with the complications that arise when a daughter switches bodies with her mother. Given that we can make movies about this situation, it seems plausible to conclude that body switches are logically possible. However, it is easy to see that according to the body theory of personal identity, body switches should be logically impossible. That does not appear to be a very convincing conclusion.

A final weakness of the body theory has to do with cases of total amnesia. It seems reasonable to say that a person who suffers from complete amnesia has lost his sense of self and is not the same person anymore. This indicates that our sense of personal identity is dependent on there being psychological continuity. If the psychological continuity is broken, it is hard to see why we should maintain that we are still the same person. However, if we subscribe to the body theory, then a person who suffers from complete amnesia is still the same person as long as he has the numerically same body. This might strike many people as a rather unorthodox conclusion.

The Soul Theory of Personal Identity

The Case for the Soul Theory

The soul theory of personal identity follows a similar philosophical strategy as the body theory. Both theories attempt to tie our personal identity to an enduring entity. The body theory focuses on the physical body; the soul theory is centered around the idea of a nonphysical soul. The key principle of the soul theory is then: Same soul, same person!

The great advantage of the soul theory over the body theory is that it can easily explain how life after death is logically possible. According to the soul theory, our personal identity is not affected by the death of our physical bodies. When our heart stops beating and our brain stops functioning, our nonphysical soul simply continues to exist and allows us to continue on. Moreover, the soul theory is also firmly grounded in popular culture. Singers and songwriters frequently talk about the soul as the center of our self. Religious texts support these sentiments as well by using the concepts "soul" and "self" interchangeably. It is therefore no surprise that many people feel very comfortable embracing the soul theory of personal identity. Unfortunately, the soul theory also leads to some serious philosophical difficulties. We will discuss these in the following section.

FOOD FOR THOUGHT

The soul theory has been around for a long time. The philosopher Plato is one of the first thinkers to develop the soul theory in greater detail. According to Plato, the soul has no gender, that is, it is possible that one and the same soul could have a male body in one life and a female body in another reincarnation. Do you agree on this point with Plato? Do you think that you could be the same person even if you changed your gender?

Problems for the Soul Theory

Good philosophical theories should not only appear plausible, but they also need to help us to explain the world. The soul theory of personal identity seems plausible to many people, but it runs into difficulties when it comes to offering explanations for our beliefs and our judgments about personal identity. Consider an example from college life. Suppose you are enrolled in a Monday, Wednesday, and Friday philosophy class. Your teacher is a brown-haired, 5'8" tall woman with a British accent. Suppose it is the second class meeting of the semester. The student who sits next to you and who missed the first class session asks you: "Is she the same person who taught this class on Monday?" You answer: "Yes, she is." Suppose the student does not quite trust you. He continues: "Do you know this for sure?" You answer: "Yes, she has the same accent, the same brown hair, and she is of the same height. She is the same person." Notice how, in justifying and explaining your knowledge that you are dealing with the same person, you made reference to the person's body. Imagine what would happen if you are a firm believer in the soul theory. In that case you would have to respond to the second question of your classmate as follows: "Well, I am not entirely sure whether that is the same person who taught the class on Monday. I am after all not able to check whether she has the same soul as the person on Monday." That answer seems peculiar. Most of us would feel very confident to assert that we do indeed *know* that the teacher was the same as on Monday. But it is hard to see how a supporter of the soul theory could ever explain why this judgment is justified. It follows therefore that the soul theory of personal identity leads to a form of skepticism. We can never be sure whether we deal with the same person because we have no means of checking whether they continue to have the same soul. Souls are, after all, invisible, nonphysical substances that cannot be seen, heard, or tasted. The skepticism even extends to judgments about our own selves. By what means can I verify that I have the same soul as yesterday? Perhaps my soul has disintegrated, or it has multiplied. There seems to be no way of making sure that this has not happened. If we want to avoid such thoroughgoing skepticism about personal identity, we need to look for an alternative to the soul theory.

FOOD FOR THOUGHT

The soul theory also leads to certain theological difficulties. If the soul theory is correct and our self consists in an immaterial non-physical substance, then we actually never die. What happens at death is then simply the separation of our soul from our body. But we never really vanish. We continue to exist. The theological difficulty of this view is to make sense of the concept of resurrection. If we never die, we consequently do not need to be resurrected. However, many religions are founded on the idea of resurrection. Can you think of a way in which we can make the soul theory of personal identity compatible with the idea of resurrection?

In addition to these skeptical worries, the soul theory is also confronted with some serious metaphysical challenges. These metaphysical questions are normally discussed in the context of the mind/body problem, and therefore we will discuss them in the next chapter.

The Memory Theory of Personal Identity

The Case for the Memory Theory

The body theory and the soul theory attempt to provide an account of personal identity that assumes that our personal selves are substances. The body theory claims that we are physical substances and the soul theory claims that we are immaterial substances. Since both theories run into problems, it is tempting to look for alternative accounts of personal identity. A promising alternative is to explain personal identity in terms of a psychological connection between different life stages. The best-known theory that defines personal identity in terms of a psychological connection between life stages is the memory theory. The English philosopher John Locke was the first to develop a version of the memory theory in some detail. He writes:

> For since consciousness always accompanies thinking, and 'tis that, that makes every one to be, what he calls *self*; and thereby distinguishes himself from all other thinking things, in this alone consists *personal Identity*; *i.e.* the sameness of a rational Being: And as far as this conscious-

ness can be extended backwards to any past Action or Thought, so far reaches the Identity of that *Person* . . .[2]

The basic idea behind the memory theory of personal identity is therefore the following. I am identical to a person who existed in the past as long as I can remember at least some events that were experienced by that person. This seems plausible. Right now, for example, I can remember what it felt like to receive a failing grade on a Latin examination in 8th grade. If I can remember this experience, then it is clear that the person who received the failing grade in 8th grade is I. Nobody else can possibly remember what it felt like to fail that Latin exam. My self therefore extends back as far as I can remember experiences of the past. We are connected with the past as long as the past is somehow present within us, and we will be connected with our present in the future, as long as we are able to remember this present.

It is easy to see that the memory theory can solve the problems that undermined the body and the soul theory of personal identity. First, according to the memory theory, it is easy to explain how it is logically possible to survive one's death. If after my death a person in heaven can remember what I did on this Earth, it seems plausible to conclude that this person is identical to the person I am today. It is of no consequence whether that person should have a spiritual body or whether it is simply a nonphysical soul that exists in a different sphere. As long as my memories are around, I myself will be around.

Moreover, unlike the soul theory, the memory theory can also explain how we can know that the person we see today is the same person we knew in the past. For if we are in doubt, we can simply ask the person questions about their memories. Consider the example of a 20-year class reunion. Suppose you see a person who looks somewhat like your old buddy Alexis. However, you are not quite sure whether she is indeed your old buddy. According to the memory theory, all you need to do is start a conversation and ask that person a couple of questions about the past. If the person can remember some of the adventures you and Alexis survived together, you have excellent reasons for thinking that the person is indeed the same Alexis, no matter what she looks like. The memory theory, therefore, can do something the soul theory failed to do: it can explain how we can know that we are dealing with the same person we knew in the past.

There are further reasons that support the memory theory. The German philosopher Gottfried Wilhelm Leibnitz (1646–1716) suggested the following thought experiment. Suppose that you are offered the chance to become the King of China (i.e., a person with unlimited wealth and every opportunity to fulfill all of his desires) on the condition that you have to undergo a brainwashing that will destroy all and every memory you currently have. Would you accept that offer? Most of us, I suppose, would decline. What good is it to become rich and powerful if we have to sacrifice our memories? Our sense of self seems essentially connected with our ability to remember our past. If a person who does not know my name, my parents, nor any of my past experiences should happen to become the King of China, that person does not seem to be me, even if he should happen to have the same body I currently have.

Problems for the Memory Theory

Although the memory theory is well compatible with common sense and is able to solve many of the difficulties that plagued the body and the soul theory, it leads to some difficulties as well. The Scottish philosopher Thomas Reid (1710–1796) pointed out that the memory theory leads to potential inconsistencies. Reid imagined the following scenario. Suppose that there is an old retired general who still has vivid memories of his experiences as a middle-aged officer but who has completely forgotten everything about his childhood. Suppose further that when he was a middle-aged officer, the general still had a very detailed recollection of his childhood. The situation can be visually represented as follows:

The logical problem that arises in this situation for the memory theory is the following. Since M can remember his life as a young boy, we have to conclude that M is identical to Y. Moreover, since G can remember his life as a middle-aged officer, we also need to conclude that G is identical to M. However, since the old general has absolutely no recollection of his life as a young boy, we also need to hold that G is not identical to Y. It follows therefore that the memory theory seems to entail the following set of inconsistent propositions.

1. M = Y
2. G = M
3. G ≠ Y

Any philosophical theory that leads to inconsistencies is in serious trouble. We can take this as a reason to abandon the memory theory completely or we can try to modify the theory such that the inconsistency can be avoided. The latter option seems more reasonable, since only a small modification of the theory will allow us to deal with these situations successfully. All we need to do is to distinguish between **indirect** and **direct memories.** A direct memory is a memory that one can recall consciously right at this very moment. For example, I have a direct memory of what I ate for breakfast this morning. However, I have no direct memory what shirt I was wearing ten days ago. When I try to think about it, I simply draw a blank. **Indirect memories** are memories that I cannot recall directly, but which a former version of my self used to be able to recall directly. For example, I cannot directly remember the name of my first English teacher in high school. However, there was a time in my life when I was able to recall this easily and I am linked to that time via direct memories that I can recall right now.

FOOD FOR THOUGHT

Decide whether you have direct or indirect memories of the following events in your life:

1. Your 16th birthday.
2. The name of your best friend in 4th grade.
3. The name of the lead singer in your first favorite music group.
4. Your 10th birthday.
5. The title of the first book you ever read.
6. The name of your favorite elementary school teacher.

This distinction between indirect and direct memories puts us in a position to solve the difficulty that was raised by Thomas Reid. Although the old general cannot directly recall his experiences as a boy, he has an indirect memory of these events, since a former version of himself (the middle-aged officer) is able to recall these experiences directly. If we modify the memory theory such that being the same self only requires that we have an indirect memory link to the past, then we can successfully avoid the prior inconsistency. In that case we can say that the old general is still the same person as the young boy, because the old general has indirect memories of his childhood.

This modification of the memory theory also helps us to deal with cases of Alzheimer's. Consider the following situation. Suppose that one of your close relatives has a serious case of Alzheimer's. You visit him in the nursing home at the beginning of the week and you have a great conversation. A couple of days later, during your next visit, the situation of your relative has deteriorated. When you enter his room, he greets you with the words, "Who in the world are you?" In this situation it would be odd to say that your relative is no longer the same self as he used to be several days ago. According to the original memory theory, however, this conclusion would be forced upon us since your relative has no direct memories of your conversation at the beginning of the week. Stating the memory theory in terms of indirect memories resolves this problem. In this case, we can argue that your relative probably has some direct memories that link him back one or two days ago when he could still directly remember the conversation. We are therefore able to conclude that your relative, in spite of his shaky memories, is still the same person.

A more serious challenge to the memory theory is raised by the problem of false memories. It is well known that memories can be deceiving. I seem to remember, for instance, that as a 3-year-old child I got lost in a crowded shopping mall for several hours. However, I am not quite sure whether this is really a genuine memory or simply something I seem to remember because my mother told me about the incident later on in my life. Let us call memories that are not caused by actual experiences false memories. It is obvious that false memories can lead to a false sense of self. Suppose that I seem to remember the experiences of Napoleon. I am obviously not justified to claim on the basis of these memories that I am identical to Napoleon unless I can be sure that these memories are genuine and true.

FOOD FOR THOUGHT

The problem of false memories is especially pressing when people seem to remember experiences from past lives. Take a look at the following experience that was anonymously described on a Web page with the title *Practical Guide to Past-Life Memories:*

> My husband and I went on a camping trip last summer. We had never done anything like it before, and I found it hard to fall asleep outdoors under the stars. It was beautiful lying there in my husband's arms, but once he fell asleep I'd lie there for hours, half expecting an attack at any moment. Three days into the vacation I managed to fall asleep in the middle of the night and dreamt that I was a young American Indian boy lost in the same area we were camping in. I could feel the young boy's nervousness and fear as he struggled to find food and make his way home. He lay on the ground at night, just as I was doing, and he wasn't able to sleep either as he was aware of every sound and movement. He seemed to think he was being followed or pursued, and all day long he kept looking behind him. He did this day after day. Eventually, it all got to be too much for him and he began to run. He caught his foot in the root of a tree and fell, breaking a leg. He couldn't move, and he lay on the ground waiting for death. When I woke up, I was sweating and my heart was racing. I'm convinced that I was that boy. It was far too vivid and real to be a dream.

Would this person be justified to believe that she is the same person as the young American Indian boy?

Similar problems are raised when people seem to remember (often under hypnosis) certain dramatic events from their early childhood. This shows that in order to provide an accurate account of personal identity on the basis of memories, we need to distinguish between false and genuine memories. The easiest way to draw this distinction is to define genuine memories as follows. A genuine memory is a memory of an experience that in fact happened to **me.** Although this definition seems natural, it creates a serious logical problem for the memory theory. The memory theory explains personal identity in terms of genuine memories. If we now turn around and define genuine memories as memories of experiences that in fact happened to me, we are involved in a vicious circle.

For we define who we are in terms of genuine memories and then turn around and define genuine memories in terms of who we are. This is logically not acceptable.

To avoid this difficulty, the Australian philosopher Sydney Shoemaker introduced the concept of a **quasi-memory**. A quasi-memory is an experience

1. That we seem to remember,
2. That somebody actually had, and
3. That is caused in the right way by an actual experience.

It is not important to understand this rather technical concept precisely. What is important is to understand that this concept of a quasi-memory allows us to state the memory theory of personal identity without presupposing that we already understand the concept of self. We can say now that a person at time t_1 is identical with a person at time t_2 if and only if the person at time t_2 quasi-remembers the experiences of the person at time t_1. Introducing the concept of a quasi-memory has some drawbacks, however. Take a look at the third condition of the definition. We quasi-remember something only if it is caused by actual experiences. This condition makes sure that mere illusions and false memories do not count as quasi-memories. However, the condition raises an epistemic problem. How can we know that condition 3 applies to our memories? We obviously cannot know this directly. The philosopher John Perry has concluded, therefore, that causal memory theories can successfully avoid the charge that they offer a circular account of personal identity, but they do so "at the cost of making 'the self' an inferred entity."[3] This is not an entirely satisfactory result.

FOOD FOR THOUGHT

The philosopher Bernard Williams suggested the following thought experiment as an objection to the memory theory. Suppose someone informs you that at a future time t, you will be tortured. Upon hearing this you are scared and fearful. But then you are told that prior to t, all your memories will be erased as well. Will this alleviate your fears? Williams argues that this additional information will do nothing to quell your fears of torture. Do you agree with

Williams? If yes, what theory of personal identity is supported by this answer?

A third difficulty for the memory theory of personal identity is that it does not seem to be a sufficient condition for being the same person. Consider the example of college freshman José. In high school José was a melancholic, introverted person who never talked to his classmates. After going to college, José changed his ways. Now, he is friendly, outgoing, and goes out of his way to talk to other students. It seems tempting to say that José has become a different person. However, it is also obvious that the memory theory cannot explain why this should be so. This example suggests that being the same person not only requires that we remember our past, but also that we retain at least some of our psychological characteristics. Having overlapping memories might only be a necessary but not a sufficient condition for remaining the same person.

Final Remarks on Personal Identity

The problem of personal identity, similar to the problem of free will, does not lead to a clear-cut solution. The illusion theory is theoretically elegant, but we have seen that it leads to pragmatic difficulties. The body and soul theories both run into serious logical or epistemic difficulties. The memory theory, if it is to avoid the charge of being circular, seems to turn the concept of self into a highly abstract concept. In recent times, philosophers have become less interested in providing a clear analysis of what personal identity consists in, but instead have been discussing whether the concept of personal identity is very important for our understanding of the world. This shift in emphasis was mainly caused by the work of the philosopher Derek Parfit (1942–). Parfit pointed out that the relation of personal identity is, from a logical point of view, a very rigid relationship. It is, for instance, logically impossible that a person at time t_1 is identical with two numerically distinct persons at time t_2. In a famous thought experiment, Parfit imagined what would happen if a teletransporter were to produce two exactly similar copies of me, while destroying the original. Would I still be around? If yes, which of the two copies is identical with me? According to the memory theory, I have equally good reasons to pick any of the two. But it is, as we have seen, logically impossible that I am identical with both of them. As a solution, Parfit suggested that we entertain the idea that we can survive without being strictly identical to anyone. Many philosophers have found this result questionable. The debate about the importance of personal identity is still in full swing and will not be resolved anytime soon. Although there is no clear-cut solution to the problem of personal identity, our discussion has shown once more that the nature of our own self is mysterious. We will therefore continue our exploration of the self by clarifying the relationship between our bodies and our minds.

Endnotes

1. James, William. The Stream of Consciousness. In: *Psychology*, Chapter XI. New York: Henry Holt and Co., 1910, pp. 151–175.
2. Locke, John. *An Essay Concerning Human Understanding*. Oxford: Clarendon Press, 1975, p. 332.
3. Perry, John. The Importance of Being Identical. In: Rorty, Amelie (ed.). *The Identities of Persons*. Berkeley: University of California Press, 1976, p. 69.

For Further Reading

Parfit, Derek. *Reasons and Persons*. Oxford: Claredon Press, 1984.

Perry, John. *A Dialogue on Personal Identity and Immortality*. Indianapolis: Hackett, 1978.

Rorty, Amelie (ed.). *The Identities of Persons*. Berkeley: University of California Press, 1976.

Shoemaker, Sydney, and Swinburne, Richard (eds.). *Personal Identity*. Oxford: Blackwell, 1984.

Williams, Bernard. *Problems of the Self*. Cambridge: Cambridge University Press, 1973.

CHAPTER FIVE

THE MIND/BODY PROBLEM

What Is the Problem?

The problem of personal identity has introduced us to the idea that our selves have a physical as well as a psychic component. In this chapter, we will explore this relationship between our bodies and our minds in more detail. Initially, you might be surprised to hear that philosophers find the relationship between body and mind problematic. Humans like you and I have a body, and we also have a mind. What in the world is so mysterious about this? At first glance very little, but certain questions begin to emerge as soon as we describe the features of bodies and minds in more detail.

Let us start by describing some characteristics of human bodies. Since I am not sure who is reading this book right now, I will simply pick my own body as an example. My body is 5'7" tall and weighs 160 pounds. It has brown hair and blue eyes. Its nose is rather crooked since I broke it several times in my youth, and its feet are rather small. I could go on like this and describe additional properties of my body, but I am sure that you get the point. It is not particularly challenging to describe bodies. Bodies have **physical properties** just like any other physical object. They have color, shape, size, and texture. We can see them with our eyes, measure their weight, and take pictures of them. Moreover, human bodies are also subject to the laws of physics. If you take my body and throw it through a second-floor window, it will crash to the ground like a rock. A physicist would be able to calculate the impact velocity without any difficulty. Moreover, in that case we would also be able to predict that my body would not survive such a fall without damage. Human bodies are similar to complex machines. If we treat them without proper care, they fall apart, and sooner or later (even with proper care) they will stop functioning.

Let us now turn to a description of minds. Initially, it might seem as if human minds are more difficult to describe than human bodies. It's obvious that we cannot take pictures of them or measure their size or weight. Notice that if I say, "My brain is a gray organic mass that weighs 4 pounds," I haven't told you anything about my mind, but something about the internal structure of my body. My brain is part of my body, and the fact that my brain is perhaps smaller than yours would not entitle you to draw the conclusion that you have a bigger and better mind than I have. So, when we want to develop a description of our minds, we cannot simply give a description of our brains.

Although minds cannot be described in the same way we describe our bodies, it is nevertheless far from difficult to say something about our minds. After all, we are aware of what thoughts and sensations happen within them. Right now, for example, I am thinking that later today I have to buy a present for my mother's birthday. This thought is something that happens in my mind. Having thoughts and beliefs is part of my mental life. But there is more to the mind than that. Another key ingredient of the mind is sensations and feelings. If somebody told me that I am an incompetent teacher of philosophy, I would feel sad and disappointed. These feelings are also part of my mental life. If all I had was a body without a mind, my life would certainly be less cumbersome. There would be no feelings of fear or regret. I would never be depressed, but on the other hand, life would also be rather dull. For just as I would be unable to feel these sad feelings, I would also be unable to feel joy and happiness. Without a mind there would be no dreams and hopes. A steak would have no flavor, and a kiss would be without passion.

FOOD FOR THOUGHT

In order to come to terms with the role minds play in this universe, it may be useful to engage in this thought experiment: Imagine, as clearly as you can, a universe that consists only of physical objects and physical properties but which lacks minds and mental properties. Would this universe contain colors and sounds? Would there be space and time? Would pineapples still taste sweet and the sea salty? Would roses still be beautiful? Make a list of those features of the world which would vanish if all minds were suddenly wiped out.

A good way to approach the mind is to understand it as something that allows us to engage in a wide range of activities; these are shown in the following illustration:

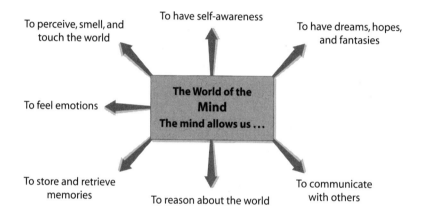

We have seen that bodies have physical properties; minds, on the other hand, can be described in terms of **mental states.** When I am thinking about my twelfth birthday party, my mind is in a certain memory state. Memories, sensations, beliefs, and dreams are all examples of mental states. Using one general term to refer to all mental phenomena might suggest that all mental states share common characteristics. However, it is notoriously difficult to find a universal feature that is essential to all mental states. Mental states are diverse and varied. The following exercise illustrates this point.

FOOD FOR THOUGHT

Take a look at the following examples of mental states and try to determine whether they can be grouped into a number of larger categories.

Continued

1. Feeling a sharp pain.
2. Being convinced that the Red Sox are going to win the World Series in 2007.
3. Knowing that 2 + 2 = 4.
4. Smelling freshly brewed coffee.
5. Seeing a lunar eclipse.
6. Dreaming of winning the lottery.
7. Remembering to buy some milk at the grocery store.
8. Imagining a perfect vacation.
9. Fearing that the war on terrorism will never be over.
10. Knowing that there are nine planets in the solar system.
11. Perceiving a yellow sunflower.
12. Thinking that the world is round.
13. Experiencing great frustration.

Now that we have developed a rough description of human bodies and minds, it is easy to appreciate the emerging puzzle: human bodies and minds are intimately tied to each other. Physical states (like a cut on my finger) can produce mental states (such as a feeling of pain), and mental states (like feeling embarrassed) can produce physical states (such as blushing). However, in spite of this close interaction, mind and body are also quite dissimilar. When we talk about our bodies we describe them as exhibiting **physical properties.** Physical properties are **public** in the sense that others can observe and measure what kind of physical state my body is in. A medical doctor, for example, can easily measure a wide range of physical properties of my body (e.g., temperature, weight, size). However, when we talk about our minds we describe **mental states** and **mental properties** and thus talk about beliefs, desires, and wishes. These mental states are experienced from a **first-person perspective** and are inherently **private.** Others cannot tell from the outside what it feels like to have my desires or sensations. Although a medical doctor can tell me that my body is running a fever, she cannot tell me what it feels like to have this fever. The experience of having this fever happens in my mind and seems inaccessible to anybody but myself. This realization leads us to the central question of the mind/body problem: **How exactly are the physi-**

cal states of human bodies related to the mental states of human minds?

In this chapter we will study and evaluate how various philosophers have tried to respond to this question. We will see that philosophers and scientists have made considerable progress in recent years, but the question remains an open one.

FOOD FOR THOUGHT

Before we discuss several solutions to the mind/body problem in more detail, it may be interesting for you to record your own initial beliefs and ideas about the relationship between mind and body. Answer the following questions with T/F:

1. It is possible for my mind to survive the death of my body.
2. Someday in the future it will be possible to build machines that have a mind just like mine.
3. The best way to treat depression is to change the chemical reactions inside my brain.
4. Sometime in the future, it might be possible for a crazy scientist to create false memories in my mind by simply injecting certain chemicals into my brain.
5. Although scientists can understand the composition and nature of clouds, planets, black holes, and other physical objects, they will never understand the true nature of emotions like anger, love, or hate.
6. Dogs and cats have beliefs and hopes just like humans do.
7. Sometime in the future computers might have consciousness and self-awareness.
8. My thoughts and ideas are the product of my environment and my upbringing.
9. There might exist conscious beings on other planets who do have beliefs and self-awareness but who do not have brains like ours.
10. It is impossible for machines to be creative or funny. Even the most advanced robots, therefore, could never be stand-up comedians.

Possible Solutions to the Mind/Body Problem

Our previous discussion has helped us clarify the nature of minds and bodies. It is now time to explore in greater detail how the physical states of our bodies are related to the mental states of our minds. Theories about the relationship between physical states and mental states fall into three broad categories: **physicalism, dualism,** and **idealism.** The basic idea behind these theories is explained in the following chart.

How Are the Mental States of My Mind and Physical States of My Body Related to Each Other?

Physicalism	**Dualism**	**Idealism**
Mental states can be completely explained in terms of physical states. Physical states are more fundamental than mental states.	Mental states and physical states are equally "real" and ontologically independent.	Mental states are more fundamental than physical states.

Let us take a closer look at each of these theories. Supporters of **physicalism** believe that the physical states of the body are more fundamental than the mental states of the mind. But what exactly does that mean? Let us clarify this idea with the help of an analogy. Consider the relationship between Huckleberry Finn and Mark Twain. Each of them has various properties. Huckleberry Finn is a young boy who runs away from home and travels on the Mississippi River. Mark Twain is a well-known American author who was born in Florida, Missouri. It is easy to see that Mark Twain is a more fundamental entity than Huckleberry Finn. If we want to explain why Huckleberry Finn has certain features, we need to appeal to the ideas of Mark Twain. It would be silly to reverse this explanatory relationship. Huckleberry Finn is, after all, a fictional character that would not exist if Mark Twain had never been born. Philosophers use the term **ontological dependence** to describe the relationship between Huckleberry Finn and Mark Twain. In general, we can say that one entity ontologically depends on another entity if it cannot exist without the other.

FOOD FOR THOUGHT

In order to understand the term "ontological dependence" better, answer the following claims with T/F:

1. Tigers are ontologically dependent on lions.
2. Rainbows are ontologically dependent on water and light.
3. Wood is ontologically dependent on trees.
4. Oranges are ontologically dependent on apples.
5. Children are ontologically dependent on their parents.
6. Birds are ontologically dependent on dinosaurs.
7. Heat is ontologically dependent on the velocity of molecules.

Physicalists believe that the relationship between body and mind is similar to the relationship between Mark Twain and Huckleberry Finn. They believe that we can explain the nature of mental states in terms of the physical states of our bodies. Although there is some controversy among physicalists about exactly how mental states depend on physical states, they all agree that physical states are more fundamental entities than mental states.

Dualism rejects the idea that our minds and mental states are less fundamental than our bodies and physical states. According to dualism, the universe contains two different and equally real substances: mind and body. The relationship between these two substances is in some ways similar to the relationship between apples and oranges. Just as oranges can exist without apples and apples without oranges, so minds, according to dualism, can exist independently of the body. Although many dualists accept the idea that minds and bodies can interact with each other, they maintain that minds are **ontologically independent** from bodies. Dualists reject the idea that minds can be explained in terms of the body. Critics of dualism sometimes have dubbed it the doctrine of the *"ghost within the machine"* because dualists believe that there is something irreducibly nonphysical within conscious beings.

Idealism is a third fundamental theory that explains how minds and bodies are related to each other. We have already encountered a version of idealism when we talked about George Berkeley's defense of an empiricist theory of knowledge. Idealism is the reverse of physicalism because idealism holds that minds are more fundamental than physical bodies. At first encounter, idealism seems outlandish. How can anybody think that the existence of my leg, for example, is ontologically dependent on the fact that I think that I have a leg? We normally think that legs, tables, cars, and other physical objects exist regardless of whether there are minds or not. Recall, however, the Food for Thought exercise on pages 136–137. I asked you to imagine what the universe would be like if we were to eliminate all minds from it. An idealist believes that such a universe would be empty, since minds rather than matter are the fundamental building blocks of the universe. This is a fascinating idea, but since idealism plays no significant role in the contemporary philosophical debate about the mind/body problem, I will omit a fuller discussion. In the remainder of this chapter, we will focus exclusively on the debate between dualism and physicalism. We will try to determine which of these positions appears more reasonable in light of the evidence available to us.

Substance Dualism

The classical version of dualism is **substance dualism.** Its most famous proponent is the French philosopher René Descartes (1596–1650). According to Descartes, minds and bodies are different kinds of entities. Bodies are physical substances that are located in space and time and are subject to the laws of physics. Minds, on the other hand, are nonextended thinking substances. Mind-substance is much more difficult to describe since it lacks, by definition, physical properties. However, we can at least describe it negatively as a substance that is not subject to the laws of physics. Is substance dualism a plausible theory? In order to determine that, we need to see how compelling the arguments in defense of substance dualism actually are.

Arguments for Substance Dualism
Near-Death Experiences   Consider this popular, though often neglected, argument in support of substance dualism:

1. If substance dualism is false, then my mind cannot exist independently from my body.
2. My mind can exist independently from my body.

Therefore: Substance dualism is true.

This argument is an instance of the deductive argument form **modus tollens,** and is therefore valid. Let us try to determine whether it is also sound. Premise 1 seems to be true, but how plausible is premise 2? Many religions support the idea that our minds will survive our bodily deaths and that our minds (on their own or with a new spiritual body) have the chance to enter heaven. Although this religious conviction can help us to see why the idea of life after death is attractive, it alone cannot determine whether it is rational to believe that minds can exist separately from bodies. Since philosophers are committed to adopting the most rational beliefs about the universe, we need to go beyond religion to determine whether the belief that our minds can exist without our bodies is reasonable. Can we find any evidence in support of the claim that minds can exist without bodies? The best evidence in support of this idea are so-called near-death experiences. Consider what Gloria G. experienced during brain surgery:

> As I was lying on the table I heard the doctors pronounce the operation a failure and pronounce me dead. I then remember them frantically trying to resuscitate me. While they were trying to bring me back to life, I was just floating up near the ceiling. It was a weird feeling because I was up there and this body was below . . . Then I seemed to wander up through the floors of the hospital. I saw plainly, for instance, a young man who had been injured in an automobile accident . . . Then everything began to get dark: I passed through a spiraling tunnel until I seemed to come to a place illuminated by an immensely bright light . . . A tremendous peace overcame me. My grandmother, who had died nine years before, was there. I couldn't see her—for she seemed behind me—but I could feel her presence and hear her voice . . . Suddenly, I was thrust back into my body. I don't know how or why. My next recollection is of the nurse standing near me in the recovery room.[1]

Gloria's experience is rare, but not unique. Other people have reported very similar near-death experiences, which corroborate crucial elements of Gloria's report. It is obvious that Gloria's experiences support the claim that minds can exist without bodies, for while it seemed to her that she was floating without her body above the operating table, she had feelings and perceptions. This suggests the following argument:

1. Some people report that they had experiences while being outside of their bodies.
2. The best explanation for these reports is that minds can indeed exist without bodies.

Therefore: Minds probably can exist independently from bodies.

This is an inductive argument, and it therefore cannot establish its conclusion with absolute certainty. However, we need to determine how strongly this best-explanation argument supports its conclusion. Remember what we learned in Chapter 1: in order to find out whether a given explanation is indeed the best, we need to compare the explanation to other available explanations of the same fact. How else can we explain Gloria's experiences? It is certainly possible that Gloria's experiences were caused by oxygen deprivation. We know that Gloria's heart stopped beating while she was lying on the operating table. This means that very little oxygen reached her brain for a while. But people whose brains are deprived of oxygen have been known to report visions and unusual experiences. Moreover, recently, neurologists who studied the brain of a patient who reported out-of-body experiences have found that a part of the patient's brain known as the angular gyrus was very active during these experiences. This suggests that out-of-body experiences might be caused by neurological processes in the brain. It is therefore possible to explain Gloria's experiences without accepting the claim that her mind left her body. These alternative neurological explanations have the advantage of being relatively simple since they only refer to physical entities (e.g., brains, neurological processes, angular gyrus) and avoid any reference to nonmaterial minds. Moreover, they also appear to be more conservative, since many people find the idea that the world consists only of physical entities to be in agreement with their overall picture of the world. It follows therefore that if we accept the principle of Ockham's Razor and the principle of conservativism, we have to conclude that the above best-explanation argument is not very strong. Gloria G.'s near-death experience does not provide sufficient evidence to make the conclusion that minds can exist independently from bodies very likely to be true.[2]

Does Gloria's near-death experience convince you that mind and body are separate entities? If yes, can you think of further reasons that support the conclusion that Gloria's mind has indeed left her body? What, for example, should we say to those researchers who claim that Gloria's experiences were caused by neurological activity in the angular gyrus?

The Conceivability Argument   Since the above best-explanation argument is not conclusive, let us explore some other arguments in support of substance dualism. Actually there are several, but I will focus only on one very prominent one: the **conceivability argument.** To understand the conceivability argument clearly, we need to know more about what philosophers have to say about the relation "x is identical with y." We can acquire this background knowledge by looking at the following hypothetical story.

Suppose you have a conversation with Paul, who is a big fan of conspiracy theories. Among other things, Paul believes that George W. Bush is not really who he claims he is. Paul is convinced that George W. is actually the same person as Dan Quayle. According to Paul, Dan Quayle realized that he could never win the presidency as long as people recognized him as Dan Quayle, so he proceeded to pass himself off as the oldest son of his mentor, George Bush. According to Paul, the rest is history, for Dan Quayle (disguised as George W. Bush) reached his ultimate goal and became president of the United States. Paul's theory that George W. and Dan Quayle are the same person is, of course, rather silly. But how can we refute him? The answer is pretty straightforward: A and B are identical with each other only if they have all properties in common. This principle is known as **Leibniz' law,** and it plays an important role in many areas of philosophy. If we apply Leibniz' law to Paul's theory, it follows that George W. and Dan Quayle can only be identical with each other if they have all properties in common. Suppose that I find out that Dan Quayle is 5'9" tall, whereas George W. is 6'1". This is sufficient evidence to refute Paul's theory, for I have now shown that Dan Quayle has at least one property (being 5'9" tall) that George W. lacks. This fact, together with Leibniz' law, establishes that Quayle and George W. cannot be the same person, and that Paul's conspiracy theory is false.

The Quayle/Bush story illustrates a general argumentative strategy in support of substance dualism. If we can find at least one property of minds that bodies do not have, we are entitled to draw the conclusion that minds and bodies cannot be one and the same thing. This is the basic strategy of the conceivability argument, which was first introduced by René Descartes. In standard form, we can present this argument as follows:

1. I can conceive that I exist without a body.
2. I cannot conceive that I exist without a mind.

Therefore: 3. My mind is more intimately connected with me than my body, and thus my mind has a property (the property of being essentially connected with me) that my body lacks.
4. If my mind has at least one different property than my body, then my mind cannot be identical to my body.

Therefore: My mind is not identical to my body.

At first glance, all premises of the conceivability argument appear to be true, and the argument therefore seems to makes an impressive case for substance dualism. However, many philosophers have expressed reservations toward it. First, consider premise 1. Can I really conceive that I exist without a body? If I have no body whatsoever, then I also have no eyes, and no ears, and no tongue. But how can I be myself without being able to smell, see, or hear? It is easy to imagine that I exist with a different body than the one I have right now. I could be 7 feet tall and weigh 400 pounds, but this is not enough for the argument to go through, for I can equally well imagine that I exist with a different mind. So, in order to draw the necessary distinction between body and mind, I need to make sense of the idea that I can exist without any body at all. Some thinkers have doubted that it is logically possible for a human person to be identical to a disembodied being.

FOOD FOR THOUGHT

According to many religions, we can exist in heaven with a spiritual body. But this raises the question of what spiritual bodies would be like. Would all spiritual bodies look alike? Would there be a male spiritual body and a female spiritual body? Would my spiritual body be similar to the body I used to have when I was 18, or would it be more like the body I'll have when I am 75? How would you answer these questions?

The second problem with the conceivability argument is that the concept of "conceivability" is not sufficient to justify the conclusion that entities are not identical to one another. Consider the following, obviously flawed, argument.

1. I can conceive that Clark Kent is an ordinary human being.
2. I cannot conceive that Superman is an ordinary human being.

It follows therefore that Clark Kent has a property that Superman lacks and that entails by Leibniz' law that Clark Kent is not the same person as Superman.

This argument demonstrates that we need to be very careful when we apply Leibniz' law to properties that are a result of our beliefs. There is a crucial difference between the sentences "The car in the yard is red" and "I believe the car in the yard is red." The latter sentence can be true even if the car in the yard is in fact orange. This shows that *conceiving* of objects A and B differently does not warrant the conclusion that A and B are in fact different objects. The differences might be caused by the fact that we *describe* A and B differently and that these different descriptions cause us to have different beliefs about these objects. But one and the same object—for example, the planet Venus—might be described in two different ways (as Evening Star or Morning Star), and we therefore might have different beliefs about the same object if we encounter it under different descriptions. For example, I might believe that the Morning Star is a planet, whereas I believe that the Evening Star is an actual star. This suggests that our inability to conceive that we exist without our minds might only reflect that we describe minds and bodies differently. The observation that we conceive of the relationship between our selves and our bodies and minds differently is not strong enough to establish that minds and bodies are ontologically independent entities.

Intentionality   Although the conceivability argument fails, the general strategy of the argument is promising. The best arguments in defense of dualism rest on the attempt to find properties that distinguish minds from bodies. In the contemporary discussion, many philosophers focus their attention on **intentionality.** "Intentionality" is a technical philosophical term and refers to a property of mental states. Some mental states, for example, the thought that I should buy a present for my grandmother, are *about* something else. In this case, the mental state is about my grandmother and the present I want to buy. To say that mental states have intentionality is to say that mental states represent something else. Notice, however, that it is not clear how ordinary physical objects like trees, cars, or brain states can be *about* other things in the same way as mental states are. A tree and any other physical object are what they are, and it is hard to see in virtue of what they could represent something else. It would be strange to say that a tree is about my grandmother. This has prompted some philosophers to resurrect the general strategy of the conceivability argument in a different form. They argue that it is in principle impossible for physical states of the body to have intentionality. But since mental states do have this property, it seems to follow that bodies and minds are different kinds of entities. The debate about intentionality is still ongoing, with no clear resolution in sight. It is therefore not possible to assess the strength of these arguments for dualism conclusively.

Arguments Against Substance Dualism

The Problem of Interaction   We have seen that the arguments in defense of dualism are open to objections. When one fails to establish a philosophical position, it is always advisable to check whether it might not be easier to disprove the theory instead. Let us turn our attention, therefore, to some of the more serious objections to dualism. Substance dualists like Descartes do not only believe that minds and bodies are independent substances, but they also believe that mind and body interact with each other. Let us see in more detail why it is plausible to think that mind and body interact with each other.

When you raise your arm up into the air, the physical movement of your body was probably preceded by a mental event: the decision to raise your arm. In situations like this, it seems very natural to say that our mind caused our body to move. On the other hand, there are instances when your body seems to influence your mind. Suppose, for example, that you expose your body to 8 hours of intense sunlight. The chances are high that the resulting state of your body will lead to a considerable amount of pain sensations. This is a paradigm example of a situation in which physical states (burned skin) cause mental states (sensations of pain). Once we realize that mind and body interact so closely with each other, we can also see that substance dualism faces a serious problem. Given that minds and bodies are different substances, how is it possible for them to influence each other? The following hypothetical situation might help you to understand this impasse more clearly.

Suppose you are playing a game of pool with Joe Shark. Joe is more skilled than you, and he is already working on the eight ball while you still have most of your balls on the table. Suddenly Joe stops and puts down his cue. He closes his eyes and stands very still. At first you think that Joe is simply concentrating before he attempts to sink the eight ball. But after several minutes, you become irritated and ask him: "Hey, Joe what are you doing? You're supposed to take your shot." Joe responds, "I'm in the process of taking my shot. I have decided to sink this last ball with my mind. Just give me a couple of minutes to focus all of my mental energies on the ball." What would you say to Joe in this situation? Would you say, "Well Joe, that's quite an interesting mind you have there." Or, would you say, "Joe, you can stand there and think about sinking the eight ball until you are blue in your face, but I can tell you one thing for sure: It's not going to go anywhere. In order to move the eight ball you need another physical object like a stick or a hand. Minds are not sufficient to move matter." Isn't it clear that you are going to say something like the latter? And if Joe does not accept your explanation, wouldn't you conclude that he has a rather bizarre picture of reality?

This hypothetical story illustrates that substance dualism cannot explain how material bodies can causally interact with immaterial minds.

The basic structure of the problem can be illustrated with the following *reductio ad absurdum*-style argument:

1. Assume that substance dualism is true.
2. If substance dualism is true, then the mind is an immaterial, nonextended thinking substance and the body is an extended physical substance.
3. Immaterial nonextended substances cannot interact with extended physical substances.
4. Mind and body interact with each other.

Therefore: Substance dualism is false.

This argument is valid, and all of its premises seem to be true. You might wonder on what grounds people accept premise 3. Can we be sure that immaterial and nonextended substance cannot causally interact with extended physical substances? In defense of this premise, one can point to a fundamental physical principle that physical energy is neither created nor destroyed. This principle is known as the *conservation of energy*. Premise 3 therefore is well established.

FOOD FOR THOUGHT

We have seen that substance dualism is in conflict with a fundamental principle of physical science: the conservation of energy. However, not everybody would agree that this is a devastating objection to dualism. Some people believe that there exist phenomena that are not explainable by the common physical laws of matter and energy. One such possible phenomenon is **telekinesis,** the ability to move objects from a distance with your mind. What do you think about telekinesis? Do you think we should take seriously reports from people who claim that they can move physical objects from a distance? Recall the movie *Star Wars*, when Luke Skywalker uses the *Force* to pull a spaceship out of the swamp. Do we have any reasons to think that this might be causally possible in our universe?

Some dualists (those who embrace a position known as **Parallelism**) have tried to save their theory from this argument, by denying premise 4. They claim that minds and bodies exist in parallel worlds and thus never interact with each other. But Parallelism faces the difficult task of explaining why mental events and physical events, although disconnected, are so well coordinated with each other. Some thinkers have tried to explain this harmony by arguing that God himself intervenes and assures that mind and body are appropriately linked. This solution is known as **Occasionalism.** But it is easy to see that Occasionalism is a rather convoluted theory that is in conflict with Ockham's Razor. Overall, there seems to exist no easy way for a dualist to escape the problem of interaction.

Do Dualists Commit a Category Mistake? The Oxford philosopher Gilbert Ryle (1900–1976) developed a further objection to dualism. Ryle claims that dualists put the term "mind" into the wrong logical category, and thus commit a "category mistake." To explain the logical framework of category mistakes, Ryle asks us to imagine the following hypothetical situation: suppose your parents come to visit you for the first time on campus. They are eager to see the university, so you take them on a little tour of the campus. You show them the library, the dorms, the lecture halls, and the auditorium. After the tour you can see that your parents are disappointed, so you ask them why they are not enjoying themselves. They say: "We came here to see the university, but all you have shown us are the lecture halls, the dorms, and the library. That's great! But would you now please show us the university itself?" It is easy to see that your parents have committed a semantic mistake. They think that the university is a specific building like the library or the dormitory. They do not realize that the term "university" refers to a whole group of buildings. They have put the term into the wrong logical category. This is a good example of a category mistake.

FOOD FOR THOUGHT

Category mistakes occur not only in the context of the mind/body problem, but also in many other fields. Take a look at the following claims and explain why one might want to say that they too entail a category mistake:

Continued

1. The world spirit helped Napoleon to conquer Europe.
2. Nothingness stared into his eyes and made him jump from the bridge.
3. The American Revolution was caused by the Enlightenment.
4. The average American lives next door.
5. Love is my best friend.

According to Ryle, substance dualists are also guilty of committing a category mistake. Dualists classify minds as substances. They say, for instance, that minds can leave the body and that minds can cause the body to move. Dualists therefore attribute properties to minds that we normally only attribute to separately existing physical things. According to Ryle, dualists fail to realize that the term "mind" does not refer to a specific entity like our body, but rather refers to certain aspects of our bodies. Defenders of dualism can accuse Ryle of simply begging the question. By insisting that minds should not be classified as substances, Ryle seems to assume what he is trying to prove. However, Ryle's criticism of dualism shows that it might be fruitful to think about the mind as something other than a nonphysical substance. Let us therefore take a serious look at nondualistic solutions to the mind/body problem. We will do this in the following sections.

Varieties of Physicalism

The basic tenet of physicalist theories about the mind is the idea that we can explain mental states in terms of physical states of the body. This idea is especially attractive in light of recent advances in neuroscience. We know, for example, that injuries to the frontal lobe of the cerebral cortex affect language capabilities in most people. We further know that chemicals like cocaine, alcohol, or anesthetics can affect our emotions and thoughts. Moreover, we have learned that memory loss can be caused by the degeneration of nerve tissues in the brain. All of these findings suggest that our mental life is dependent on physical processes within our bodies (especially the brain). To develop a satisfactory physicalistic theory of the mind, however, we need to do more than simply state the fact that our minds are dependent on our bodies. In addition, we need to say precisely what kind of physical states constitute mental states like pain or the feeling of love. It is at this point where thinkers who are attracted to physicalism begin to disagree and develop different kinds of physicalistic theories about the mind. The following chart provides an overview of some basic physicalistic theories.

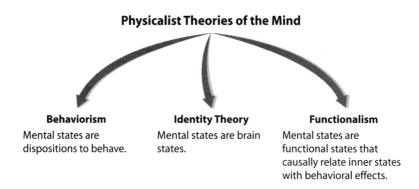

Physicalist Theories of the Mind

Behaviorism	**Identity Theory**	**Functionalism**
Mental states are dispositions to behave.	Mental states are brain states.	Mental states are functional states that causally relate inner states with behavioral effects.

In order to determine whether physicalism is a plausible solution to the mind/body problem, we need to see whether any of these theories provides a satisfactory account of the relationship between body and mind.

Behaviorism

Behaviorism is closely tied to the development of psychology. Psychology is not a very old scientific discipline. It was only at the start of the twentieth century that psychology gradually established itself as an independent scientific field of study. The main challenge for psychology was to develop a satisfactory scientific methodology with which to study the human mind.

Every science relies heavily on observations and measurements. However, it is far from trivial to observe and measure what happens in the mind of human beings. At first, psychologists tried to solve this problem by asking subjects to report on their sensations, feelings, or thoughts in experimental situations. The results of this approach were disappointing. Psychologists found out that many people have a hard time reporting reliably what happens in their minds. This might be surprising, but the basic problem is easy to grasp. Suppose Susan is a psychologist who wants to study pain. Among other things, she wants to develop a classification of different types of pain. To this end, she creates experimental settings that should help her to determine whether experiences of type X are more painful than experiences of type Y. She starts her investigation with a relatively ordinary experiment. She wants to investigate whether it is more painful to pierce one's nose or one's navel. Suppose now that you participate in her study, and that, under Susan's supervision, you pierce your nose as well as your navel. After the procedures, Susan asks you to compare your pain experiences. It certainly would be challenging for you to report with a high degree of confidence that one pain sensation was more intense than another one. It is not easy to compare sensations. But even if you were sure that piercing your navel was more painful than piercing your nose, it would certainly not follow that this would be true for other subjects as well. Introspective reports about sensations and mental content are idiosyncratic and cannot generate and support general laws about the human mind.

After realizing that introspective reports did not lead to a secure scientific foundation for psychology, psychologists started to look for a way to study the mind in a different way. The solution to these difficulties was to study human behavior. How, you might ask, can human behavior tell us anything about human minds? Consider the following examples. Suppose I want to find out whether your belief in God is stronger today than it was last year. To find the answer to this question, I could simply ask you. However, we have already seen that this not only leads to certain methodological difficulties, but it might also be the case that you yourself do not know whether the degree of your belief has increased or decreased. A good way to find an answer to this question might simply be to study how you behave. If you used to go to church weekly and read the Bible every evening—whereas now you go to church only occasionally and have stopped reading the Bible—it is quite reasonable to conclude that your belief in God has decreased. Studying your behavior (going to church, reading the Bible, talking about God) is an excellent way to gain knowledge about your mind (the degree to which you believe in God).

FOOD FOR THOUGHT

Consider one more time the research project of Susan the psychologist. Would she be able to find an answer to the question whether piercing one's navel is more painful than piercing one's nose if she were to study behavior rather than introspective reports? What do you think?

Logical Behaviorism

This general idea of observing behavior as a way of studying the mind is known as **methodological behaviorism**. It is the cornerstone of a scientific study of the mind. Methodological behaviorism proved to be pretty successful, and this caused several philosophers to push the behavioristic approach to the mind even further. They developed so-called **logical behaviorism**. The key idea of logical behaviorism, which was most prominently defended by B. F. Skinner (1904–1990), is the claim that we can eliminate all mental terms like "pain," "belief," or "hope" from our scientific discourse by translating these terms into claims about human behavior. Consider the sentence "John loves Lucy." According to Skinner and other logical behaviorists, this sentence should not be part of a good scientific language since we cannot determine clearly under what conditions this sentence is true or false. In order to make progress, we first need to translate the sentence into a statement about John's behavior. We should therefore say something like this: the sentence "John loves Lucy" is equivalent to "John has a tendency to bring flowers to Lucy, and he has a tendency to hug her repeatedly, and he has a tendency to tell her 'I love you.'" These latter sentences about John's behavior can be verified to be true or false, and so are an acceptable part of scientific discourse. In general, logical behaviorists suggest that *all mental phenomena like beliefs or sensations can be understood as dispositions to behave in certain ways.* Logical behaviorism is therefore an eliminative theory about mental terms because it holds that in the final analysis of the world we do not need to make reference to terms like "pain" or "belief." All of these terms can be replaced by descriptions that only refer to behavior.

FOOD FOR THOUGHT

How would a logical behaviorist transform the following sentences, so that they become a legitimate part of scientific discourse?

1. Henry is angry with Maud.
2. Torsten believes that he is ugly.
3. Nikisha wants to become rich.
4. Tonya is in severe pain.
5. Avrindam has learned Spanish well.

Logical behaviorism is a rather economical theory of the mind. It solves the mind/body problem by explaining minds in terms of behavior. It does not face the problem of interaction, which created such severe problems for dualistic thinkers. For logical behaviorists, our talk about minds is just a convoluted way to talk about our behavior. Minds *are not* fundamental entities in the world and the questions of how minds can interact with bodies is thus eliminated. Logical behaviorism also provides a theoretical framework for psychological research. Since human behavior can be understood in terms of **stimuli, conditioning,** and **responses,** behaviorism allows us to learn about the mind by constructing theories centered upon these observable terms as well. According to behaviorism, our "mental life" is simply a set of learned behavioral responses to various stimuli and reinforcements from our environment.

Arguments Against Logical Behaviorism

In spite of its elegance and simplicity, logical behaviorism is open to some serious objections. One fundamental problem can be illustrated with the help of a hypothetical story. Suppose your best friend Sara arranges a blind date for you with her old love, Bill. Sara is convinced that the two of you will be a perfect fit. However, when you meet Bill for the first time in person, you can see right away that Bill is the date from hell. He is boring, ill mannered, and simply ugly. Since you do not want to hurt the feelings of your friend Sara, you pretend to have a good time with Bill. You laugh at his dull jokes and pretend to take an interest in his life stories, but in reality you are dreading every minute of this first—and last—date with Bill. Suppose now that Bill is a behaviorist.

What would Bill say about your feelings for him? It is clear that Bill feels entitled to say that you like him. After all, you did display all the necessary "liking behavior." However, it is quite clear that Bill has been fundamentally wrong about you and your mental states. Your real feelings did not correspond to your behavior at all.

This is not a knockdown argument against behaviorism, since a behaviorist can save his theory by claiming that you would have acted differently if the circumstances had been different (i.e., if you had not wanted to pretend to like Bill for the sake of your friend Sara). A behaviorist might therefore still maintain that you had a disposition to display "non-liking" behavior toward Bill. You simply chose not to act on this disposition. The story nevertheless illustrates two weaknesses of logical behaviorism. First, to explain why you chose not to display your "non-liking" behavior toward Bill, one must refer to the fact that you believe this behavior would hurt the feelings of your friend Sara. A behaviorist, however, cannot refer to mental states (since for him mental states reduce to behavior), and must therefore offer an inadequate and incomplete explanation for why you displayed "liking behavior" toward Bill. Second, the story also illustrates that displaying a certain type of behavior is neither a necessary nor a sufficient condition for being in a certain mental state. Mental states seem to be the cause of behavior, but they are not the same things as behavior or dispositions to behave.

FOOD FOR THOUGHT

Can you think of situations in your own life in which your behavior did not correspond to your feelings and thoughts? Compare some of these examples with others in the class. Do you think that these examples are sufficient to disprove logical behaviorism?

The linguist Noam Chomsky developed a further objection against logical behaviorism. According to logical behaviorism, it is possible to explain our future behavior (and thus our mind) in terms of past conditioning and responses. Behaviorists believe that there are lawful connections between our past behavioral experiences and our dispositions to behave in certain ways in the future. However, this explanatory model makes it impossible to explain why we sometimes display completely

novel verbal behavior. When we speak or write in a language we sometimes express propositions that nobody (to our knowledge) has uttered
before. Right now, for example, I am writing a sentence I have probably
never written or read before. The most natural explanation for my behavior is that I have certain ideas in my mind that I want to express. But
a behaviorist cannot make use of this explanation, because, according to
him, mental states cannot play any role in explaining our behavior. Logical behaviorism faces the problem that it cannot explain how people
manage to display novel (linguistic) behavior.

Although there are further objections against logical behaviorism, we
are already in a position to see that an exclusively behavioristic theory of
the mind is too restrictive. Logical behaviorism draws attention to the
fact that our behavior is closely linked to what happens in our minds
and that the study of behavior can help us to develop a scientific theory
of the mind; however, it is problematic to reduce all mental states to dispositions to behave in certain ways. If we want to develop a satisfactory
physicalist theory of the mind, we need to admit that a complete account of our mental life will involve more than talk about our behavior.
Let us therefore take a look at alternative physicalistic theories.

The Identity Theory

Behaviorism is not a very natural theory about the mind and mental
phenomena. Few people would think that their mental life can be reduced to talk about behavior. The **identity theory,** on the other hand, is
a very intuitive theory that seems immediately plausible. The basic
thrust of this theory can be illustrated with respect to a historical example. In 1848, in a small town in Vermont, the railroad worker Phineas
Gage was seriously injured while setting a charge of dynamite. The explosion was set off early and sent a steel bar right through his head. Surprisingly, Phineas Gage survived the accident and recovered from his
head injuries. However, the accident caused serious repercussions. After
Phineas Gage had recovered from his injuries, his behavior changed
dramatically. Whereas he used to be easygoing and polite, he became
obnoxious and ill mannered. Friends who knew Phineas Gage before
claimed that the accident had turned him into a different person. How
can we explain what happened to Phineas Gage?

According to the identity theory, the answer is simple and straightforward. Although Phineas Gage's body survived the accident, his brain was

significantly altered by the steel bar. If we assume that mind and brain are the same thing, then we can explain Phineas Gage's change in behavior without problems. For in this case, we can claim that the steel bar injured not only Phineas Gage's brain, but his mind as well. **The general claim that mental states are ultimately brain states is the central thesis of the identity theory.** The identity theory is well supported by recent advances in neuroscience. Neuroscience has discovered that much of our mental functioning can be associated with specific parts of the brain. For example, an identity theorist has no problems explaining that damage to the posterior sectors of the left-brain hemisphere is associated with impaired reading, writing, and speaking abilities. He also has no problems explaining why persons who suffer strokes in the right cortex experience difficulties with three-dimensional thinking or pattern recognition. If mind and brain are identical to each other, we should expect damages to particular parts of the brain to correspond to damages of specific mental functions. Moreover, the identity theory also provides a fruitful framework for neuroscientific research. If mind and brain are the same thing, then we can understand all mental phenomena as a physical, chemical reaction of neurons. My thought that my grandmother is a sweet old lady is in this case perhaps nothing else but the firing of neuron #27883 to neuron #30152. Feelings of depression or schizophrenic thoughts might be nothing else but chemical imbalances in the brain. The task of neuroscience is then to identify what type of physical chemical reactions correspond to what type of mental state.

FOOD FOR THOUGHT

A good way to test whether you understand competing philosophical theories well is to apply the theories to the same situation and try to determine why they lead to different explanations or predictions. Let us try this with respect to behaviorism and the identity theory. Consider the following situation. Suppose that you are going through a difficult time in your life. Each evening after you go to bed, you start thinking that your life is simply meaningless and empty. You are tired of having these thoughts and decide that you want to change your mind. You want to get rid of these depressing late-night thoughts.

Continued

1. Suppose behaviorism is true. How would a behaviorist try to change his mind in this situation?
2. Suppose the identity theory is true. How would an identity theorist go about changing his mind?

Arguments Against the Identity Theory

In spite of its attractiveness, the identity theory is open to objections. One crucial objection is well illustrated by the philosopher John Searle. Searle writes:

> Imagine that your brain starts to deteriorate in such a way that you are slowly going blind. Imagine that the desperate doctors, anxious to alleviate your condition, try any method to restore your vision. As a last resort, they try plugging silicon chips into your visual cortex. Imagine that to your amazement and theirs, it turns out that the silicon chips restore your vision to its normal state. Now, imagine further that your brain, depressingly, continues to deteriorate and the doctors continue to implant more silicon chips. You can see where the thought experiment is going already: in the end, we imagine that your brain is entirely replaced by silicon chips; that as you shake your head, you can hear the chips rattling around inside your skull. In such a situation there would be various possibilities. One logical possibility, not to be excluded on any a priori grounds alone, is surely this: you continue to have all of the sorts of thoughts, experiences, memories, etc., that you had previously; the sequence of your mental life remains unaffected . . .[3]

Searle's thought experiment points to a crucial weakness of the identity theory. The identity theory identifies mental states with brain states. It thus is committed to the general claim: *Wherever there is no brain, there is no mind!* But is this claim really plausible? The thought experiment clearly shows that it is logically possible that a being whose brain has been replaced by silicon chips has a mind. This shows that a strong version of the identity theory (sometimes called type-type identity theory), according to which mental states and brain states are necessarily identical, is false. The identity theory leads to a certain kind of chauvinism by insisting that beings without the appropriate "hardware" (i.e., brain states) cannot have a mental life. This seems problematic in light of the fact that lower animals, for example an octopus, seem perfectly capable of experiencing mental states like pain without having a brain similar to ours. It also appears problematic in light of the possibilities that advanced machines or space aliens might have minds. Suppose, for example, that we encounter an alien space creature that is made entirely of previously unknown materials. We certainly would not be entitled to conclude that it does not have a mind simply because it does not have a brain like we humans do. Although our own mental life seems intimately tied to our brains, the general claim that mental states are brain states appears suspect. This does not mean that we have to abandon the identity theory completely, but it does entail that we have to modify the theory to make room for the fact that other creatures besides humans could have minds. A functionalist account of the mind provides such a modification.

Functionalism

Functionalism developed as a response to the central weakness of the identity theory. Functionalists take the idea that minds can be realized in different physical materials seriously. They thus reject the idea that minds are necessarily tied to brains. According to functionalism, mental states are functional states. But what exactly does this mean?

Functional Concepts and "Stuff" Concepts

Consider the example of water. If somebody were to ask you to explain the nature of water, you would probably say that water is a certain kind of substance. More precisely, you might want to say that water is H_2O. Water therefore is a "stuff concept," that is, it can be defined as a particular kind of material stuff. Gold and wood are further examples of stuff concepts. Now, consider the term "money." To clarify what money is, it is not very helpful to say something about silver or printed paper. Money can come in a wide variety of different material manifestations. A credit card, for example, is also a form of money. To clarify what money is, we need to make reference to the functional role money plays in our lives. We might say approximately that everything that allows you to purchase goods is money. This functional definition of money applies to silver coins as well as to credit cards or paper money. The term "money" therefore does not refer to a stuff concept but rather to a functional concept.

FOOD FOR THOUGHT

Determine whether the following concepts are **stuff concepts** or **functional concepts:**

1. Food
2. Lion
3. Pen
4. Uranium
5. Shoes

Functionalism: Mind as Software

The basic idea of functionalism is to treat "mind" as a functional concept. We can roughly say that according to functionalism, **something is a mind if it functions appropriately.** This explains nicely why space aliens or advanced machines might have a mind although they do not have a brain. As long as an entity possesses a physical mechanism that can play the same functional role as our neurons play in our brain, that entity will have a mind. It does not matter whether the entity consists of organic tissue, silicon chips, or glass fibers. Functionalism is therefore well positioned to deal with the chauvinism objection that created so many problems for the identity theory. An analogy might be useful to illustrate the basic tenet of functionalism. We can say that, according to functionalism, the mind is similar to a software program. Notice that one and the same software program can run on very different computers. As long as the hardware of a computer is complex enough to run the program, the program can be installed. Similarly, a functionalist believes that any physical system that is complex enough to recreate the functional interactions between neurons in our brain, can have a mind.

Functionalism and Artificial Intelligence: The Turing Test

It is easy to see that functionalism supports the idea that it should be possible to create artificial intelligence (AI). If we succeed in building machines that can play the same functional role as our brains, then these machines must, according to functionalism, have a mind. Alan Turing (1912–1953), one of the founders of modern computer science, suggested a method that was intended to allow us to determine whether advanced machines indeed have minds. The test is the so-called **Turing Test.** The basic idea of the Turing Test is to put a human being, whom we will call the tester, in front of a computer terminal. The tester can type questions about any subject matter into the computer terminal and the questions are answered by somebody in the other room. What the tester does not know is whether the questions are answered by another human being or by an advanced machine. It is the job of the tester to determine whether he is interacting with a machine or with a real human being. Alan Turing suggested that if we could create a machine that could answer the questions of the tester such that the tester is convinced that he is dealing with a human being, then we should conclude that the machine has a mind. In this case we would say that the machine has passed the Turing Test.

It is easy to see that supporters of functionalism should accept the Turing Test. Being able to conduct a conversation is, after all, one of the crucial functions of minds. Since functionalists agree that anything that plays the appropriate functional role is a mind, they must also accept the idea that a machine which passes the Turing Test has a mind. Functionalism therefore supports the idea that artificial intelligence is possible.

FOOD FOR THOUGHT

The question whether advanced computers could have minds is a hot philosophical issue. One cannot deny that computers have come a long way and that they are capable of astounding things. But is it also possible that computers might someday develop consciousness and a sense of self-identity? Many people are convinced that this could never happen. They believe that no machine could ever have a mind. However, not all arguments in defense of this conviction are very convincing. Take a look at the following arguments and decide whether they are compelling or not:

1. Computers are not alive. Only living things can have a mind. Therefore: Computers cannot have minds.

2. Computers only follow programs and thus do not act creatively or in unpredictable ways. In order to have a mind, one needs to be able to act creatively and unpredictably. Therefore: Computers cannot have minds.

Continued

3. Computers cannot have feelings and emotions. A thing without emotions and feelings cannot have a mind. Therefore: Computers cannot have minds.

Arguments Against Functionalism

The Chinese Room Argument   A number of thinkers have objected to the idea that machines could have minds simply by enacting the appropriate functional program. John Searle is perhaps the best-known philosopher who has attacked functionalism on this point. To refute functionalism and the related idea of artificial intelligence, Searle presented the "Chinese Room argument." Searle writes:

Consider a language you don't understand. In my case, I do not understand Chinese. To me Chinese writing looks like so many meaningless squiggles. Now suppose I am placed in a room containing baskets full of Chinese symbols. Suppose also that I am given a rule book in English for matching Chinese symbols with other Chinese symbols. The rules identify the symbols entirely by their shapes and do not require that I understand any of them. The rules might say such things as, "Take a squiggle-squiggle sign from basket number one and put it next to a squoggle-squoggle sign from basket number two."

Imagine that people outside the room who understand Chinese hand in small bunches of symbols and that in response I manipulate the symbols according to the rule book and hand back more small bunches of symbols. Now, the rule book is the "computer program." The people who wrote it are "programmers" and I am the "computer." The baskets full of symbols are the "data base," the small bunches that are handed in to me are "questions" and the bunches I then hand out are "answers."

Now suppose that the rule book is written in such a way that my "answers" to the "questions" are indistinguishable from those of a native Chinese speaker. For example, the people outside might hand me some symbols that unknown to me mean, "What's you favorite color?" and I might after going through the rules give back symbols that, also unknown to me, mean "My favorite is blue, but I also like green a lot." I satisfy the Turing Test for understanding Chinese. All the same, I am totally ignorant of Chinese. And there is no way I could come to understand Chinese in the system as described, since there is no way that I can learn the meanings of any of the symbols. Like a computer, I manipulate symbols, but I attach no meaning to the symbols.[4]

Searle's Chinese Room argument is supposed to show that computers are, in principle, not capable of understanding the meanings (semantics) of words and symbols. They are limited to processing symbols on the basis of their shapes (syntax). Genuine minds, on the other hand, are capable of understanding the meanings of words. Searle concludes therefore that computers only appear as if they have minds; in reality, they have none. Passing the Turing Test is not a sufficient condition for mentality.

Defenders of functionalism and artificial intelligence are normally not impressed by the Chinese Room argument. They point to several weaknesses. First, Searle's argument is built around an analogy between the Chinese Room and the inner workings of computers. This analogy might not be as close as Searle makes it out to be. Currently, computers process information in a sequential, step-by-step manner that is roughly analogous to what happens in the Chinese Room. But current computers also cannot pass the Turing Test. This suggests that computers that actually pass the Turing Test might function differently than Searle describes them. Computers that pass the Turing Test might, for example, be based on parallel distributive processing rather than sequential processors. The central analogy between computers and the Chinese Room might therefore be misleading. The second objection to the Chinese Room argument is called the **systems reply.** The Chinese Room argument shows that the *person* in the room does not understand Chinese. The *person*, however, is only one part of the system. What would happen if we were to consider the system as a whole? Could not the system as a whole understand Chinese? Consider the workings of my brain for a moment. It is quite plausible to think that no part of my brain understands the meaning of English sentences. Understanding and consciousness might be a result of my whole brain working together. This suggests that Searle overlooks the possibility that the whole Chinese Room together is capable of understanding Chinese. Searle himself has responded to these objections at considerable length. At this point, it would be too much to explore the debate about the Chinese Room argument in full. For our purposes, it is sufficient to note that the Chinese Room argument is by no means a knockdown argument against functionalism. However, if you agree with John Searle and believe that even the most advanced computers cannot have minds, it might be interesting to explore how the Chinese Room argument can be strengthened.

Problems with Qualia A more serious objection against functionalism is raised by so-called inverted spectrum cases. Consider two twin brothers, Alf and Tony, who experience the same colors differently. Tony sees red and green as normal people experience these colors. Alf, on the other hand, experiences red as Tony experiences green, and green as Tony experiences red. Notice that neither Tony nor Alf (nor anybody else, for that matter) will ever discover that they have different sensations with respect to the same colors. When Tony sees a ripe tomato, he will say: "Look at that great red tomato!" And Alf, who has learned to associate his experience of green with the word "red," will say the same thing. Alf is perfectly capable of picking out red things. It is just that what people call red causes a green sensation in him, and what people call green causes a red sensation in him. This thought experiment raises a fundamental problem for functionalism. Notice that from a functional perspective Alf and Tony appear to be equivalent. They can do the same things (e.g., recognize green and red) and they display the same verbal behavior in similar circumstances. So, according to functionalism, both are in the same mental state when they see and experience red things.[5] This, however, is clearly not the case. For Alf and Tony experience the same color differently, and they thus have different color sensations.

Inverted spectrum cases show that functionalism has a difficult time to make room for what philosophers have called **qualia**. The term "qualia" refers to the phenomenal aspect of mental states. The philosopher Frank Jackson gives the following examples of qualia: "the itchiness of itches, pangs of jealousy, . . . the characteristic experience of tasting a lemon, smelling a rose. . . ."[6] It is hard to deny that some of our mental states, especially sensations, have a characteristic, phenomenal feeling (qualia) when we experience them. When I smell freshly brewed coffee, run my fingers over sandpaper, or see a bright red, I am the subject of mental states with very distinctive phenomenal characteristics (qualia). But it is problematic to explain qualia in functional terms, because it seems possible that functionally equivalent mental states are associated with completely different subjective qualia. The philosopher David Chalmers puts this point as follows: "Nobody knows why physical brain processes are accompanied by conscious experiences at all. Why is it that when our brains process light of a certain wave-length, we have an experience of deep purple? Why do we have any experiences at all? Could not an unconscious automation have performed the same task just as well?"[7] Chalmers argues in this context that it is logically possible that there are beings who act like us in every respect and who process information like we do, but who lack any kind of subjective consciousness (and hence any qualia). Chalmers calls these beings "zombies" (not to be confused with Hollywood zombies). Since Chalmers' zombies are functionally equivalent to us (i.e., they do and say the same things as we do), but lack subjective phenomenal qualia, they seem to illustrate that functional accounts of the mind are incomplete. Philosophers have called this problem the problem of the "explanatory gap." It seems as if functionalism could never close this gap, and that functionalism—and perhaps any purely physicalistic theory of the mind—seems to provide an incomplete account of what minds really are.

FOOD FOR THOUGHT

Are Chalmers' zombies really logically possible? Some philosophers have doubted the coherence of the idea that there could be beings who do all the things we do without having any feelings at all. Consider specific activities in your life and decide whether a zombie could participate in these activities without any subjective feelings.

Final Remarks on the Mind/Body Problem

The relationship between body and mind is today as mysterious as it was in the past. From a commonsense perspective, Descartes' **substance dualism** seems very attractive. Although substance dualism is supported by religious beliefs and near-death experiences, it leads to a number of prominent difficulties: the **problem of interaction** and Ryle's charge of a **category mistake.**

Physicalist theories about the mind are attractive in light of recent advances in neuroscience. We have seen, however, that a purely **behaviorist approach** to the mind cannot produce a satisfactory theory. The **identity theory** is more promising, but it too leads to a central problem: the possibility that mental states can be realized in multiple physical systems. **Functionalism,** on the other hand, is well suited to deal with this difficulty, but it has a hard time accounting for the subjective qualitative character (**qualia**) of mental states.

It is not quite clear yet how serious the qualia problem really is. Some contemporary philosophers simply deny that inverted spectrum cases or Chalmers' zombies raise fundamental problems for physicalistic theories of the mind. They argue that a closer analysis of these cases reveals that inverted spectrum cases as well as "Chalmers' zombies" do not present genuine logical possibilities. Others have taken the qualia problem as a reason to reintroduce a version of dualism: **property dualism.** Property dualism is a mixture of physicalism and dualism. Property dualists reject substance dualism and agree with the physicalists that our minds have a purely physical foundation. However, property dualists deny that every mental property can be reduced to physical processes. This puts property dualists in a position to accept that qualia are irreducible mental properties. Whether property dualism is a fruitful theory is not quite clear yet. Philosophy of mind is one of the most active fields in contemporary philosophy. Our present discussion is only a very preliminary introduction to the main positions and questions. However, the discussion should be rich enough to give you a chance to think about the relationship between body and mind on your own. In the course of reading this chapter, you might have revised some of your own ideas about how minds and bodies are related to each other. It might therefore be interesting to go back to the Food for Thought exercise on page 139 and check whether you would now answer the questions there differently.

Endnotes

1. This near-death experience is described in Graham, George: *Philosophy of Mind: An Introduction.* Oxford: Blackwell, 1998, pp. 22–23.
2. For a more complete discussion of the significance of near-death experiences see Blackmore, Susan: *Dying to Live.* London: HarperCollins, 1993.
3. Searle, John. *The Rediscovery of the Mind.* Cambridge: MIT Press, 1992, p. 65.
4. Searle, John. "Is the Brain's Mind a Computer Program?" *Scientific American* 262 (Jan. 1990):26.
5. A convinced functionalist will probably deny that Alf and Tony are in functionally equivalent states. This is not implausible. Since Alf and Tony represent the color red differently, one might argue that there also *has* to be a functional difference between Alf and Tony. This points to the best response a functionalist can muster in response to inverted spectrum cases. A convinced functionalist will simply deny that these cases are logically possible.

6. Jackson, Frank. "Epiphenomenal Qualia." *Philosophical Quarterly* 32 (1982):127–136.

7. Chalmers, David. "The Puzzle of Conscious Experience." *Scientific American* 237 (Dec. 1995):53.

For Further Reading

Chalmers, David. *The Conscious Mind: In Search of a Fundamental Theory.* New York: Oxford University Press, 1996.

Churchland, Paul. *Matter and Consciousness.* Cambridge: MIT Press, 1988.

Graham, George. *Philosophy of Mind: An Introduction.* Oxford: Blackwell, 1998.

Dennett, Daniel. *Brainstorms: Philosophical Essays on Mind and Psychology.* Cambridge: MIT Press, 1981.

Guttenplan, Samuel (ed.). *A Companion to the Philosophy of Mind.* Oxford: Blackwell, 1994.

Ryle, Gilbert. *The Concept of Mind.* London: Hutchinson, 1949.

Searle, John. *The Rediscovery of the Mind.* Cambridge: MIT Press, 1992.

Tye, Michael. *Ten Problems of Consciousness.* Cambridge: MIT Press, 1995.

CHAPTER SIX

DOES GOD EXIST?

God, Faith, and Reason

Some philosophical problems seem far removed from the way we live our day-to-day lives. However, this is not true when we deal with questions about God. If God exists, we must understand ourselves and the universe in terms of a relationship to a perfect and ultimate being. Part of our lives, then, should be devoted to building this relationship through prayer, the observance of religious rituals, or the reading of holy books like the Bible or the Koran. If, on the other hand, we conclude that God doesn't exist, we are faced with a different situation. While we are then free to dismiss religious activities as nonsense, we consequently have to accept the idea that we are finite beings who live in a universe without ultimate meaning or purpose.[1] The question of whether God exists is therefore of obvious interest, and the answer we give to the question has an immediate impact upon our lives and our understanding of the world.

It is nevertheless frequently difficult to engage people in a thorough discussion about God's existence. Many people hold that religious beliefs are only a matter of faith and should not be scrutinized with the help of reason. For them religious beliefs are a matter of the heart (faith) and not a matter of the head (reason). There is something to be said for this position—some well-known philosophers such as Kierkegaard (1813–1855) have defended it—but extreme versions of this so-called **fideistic** approach to religious beliefs are nevertheless difficult to justify. To illustrate this, consider the following example. Suppose you find out that a friend of yours has joined a radical religious group that considers higher education as a work of the devil and consequently advocates the destruction of all college campuses. The next time you meet your friend he is on his way to class with dynamite strapped to his body. You feel a strong moral obligation to stop him, but how could you do it? If you are stronger than he is, you might try to wrestle him to the ground or you might try to get the help of a nearby policeman. But suppose that there is no policeman, and that you weigh 125 pounds while your friend is the star running back of the football team. At this point your only option is to try to convince your friend—with the help of arguments—that he is mistaken to think that God wants all college campuses to be destroyed. Of course, this is an extreme example, but it illustrates that all of us— whether we are Christians, atheists, Jews, Muslims, Hindus, Buddhists, or advocates of some other religious perspective—have an obligation to test and analyze our religious beliefs by means of reason. Reason might not be able to solve all religious questions, but it can provide a framework that prevents people from misusing religious sentiments for dangerous ends. Therefore, it is a vital task to analyze our religious beliefs. In this chapter, we will limit ourselves to exploring the most fundamental religious belief: the question of whether God exists.

What Do We Mean by the Word "God"?

At first glance, it might seem as if we can respond to the question of whether God exists in only two ways: either we answer with a "yes" and embrace a **theistic** position or we answer with a "no" and support a version of **atheism.** However, there are more than two options here. For one, we may decide to subscribe to an **agnostic** position. An agnostic believes that while it is possible for God to exist, we humans can never know this with any certainty. A further complication is raised by the inherent ambiguity of the term "God." Consider, for example, what actress Heather Headley said in a recent interview with the magazine *Glamour:* "God surrounds everything I do. I use God to get me down red carpets and when I am singing onstage. God got me that Tony Award on my desk!"[2] In the same article actress Edie Falco describes her own position about God as follows: "God defies specific description—it's universal energy . . ."[3] What is interesting to note is that both Heather

Headley and Edie Falco answered the question of whether they believed that God exists affirmatively. Yet it is far from clear whether they both share the same idea what kind of being God is. For Edie Falco God is "universal energy," whereas Heather Headley's God "[gets her] Tony Award[s]."

Although most people (approximately 75 percent of the American population) agree that God exists, many people have conflicting ideas what kind of being God is. It is therefore important to clarify what we mean by the term "God" before we can investigate whether there are any good reasons to believe that God exists.

FOOD FOR THOUGHT

What properties are essential to God? Decide whether you believe that the following assertions about God are true or false.

1. God is eternal.
2. God knows what is going to happen in the future.
3. God is male.
4. God has a physical body.
5. God is all-powerful (omnipotent).
6. God knows everything (omniscient).
7. God appears differently in different cultures.
8. God is all-good (omnibenevolent).
9. God is the greatest being that we can think of.
10. God and Jesus are one and the same person.
11. God is everywhere in nature.
12. God helps those who deserve help.
13. God causes miracles.
14. God is sometimes really mad at human beings.
15. God loves all humans equally.
16. God is so different from us that we have no idea what God is like.
17. God is infinite.
18. When I talk to God I know that he listens.

As you can see from the previous Food for Thought exercise, there can be much disagreement about which properties are essential to God.

To gain some point of reference, we can divide the various conceptions of God into three broad categories: classical theism, pantheism, and "new-age" conception. This threefold distinction is illustrated by the following diagram:

Different Conceptions of God

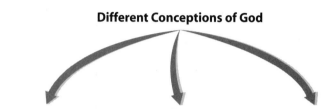

Classical Theism	**Pantheism**	**New-Age Conception**
Classical theism is embraced by three monotheistic world religions: Judaism, Christianity, and Islam. According to this conception, God is separate from the universe (i.e., is the creator of the universe). God is a person and performs acts (miracles). Moreover, God is seen as omniscient, omnipotent, and omnibenevolent.	According to this conception, God is everywhere. Nature and God are one. God is not separate from the universe. This conception is especially popular among the romantics and some Eastern religious systems.	A broad category that refers most prominently to those who think that God is a spiritual, personal guide. Writers in this group tend to draw a distinction between religion and spirituality. More recent, more personal writings play a more prominent role than traditional religious texts.

This classification is somewhat simplistic, but it nevertheless helps us to see that classical theism, the view of God supported by the three major theistic religions of the world, is not the only conception of God. Notably, Eastern religions embrace a quite different perspective. In the Western philosophical tradition, however, most thinkers have embraced a classical theistic conception of God, and we will focus our discussion on their standpoint. However, this does not mean that we will disregard nonclassical conceptions of God completely. Later in this chapter, we will see that certain philosophical puzzles might be approached differently if we revise the "classical" conception of God. Let us begin by clarifying classical theism in more detail.

According to classical theism, God has several key features: God is the creator of the universe and he is omnipotent, omniscient, and perfectly good (worthy of worship). He is infinite, everlasting, and not dependent on anything other than himself (i.e., he is self-existent and necessary). Most importantly, the classical theistic God of the Torah, the New Testament, and the Koran is a person. That means that God is the kind of being who can act, who is capable of love and creativity, and who can enter into relationships with humans. It is in virtue of God's personhood that God can be our friend or helper.

Classical theism does not yield a completely unified conception of God. There are many questions that are hotly debated within this broad tradition. For example, is God capable of having emotions or is he impassible? To what degree does God know the future? What is the relationship between God, the Holy Spirit, and Jesus? Which—if any—is the true word of God: the Koran, the Torah, or the Bible? In spite of these difficulties, it is nevertheless possible to extract a fairly coherent conception of God from these three theistic religions. From now on, we will understand the question of whether God exists as the question whether an omnipotent, omniscient, omnibenevolent, and personal creator of the universe exists.

FOOD FOR THOUGHT

Take a look at the following statements about God given by various celebrities and thinkers. Decide whether the statements are best classified as a form of classical theism, pantheism, or new-age conception of God:

HEATHER GRAHAM: "I especially feel God when I'm in nature, where I can sense that something more powerful than we are is out there. I love the feeling of being with earth and all that goes with it."

DEBORAH GIBSON: "I believe there is a higher power when melodies pop into my head seemingly from nowhere. I feel that ideas come to me when they are supposed to—I am simply there to channel them."

JAMES DIETZ: "God is merciful and His Mercy finds expression as divine openness and patience with the human estate. . . . It is through God's Mercy that man has the unlimited opportunity to develop and maintain a viable, fulfilling relationship with Him."

CARMEN ELECTRA: "My relationship with God is one-on-one. My faith has affected my life tremendously, especially in this last year. I lost my mom and sister and had a disastrous marriage. Instead of going out to party to take the pain away, I'd spend time alone. I still pray to God every night."

GLORIA STUART: "I certainly think there is a force, because how does a butterfly know it's supposed to be yellow or white? How, of the billions of trees in the world, is every one an individual shape? Why did the dinosaurs disappear?"

Arguments in Defense of Classical Theism

Arguments from Religious Experiences

Some of the most effective arguments in defense of the existence of God are based on religious experiences. The basic idea of these arguments is easy to grasp, and can be presented in standard form as follows:

> 1. I have experiences that seem to be caused by God.
>
> Therefore: God exists.

Notice that a very similar argument can be given with respect to the existence of external physical objects. If somebody asks me to prove that tables exist, I might answer:

> 1. I have experiences that seem to be caused by tables.
>
> Therefore: Tables exist.

The second argument strikes me as a perfectly plausible argument in defense of my belief that there are tables. While the argument does not establish the existence of tables with absolute certainty (there is, after all, a small chance that idealism is true and that tables do not exist after all), it establishes its conclusion with a high degree of probability and that is all that matters for a good inductive argument. The crucial question is whether the two arguments are sufficiently similar. Are experiences of God similar to experiences of tables?

There are some reasons for doubt. First, although most people have experiences of tables, only a few people claim to have direct experiences of God. This alone does not constitute a fatal flaw of the argument, since we can restrict the scope of the argument to those who actually have had experiences of God. We might say then that although there is no universal proof for the existence of God, at least some people (those who have had the right kind of experiences) are able to show with a high degree of probability that God exists. However, the second issue is more problematic. While the experiences of common physical objects are fairly uniform and can be described without great difficulty, the same is not true with respect to religious experiences. Consider the following two examples of people who have had religious experiences.

> Now Moses was keeping the flock of his father-in-law . . . and the angel of the Lord appeared to him in a flame of fire out of the midst of a bush; and he looks, and lo, the bush was burning, yet it was not consumed . . . God called to him out of the bush, "Moses, Moses!" (Exod. 3:1–4)

> I was alone upon the seashore as all these thoughts flowed over me, liberating and reconciling; and now again, as once before in distant days in the Alps of Dauphine, I was impelled to kneel down, this time before the illimitable ocean, symbol of the Infinite. I felt that I prayed as I had never prayed before, and knew now what prayer really is: to return from the solitude of individuation into the consciousness of unity with all that is, to kneel down as one that passes away, and to rise up as one imperishable. Earth, heaven, and sea resounded as in one vast world-encircling harmony. It was as if the chorus of all the great who had ever lived were about me. I felt myself one with them, and it appeared as if I heard their greeting: "Thou too belongst to the company of those who overcome."[4]

While Moses' experience of God as a burning bush is quite similar to ordinary perceptual experiences, the same is not true for the second religious experience. This religious experience differs significantly from ordinary perceptual experiences. It can probably be best described as a mystical feeling of unity with the cosmos. Many people who have religious experiences encounter God in such a mystical way. However, if we classify religious experiences as a type of feeling, two problems seem to emerge. First, it is difficult to see in this case how mystical feelings can justify a belief in a classical theistic God. Religious feelings are compatible with a pantheistic conception of God as well as a new-age conception of God. So, if we take religious experiences to be feelings, we consequently can only claim that there is a higher power, but we are completely unable to describe the quality and character of this "power." Second, feelings are noncognitive mental states and cannot ground inferences that lead to cognitive claims about the world. To illustrate this point, consider the following argument:

1. I am feeling very scared tonight.

Therefore: A burglar will break into my house tonight.

Such an argument is obviously flawed. Feelings—no matter how powerful—do not entitle us to draw any inferences about what the world is like. This is not to say that feelings are irrelevant, but they cannot provide a foundation for arguments that establish the existence of God or anything else. Feelings only enable us to draw inferences about our own inner selves.

FOOD FOR THOUGHT

Do you agree that religious experiences are feelings? If yes, what kinds of feelings are characteristic of religious experiences? Some people have maintained that religious experiences are in essence a feeling of dependence; others claim that religious experiences are grounded in feelings of guilt or shame; others attest that religious experiences are similar to feelings of joy. What is your opinion about this?

If the argument from religious experiences is to be successful, we must focus our attention on those religious experiences that closely resemble ordinary perceptual experiences. There can be no doubt that experiences of this kind exist. Although only very few people report that God appeared to them as a burning bush, many people report having had experiences of this type. We must only think of St. Augustine (354–430) who reports hearing God's command in a child's voice, or Emperor Constantine (274?–337) who reports seeing a burning cross in the sky. Religious experiences of this type face their own difficulty. When we use our ordinary perceptual experiences of tables as a reason for thinking that tables exists, we can assume that there is a relatively close relationship between how the table appears and how it really is—if a table appears to have a smooth surface then we are justified to believe that the real table (the table that causes the appearance) also has a smooth surface. Notice, however, that this is not true with respect to religious experiences. When God appears to Moses as a burning bush, it would be implausible for Moses to infer that God actually is fire. There is a gap here between the way God appears and the way God really is. We normally do not attribute ordinary perceptual attributes to God. Although God might appear as a flame or tree, it would be silly to think that God actually is a flame or tree. The attributes that we most frequently confer on the classical theistic God (omniscience, goodness, omnipotence, infinity, etc.) cannot be perceived in any straightforward way.

Once we acknowledge that there is a fundamental gap between religious experiences that can be described in ordinary perceptual discourses and the cause of these experiences, we are in a position to raise a powerful objection: If there is no direct relationship between the way God appears in these experiences and the way God really is, then it is perfectly plausible to assume that the *cause* of these experiences is actually not God, but rather something else (perhaps a hallucination or a vivid dream triggered by lack of sleep, a fever, or "spiritual" exercises). Moreover, since advocates of different religious traditions experience God in so many different ways, it seems much more reasonable to believe that there is no universal source for these diverse experiences.

There can be no doubt that religious experiences are a powerful element in the lives of many believers, but our discussion shows that they probably cannot provide any decisive and intersubjective ground for establishing the existence of God. William James expressed the situation well when he wrote: "[Religious experiences] . . . have the right to be absolutely authoritative over the individual to whom they come. . . . [but] no authority emanates from them which should make it a duty for those who stand outside of them to accept their revelations . . ."[5]

Cosmological Argument

An alternative strategy for trying to establish that God exists is to deduce the existence of God from the existence of the world. The basic idea of these so-called cosmological arguments is the following:

> 1. If there is no God, then there can be no world.
> 2. The world exists.
> _____
> Therefore: God exists.

The primary philosophical difficulty of this type of argument is to make the first premise of the argument plausible: Why should one think that the existence of the world (cosmos) is closely linked to the existence of God? There are various ways to explicate the relationship between God and the cosmos and this allows for different argumentative strategies. In the following, I will focus nearly exclusively on the explanatory (rather than a causal) relationship between the world and God.

Suppose for a moment that you are walking through a remote forest and come across the ancient ruins of a huge city.[6] You do not know what civilization created this city, and you certainly do not know why they created a city in this particular place, but you are sure that there is some explanation for why the city exists. This seems true not only for cities in remote forests but for things in general. I might not know why I have a terrible headache, but I am sure that there is an explanation for the throbbing pain in my skull. I might not know why President Kennedy was shot in 1963, but I am certain that an explanation exists. The principle in question here is known as the **principle of sufficient reason.** The principle asserts that for everything that exists there must be an explanation of why it exists. It is easy to see that the principle of sufficient reason can also be applied to the existence of the world itself: What is the reason that the cosmos exists?

From a logical point of view, we can identify three possible answers:

1. The cosmos (in one form or another) has always existed. Nothing external to the cosmos explains its existence.

2. The existence of the cosmos is explained by a contingent physical event (such as the Big Bang).

3. The existence of the cosmos is explained by reference to a necessary being (God).

Defenders of the cosmological argument try to establish that option 3 is the only plausible answer, and that options 1 and 2 are seriously flawed.

Let us start by analyzing the first option. Even if we believe that our current cosmos originated with the Big Bang, it is still conceivable that the cosmos itself is eternal. We can imagine, for instance, that the currently expanding universe will at some point (by virtue of gravitational forces) start to contract. This scenario is called the Big Crunch. If the Big Crunch takes place, the universe ultimately will collapse back onto itself. After it has completely collapsed, the universe may restart itself with another big explosion, and begin the cycle anew. We can imagine that this process has always been going on. If so, there may be no absolute beginning to the universe; the universe in this endless state of renewal and destruction has always been around. Is there something wrong with this idea?

To accept the idea of a universe that extends infinitely back in time, one must also accept that an infinite series exists. However, defenders of the cosmological argument argue that the idea of an actually existing infinite series is incoherent. Let me illustrate this with an example. Suppose that you come across an old man in the forest who is mumbling to himself. As you approach you can hear that he is counting backwards; he says, ". . . five, four, three, two, one. Hooray, I am done! I have counted them all." You ask him what he has been counting, and he replies that he has counted all of the natural numbers. "Whoa," you exclaim, "that must have taken a long time. When did you start?" The old man replies: "You fool! There are infinitely many natural numbers, so obviously I never started."

This example illustrates that there is something suspicious about an actual existing process that extends backward into infinity. For this reason, some philosophers argue that an actual existing infinite series is an incoherent idea. But even if we should grant that the concept of an actual existing infinite series is coherent, we still face a serious problem: To grant that the universe existed forever would still offer no explanation for why it exists. As the philosopher Richard Taylor pointed out, giving the world an age—even if it is an infinite age—does not in any way answer the question of why the world exists.[7] This suggests that if we take the principle of sufficient reason seriously, we have reasons to reject the hypothesis that the universe is eternal.

This leads us directly to the second option: Isn't it possible to argue that the universe started with the Big Bang? According to this hypothesis, the universe literally started with nothingness (vacuum). Prior to the Big Bang there was neither time nor space. I stress this because people are prone to ask: What caused the Big Bang? The sensible answer to this question is that the question itself is flawed. The Big Bang cannot be caused by anything; it is a singular event that simply happened—that's all one can say! At first glance, one might be suspicious of such an answer. Does it make sense to assume that physical events simply happen in the absence of any cause? Yet surprisingly, modern physics supports this idea—especially with respect to quantum phenomena. Take the example of radioactive decay. Although we know the time when a certain amount of uranium 239 has decayed by 50 percent to uranium 238 (the so called half-life), we do not know when an individual molecule (atom) will lose its neutron. That process is due to chance. Defenders of the Big Bang hypothesis think that the Big Bang is a similar physical event without proper cause. There is a certain probability that a quantum vacuum produces the conditions for the rapid inflation that characterizes the early stages of our universe. That is all we can say. But isn't there something terribly unsatisfactory about this picture? There is nothing whatsoever, and then suddenly there is a rapidly expanding universe? If we accept the principle of sufficient reason, the Big Bang hypothesis leads to the same quandary as the eternal cosmos hypothesis: It does not offer us any satisfactory reason for the existence of the universe.

This leads supporters of the cosmological argument to the conclusion that it is only with reference to God that the existence of the universe can be satisfactorily explained. But how, one may ask, can God provide a better explanation for the existence of the universe than some random physical event or an eternally existing universe?

In order to understand this, we need to understand the distinction between contingent beings and necessary beings. For example, I am a contingent being. My existence depends upon things other than myself. For one, I would not exist if my parents had made different choices in their lives. All ordinary physical objects like table and chairs are contingent as well. God, on the other hand, is a necessary being—a being whose existence does not depend on anything else.[8] In effect, when we refer to God as a necessary being we are saying that his existence does not stand in a need of an explanation. God—if he exists—is complete. There is nothing that causes God to exist, nor is there anything that exists prior to him. God carries the reason for his existence within himself. He is, so to speak, a self-explaining entity. Once we have grasped the necessity of God's existence, we can proceed and formulate the cosmological argument in standard form:

1. The cosmos exists.
2. There must be a reason for the existence of the cosmos.
3. This reason can only be provided by a necessary being.

Therefore: A necessary being exists.

4. God is that necessary being.

Therefore: God exists.

The argument has merit, but a number of questions arise immediately. First, why should we accept the second premise and demand a reason for the existence of the cosmos? Bertrand Russell (1872–1970) once said in a famous debate with F. C. Copleston (1907–1994): "The universe is just there and that's it."[9] Why not adopt Russell's position and embrace the idea that there is no ultimate reason for the universe? Whether or not the principle of sufficient reason should be adopted, as an absolute axiom cannot be settled in a completely objective way. It is to some degree a matter of intellectual taste. Defenders of the principle can claim that we automatically rely upon it when we are trying to understand the world. But these considerations will have little effect on thinkers like Russell or Schopenhauer (1788–1860) who prefer to think of the universe as an inexplicable accident.

FOOD FOR THOUGHT

In order to decide whether you accept the principle of sufficient reason in your own thinking about the world, it might be useful to read the following debate about the principle between Bertrand Russell and Father F. C. Copleston. Decide who of the two thinkers is closer to your own thinking. Do you agree with Copleston and accept the principle of sufficient reason as a legitimate and necessary principle, or do you agree with Russell who thinks that the search for an ultimate and complete explanation is inherently misguided?

RUSSELL: So it all turns on this question of sufficient reason, and I must say that you haven't defined "sufficient reason" in a way that I can understand—what do you mean by sufficient reason? You don't mean cause?

COPLESTON: Not necessarily. Cause is a kind of sufficient reason. Only contingent beings can have causes. God is his own sufficient reason and He is not cause of himself. By sufficient reason in the full sense I mean an explanation adequate for the existence of some particular being.

RUSSELL: But when is an explanation adequate? Suppose I am about to make a flame with a match. You may say that the adequate explanation of that is that I rub it on the box.

COPLESTON: Well, for practical purposes—but theoretically, that is only a partial explanation. An adequate explanation must ultimately be a total explanation, to which nothing further can be added.

RUSSELL: Then I can only say that you are looking for something which can't be got, and which one ought to expect not to get.

Further questions arise in the context of the third premise. The premise implies that a necessary being itself does not need an explanation. Is that a reasonable assumption? If we accept the principle of sufficient reason and demand an explanation for everything, shouldn't we also insist on an explanation for the existence of a necessary being like God? The defenders of the cosmological argument would say that a necessary being like God does not need a reason for his existence. This, however, leaves room for the skeptic to inquire why the cosmos should require a reason for its existence. If it is plausible to say that God needs no reason for his existence then, by the same token, it is plausible to insist that the universe as a whole needs no reason either.

Finally, even if we accept the cosmological argument in its entirety, it is clear that it leaves the character of God undetermined. Suppose that the argument convinces us that there must be a necessary being. While secure in our conviction, we still have no idea of what further characteristic this necessary being might have. Is this being omnipotent, omniscient, omnibenevolent, and worthy of worship? These questions are left unanswered. The cosmological argument, therefore, even if successful, cannot establish on its own that the God of classical theism exists.

Design Arguments

The design argument is one of the most popular theistic arguments. It has a long and complex history, but the basic idea behind it can be illustrated with this thought experiment: Suppose that you are a space explorer on a mission to find new intelligent life forms. At this moment you are the first human to walk on planet Alpha Nu. Alpha Nu is barren, and for hours you have seen only dust. There is no sign of water or vegetation, and you decide to radio back to your crew that there is no intelligent life on this planet, and that it is time to move on. Suddenly you step on something in the dust. As you bend down to pick it up, you realize that it is a computer memory chip. At once this discovery puts planet Alpha Nu in a different category. Although the planet now seems devoid of intelligent life, the memory chip proves that some form of intelligent life must have been present there in the past. Perhaps those who left the memory chip were visitors like you, or perhaps this chip is a remnant of a lost civilization. Regardless, the discovery of the memory chip supports the following kind of reasoning:

1. There are memory chips on planet Alpha Nu.
2. Memory chips are carefully arranged and organized entities.
3. Carefully arranged and organized entities are most likely designed by an intelligent designer.

Therefore: An intelligent designer most likely must have been present on planet Alpha Nu.

This is a strong inductive argument. What is interesting to note is that a very similar argument can be made with respect to Earth. This parallel argument goes as follows:

1. There are many plants and animals on Earth.
2. Plants and animals are carefully arranged and organized entities.
3. Carefully arranged and organized entities are most likely designed by an intelligent designer.

Therefore: An intelligent designer most likely must have been present on Earth.
4. This intelligent designer is God.

Therefore: God most likely exists.

This argument is immediately plausible, and for centuries it has been one of the most dependable bulwarks of rational theology. But does it stand up to closer scrutiny?

The crucial premise of the argument is the third premise. Is it reasonable to assume that the most plausible explanation for the apparent design of living organisms that we find on Earth is the presence and influence of an intelligent designer? There are obviously other possible explanations available. Broadly, we can identify three competing hypotheses, which are illustrated by the following chart:

There Are Manifold Complicated and Well-Adapted Organisms on Earth.
This can be explained by reference to

Traditional Creationism	**Theory of Evolution**	**Intelligent Design Creationism**
Traditional creationists hold that the Genesis account of creation is literally true, that God created the world in six days. All species were created at the same time.	Life on Earth started with extremely simple life forms, which subsequently, over millions of years, developed via the forces of natural selection into the manifold different species we see today.	An intelligent design creationist accepts the basic principles of the theory of evolution but maintains that God stands behind evolution and guides it to a preestablished end.

This brief overview is a bit simplistic, of course. There are, for instance, countless other accounts of creation besides the one in the Bible's Genesis. However, we do little harm if we group them together into one logical category since the most potent arguments against the Genesis account of creation apply to other creation stories as well. Moreover, by characterizing the theory of evolution as one theory, I do not want to imply that there are not numerous theoretical differences among evolutionary biologists about the precise paths of evolutionary development or the relative importance of various evolutionary mechanisms. But for the purposes of discussing the design argument, it is sufficient if we characterize the theory of evolution as consisting of two main claims:

1. All living creatures have evolved from a few original simple life forms (Common Descent Hypothesis, which leads to the image of the "tree of life").

2. The tree of life is and was shaped by natural selection of randomly varying genetic difference among descendants.

The first claim is pretty easy to understand, but the second claim might require some further explanation. One of the key insights of evolutionary theory is that descendants of the same parents will vary from each other. If I should happen to have four children, these four children will genetically differ from each other. These differences are due to random processes and give my children differing probabilities of "reproductive success." If one of my daughters should happen to have the looks of Britney Spears, she will have quite a choice among possible mates and thus will probably be *reproductively successful*. On the other hand, if one of my sons only has one interest in his life, namely to play computer games, there is a good chance that he will be *reproductively unsuccessful*. What is true for my descendants is true for all other living beings as well. Frog and beetle parents have genetically differing offspring just as I do. And not all offspring will do well. According to the theory of evolution, these genetic differences combined with the forces of natural selection slowly, over millions of years, add up and create and shape the tree of life.

I label the third possible explanation of how the multiplicity and variety of living organisms have come about as intelligent design creationism. Again, this is an oversimplification.[10] There are in fact several creation theories that differ substantially from traditional creationism. There are, for instance, Old Earth Creationism, Theistic Evolutionism, and Progressive Creationism. However, intelligent design creationism seems to play the most central role in the current debate about the design argument, and we are therefore justified to focus our discussion on this form of nontraditional creationism. The key idea of intelligent design creationism is to reject a literal reading of Genesis and to accept (to varying degrees) the results of modern science. Intelligent design creationism accepts that the earth is billions of years old, and that species have developed over time. They insist, however, that God plays an important and necessary part in the creation of life and in the process of shaping the tree of life. Moreover, all intelligent design creationists reject the idea that a naturalistically interpreted theory of evolution provides a satisfactory explanation for life on Earth.

After introducing our three competing theories about the origins and structure of living organisms on Earth, let us now analyze how plausible these competing hypotheses are. It is relatively easy to see that the theory of evolution is more plausible than traditional creationism. Traditional creationism involves too many claims that are at odds with our scientific knowledge of the world. First, according to our current understanding of chemistry and physics, the world is roughly five billon years old and not 6000 years as traditional creationists maintain. It is, of course, possible for a traditional creationist to dismiss all results of modern science, but this is an awkward move to make.

FOOD FOR THOUGHT

Traditional creationists frequently insist that Darwin's theory of evolution is simply conjecture. It is certainly true to say that most evolutionary processes cannot be observed and verified by direct observation since they simply take too much time to take place (they often last millions of years). Does the fact that evolutionary processes are not directly observable justify the conclusion that the theory of evolution is only conjecture?

Second, we have plenty of archaeological evidence that many species (e.g., dinosaurs or saber-tooth tigers) existed in the past, but do not exist any more. This suggests that the actual number of life forms on earth changes constantly and is a result of dynamic processes. Traditional creationism, on the other hand, supports the idea that the total number of species were all created at the same time and that each species has a unique function. In the light of the archeological evidence that claim appears implausible. Third, we have plenty of evidence that many species are not "designed" in a perfect way. Many animals have rudimentary or atrophied organs. For example, whales still have teeth, although they do not use them. Humans have appendixes that play no useful role. These imperfections suggest again that there has been no perfect original design for whales or humans. It is more plausible to explain these "imperfections" with reference to natural selection. Whales, for example, have rudimentary teeth because they descend from beings that used to live on land.

Moreover, if we take a close look at different animals, as Charles Darwin did, we can discover many instances of cross-species patterns. Darwin wrote in this context:

> What can be more curious than that the hand of a man, formed for grasping, that of a mole for digging, the leg of the horse, the paddle of the porpoise, the wing of the bat, should all be constructed on the same pattern, and should include the same bones, in the same relative positions?[11]

The existence of cross-species patterns (or so-called homologies) is difficult to reconcile with the claim that an original designer created all species from scratch. For what reason could the original designer have for creating the wings of a bat or the leg of a horse from a common design? The functions of the organs are very different, so it would be reasonable to make the design different as well. The fact that the same design patterns can be found across very different species supports the idea that different species developed from the same ancestors, and thus supports the tree-of-life hypothesis.

If we take all these points together, we can safely conclude that traditional creationism is a weak competitor to the theory of evolution.

FOOD FOR THOUGHT

The Navajo Creation Story is quite different than the account we have in Genesis. According to the Navajos, the world where people first lived was deep within the world we inhabit now. It had no sun or moon, and contained only dim clouds, which moved to tell the hours. Life began peacefully, but then lust and envy took hold. The people became violent. The Navajo fled, climbing through a hole in the sky to an above world. This world also began peacefully, but the same evils happened. This process repeated itself until finally the first man and woman emerged on the present earth. The first man filled the world with the aid of a sacred bundle of medicine, transforming different items into mountains, animals, hours, and so on. Everything in this new world was balanced: four directions, four seasons, four basic colors of black, blue, amber, and white. An essential harmony, called hozho, then prevailed.

Is this Creation story any more or less likely to be true than the creation story we find in Genesis?

FOOD FOR THOUGHT

In some school districts in the United States, parents have insisted that traditional creationism should be taught in school alongside the theory of evolution. The argument for this position is that schools have a duty to introduce a variety of different theories about one topic and let students themselves decide which of the theories they would like to adopt. What do you think about this proposal? Do you agree that traditional creationism should be taught along with the theory of evolution?

However, things look a bit different if we compare intelligent design creationism with a naturalistic version of the theory of evolution. An intelligent design creationist accepts the basic tenets of the theory of evolution. She believes in the tree-of-life hypothesis, and she also believes that natural selection is responsible for shaping the pool of living creatures. However, the intelligent design creationist maintains that God still has a role to play in all this. Is this a plausible idea? Well, there are some interesting reasons in defense of intelligent design creationism. First, the classical theory of evolution presupposes that during the early stages of life on earth there existed many, albeit very primitive, life forms that competed with each other for the available resources on earth. This, however, does not explain where life itself came from. How did the first protein, the first enzyme, or the first DNA or RNA molecule come to be? An intelligent design creationist will maintain that it is only with reference to God that we can explain how life originated in the first place. The astrophysicist Fred Hoyle made the calculation that the probability that a small typical enzyme would form at random is comparable to the probability that a tornado whipping through a junkyard would stir up the scrap to form a Boeing 747. Intelligent design creationists conclude from this that it is unreasonable to believe that life originated as the result of random processes. This is a tempting line of reasoning, but naturalistically inclined defenders of the theory of evolution might reply to it as follows: The fact that a certain highly unlikely event actually has happened does not require any special explanation. After all, something or other had to happen. To illustrate this response, consider the following example: Suppose that you are in a building together with 500 other people. Suddenly, there is a fire alarm, and all 500 people leave the building one after the other through the front door. The chief of the fire department keeps track of the people who leave the building. At the end of the fire drill, the chief knows who left the building first, who left second, and so on. Notice that the probability that the 500 people who were in the building left the building in one particular sequence is very, very small. However, the fact that one particular sequence actually did obtain can be explained best with reference to random processes. The fact that the probability of one particular sequence is very small does not require any reference to supernatural forces. The defender of the theory of evolution can say something very similar about how proteins or amino acids came to exist on earth. Although the probability that random processes produced these macromolecules is very small, we cannot reject a possible explanation simply because it requires us to believe that events with a low degree of probability have happened. After all, some event had to take place, and it might as well have been one with a low degree of probability.

FOOD FOR THOUGHT

The probability that life on earth arose out of purely natural processes is very small. Does this entitle us to conclude that God must have had a hand in the creation of life? The following thought experiment by the philosopher Richard Swinburne should help you decide what you think about this:

> Suppose you are imprisoned by a mad scientist who locks you in a room with an automatic card-shuffling machine. He tells you that unless the card-shuffling machine draws ten aces of hearts from ten different decks, the machine will explode and kill you. To your amazement, the machine does indeed draw ten aces of hearts from ten different decks and you continue to live another day. Would you believe in this situation that your survival is due to pure luck, or would you conclude that the mad scientist must have manipulated the machine?

A second reason why some thinkers prefer intelligent design creationism to the theory of evolution has to do with the fact that the fossil records we have found are not complete. According to a naturalistic version of the theory of evolution, the development of new species is a gradual process. However, the fossil records we have found up to this point sometimes simply show that during certain periods (e.g., during the Cambrian era, 600 million years ago) lots of new species seem to have come into existence all of a sudden. Intelligent design creationists can interpret this as evidence that these sudden accelerated periods of evolution are signs that a conscious designer was at work. The naturalistically inclined defender of evolution will of course not be impressed by this argument. He can respond by insisting that an incomplete fossil record is not something surprising. Not all periods of evolutionary development must have left permanent traces. Moreover, sudden accelerated periods of evolutionary development can very well be explained without reference to supernatural forces. What is interesting to note in this context is that one and the same piece of evidence (the fossil findings of the Cambrian area) can be interpreted such that they are compatible with both a naturalistic version of the theory of evolution and a modified version of creationism.

Naturalistically inclined defenders of the theory of evolution have, however, a powerful argument at their disposal. They can point out that the principle of **Ockham's Razor,** which was introduced in Chapter 1, favors the theory of evolution over intelligent design creationism. Ockham's Razor claims that if we have to choose between two competing theories of equal explanatory power, it is reasonable to favor the simpler theory. Since the naturalistically interpreted theory of evolution does not make reference to supernatural beings, it is clear that it is a simpler theory than intelligent design creationism. However, Ockham's Razor is similar to the principle of sufficient reason; although we use it frequently, it is uncertain whether we have to apply it in all cases.

The debate between intelligent design creationism and a naturalistic evolutionism has long been intense and is likely to remain so for quite some time. Even if we were to establish that the intelligent design creationist has the more plausible position, we would still encounter a difficulty that we faced previously in the context of the cosmological argument. For even if we are convinced that the complexity and beauty of life on earth can be best explained with reference to a conscious designer, it is still in no way evident that the designer resembles the God of classical theism. The design argument shares the same shortcoming as the cosmological argument; we are left to wonder whether the designer is omnipotent, all good, and worthy of worship.

The Ontological Argument
Among the various arguments for God's existence, the ontological argument is probably the most intriguing and puzzling. The first thinker to

present this argument was the theologian St. Anselm (1033–1109). The central tenet of the argument is the claim that anyone who assumes that God does not exist involves himself in a contradiction. The following argument schema captures the logical structure of the argument:

1. Assume that God does not exist.
2. If God does not exist, then *triangles have four sides.*
3. But *triangles do not have four sides.*

Therefore: Our assumption must be wrong (i.e., God must exist).

You may recall from Chapter 1 that we call arguments of this type **reductio ad absurdum** arguments. The phrase "triangles have four sides" is just a placeholder for a logically impossible statement. It has nothing to do with the actual argument, but I use the placeholder to highlight that advocates of the ontological argument try to deduce a logical contradiction from the assumption that God does not exist. But how exactly can we deduce a contradiction from the seemingly innocuous assumption that God does not exist? To understand this more clearly, we need to take a closer look at the concept of God.

Advocates of the ontological argument suggest that the idea of God is the idea of the greatest possible being one can think of. This definition seems quite plausible, but we need to investigate it more closely to get some mileage out of it. What exactly does it mean to say that one being is greater than another being? An example might be helpful here. Consider, for instance, Wolfgang Amadeus Mozart. Mozart was a brilliant composer who died in his mid-30s in 1791. Although he died so young, he had already completed 41 symphonies. Now imagine another being, let's call him "Twin Mozart," who is in all respects like Mozart but who lived longer and who completed 65 symphonies. Twin Mozart has some properties that make him greater than the actual Mozart. He lived longer and he composed more symphonies. Any property that makes one being greater than the other can be called a perfection. It follows, therefore, that the idea of Twin Mozart is the idea of a being who is greater than the actual Mozart, since Twin Mozart has more perfections than Mozart. Once we understand that one being can be greater than another being, we can also see that God is the idea of a being that has all perfections. For if God lacked any perfection, God would also be lacking in goodness. But that is conceptually impossible. These considerations suggest that it is not possible to think of a being greater than God, since God by definition is the greatest and most perfect being we can conceive. Once we understand that the idea of God is the idea of the greatest possible being, we can see that the assumption that God does not exist leads us into logical difficulties. The basic nature of the trouble can be best illustrated with reference to another example. Consider the idea of Superman. The idea of Superman is the idea of a being that has a pretty long list of impressive attributes. Superman can fly, he can see through walls, he can stop bullets, and so on. The idea of Superman is clearly the idea of a being that is greater than the idea of a human being. There is, however, one particular property that our idea of Superman lacks. We conceive of Superman as a comic book hero who exists only in our imagination. What the idea of Superman lacks is the property of existing in the real world. Consider now the idea of *"Real Superman." Real Superman* is just like Superman, but he has one property added: namely, existence. Does it not seem plausible that the idea of *Real Superman* is greater than the idea of Superman? If you answer this question affirmatively, you have in effect already embraced the ontological argument.

On the basis of our discussion, we can present the ontological argument in normal form:

1. The idea of God is the idea of a greatest possible being (i.e., it is not possible to think of a being greater than God).
2. Assume that the idea of God is the idea of a being that exists only as a figment of our imagination and does not exist in reality.
3. If 2 is true, then we can form the idea of a being in our minds that is just like God but that also exists in reality; let's call this idea the idea of *Real God.*
4. The idea of *Real God* is greater than the idea of God. So, if 2 is true, it is possible to think of a being greater than God.
5. 1 and 4 are contradictory statements.

Therefore: Our assumption that God exists only as a figment of our imagination must be false (i.e., God is a being that exists in reality).

To most people the ontological argument appears—at least at first glance—like a scam. How should it be possible to deduce the existence of God from the definition of God? However, the difficulty is to say precisely where the argument goes wrong. As long as we cannot do that, the argument remains a potent force in defense of classical theism. We might, of course, object to defining God as the greatest being one can think of. However, why should this definition be rejected? It is certainly hard to see anything that is glaringly wrong with defining God in this manner. Historically, the more promising response to the ontological argument has focused on our understanding of the term "existence." If the ontological argument is supposed to work, then we need to maintain that existence is a perfection (i.e., a great-making property). Ever since Immanuel Kant (1724–1804), people have been suspicious about this claim. Let me illustrate Kant's objection with the help of an example. Suppose you are looking for a partner with the help of a computer-dating agency. Part of the process is to describe the properties you want your dream partner to have. Suppose you come up with the following list:

My dream partner has to be
- at least 6.2 feet tall
- intelligent and funny
- rich
- good looking

One thing is clear, the more properties you add to this list, the smaller the pool of potential candidates. Properties have the "power" to exclude potential candidates. However, consider what would happen if you were to add the property of existence to the list. In this case, the list would read as follows:

My dream partner has to be
- at least 6.2 feet tall
- intelligent and funny
- rich
- good looking
- existing

What is interesting to note here is that the new list does not exclude anybody who has not been already excluded. Anybody who fulfills the first set of requirements will also satisfy the second list of requirements. This observation led Kant to suggest that "existence" is not a "real" property. But how does this claim that existence is not a property relate to the validity of ontological argument? The ontological argument requires that existence is a great-making property. We need to hold that the idea of a God who exists in reality is greater than the idea of a being just like God that exists only in the imagination. However, if we agree with Kant and hold that existence is not a "real" property, we are in a position to reject premise 4 and hold that adding "existence" to our idea of God does not result in the idea of a greater being. This is a pretty powerful objection to the argument.

FOOD FOR THOUGHT

Right after Anselm presented his version of the ontological argument, Gaunilo, a fellow monk, suggested a counterexample to the argument. According to Gaunilo, the ontological argument proves too much. If it is possible for Anselm to prove the existence of a perfect being, it should, by the same token, be possible to prove the existence of a perfect island. Gaunilo tried to establish this with the help of the following argument.

1. I can think of the greatest possible island.
2. The idea of the greatest possible island is the idea of an island none greater can be thought.
3. Assume that the greatest possible island does not exist.
4. In that case one can think of a greater island which has all the properties of the original island plus the property of existence.
5. But 4 contradicts 2.

Therefore: The greatest possible island exists.

Do you think that this is a good objection to Anselm's version of the ontological argument?

Although the traditional versions of the ontological argument have been subject to very damaging criticism, the argument has made a comeback in recent years. Alvin Plantiga (1932–) is one of the contemporary philosophers who has presented a modal version of the ontological argument. The details of the modal version of the ontological argument are rather technical, and I will therefore present only the basic outline of this type of argument. The basic idea here is to focus the discussion on "necessary existence." It seems quite plausible to assume that God's existence is necessary and not contingent, that is, whether God exists is not dependent on any contingent feature of the world. If we grant this plausible assumption, then we can present the argument in the following way.

1. God's existence is either necessary or logically impossible.
2. It is not impossible for God to exist (i.e., there is no contradiction involved in assuming that God exists).

Therefore: God exists necessarily.

The argument is rather seductive and not obviously flawed. The discussion about this modal version of the argument is still in full swing, and it might be a while before universal consensus has been reached whether and why the argument is fundamentally flawed.

Pascal's Wager

The "wager argument" is due to the French mathematician and philosopher Blaise Pascal (1623–1662). The argument, if presented with care, is extremely effective, but it differs in important respects from the arguments that we have discussed up to this point. Pascal's wager is a pragmatic argument. This means that the argument does not try to establish that God exists, but rather tries to establish the weaker thesis that it is pragmatically prudent (i.e., that it is rational) to believe that God exists.

Let us explore Pascal's wager in more detail. In order to understand the argument, we first need to come to an understanding of the concept of **expected utility.** Suppose that I offer you the following bet: If you pay me six dollars, I let you throw a standard die. If you manage to get a three, you win and I will pay you twelve dollars; if you do not throw a three, you lose and I keep the six dollars you paid me. Is this a good game to play? You have the chance to win six dollars; but you also have the chance to lose six dollars. Decisions like these are quite frequently encountered in the real world, and they are called **decisions under uncertainty.** When we are facing decisions under uncertainty, we do not know what consequences we are going to face when we decide to perform certain actions. For example, when I choose to play the above game, I do not know whether I will win or lose. If I win, I am better off, but if I lose I am worse off. Both are possible outcomes of my decision to play the game. So what is the rational thing to do? In order to approach this decision clearly, it is useful to set up a decision matrix that summarizes the options and possible outcomes. The matrix looks as follows:

Options	Possible Outcomes	
Play the game	Win	Lose
Don't play	No win or loss	

It is easy to see that if I refuse to play the game I will neither win nor lose anything. The expected utility of this decision is zero. However, what is the expected utility of playing the game? In order to calculate that, we need to take into account the probability of the various events. The probability of throwing a three with a standard die is 1/6. The probability of not throwing a three is 5/6. Once we are clear on that, we can calculate the expected utility of playing the game.

$$\text{Expected Utility (playing the game)} = (1/6 \times 6) + (5/6 \times -6) =$$
$$1 - 5 = -4$$

This calculation shows nicely what most of you already suspected: One is much better off not playing the game since the expected utility of playing the game is negative. What the negative number shows me is that it is rational to expect a loss of four dollars if one plays the game. The concept of expected utility is a great tool to make rational decisions under uncertain conditions. In general, we can formulate the following guiding principle: When faced with decision under uncertainty, it is rational to choose that action that promises the highest expected utility.

FOOD FOR THOUGHT

A fair game is a game with expected utility of zero. As long as I pay six dollars for the right to play the above game, the game is obviously not fair. What price would one have to charge in order to make the game a fair game?

FOOD FOR THOUGHT

Blackjack, video poker, and roulette (in short, any game offered in a casino) are unfair games, that is, those who play these games are faced with a negative expected utility. In spite of this, these games are very popular and make huge amounts of money for the people who own the casinos. Does this mean that all those who play these games are irrational decision makers?

But what does this principle of rational decision theory have to do with God's existence? Actually there is a direct relationship. Pascal argues that many of us are not certain whether God exists or not. All we can say is that there is a certain probability that God exists and a certain probability that God doesn't exist. This suggests that we can approach the decision whether or not to believe in God as a decision under uncertainty. The matrix for this decision looks as follows:

Options	Possible Outcomes	
Believe in God	God exists and you go to paradise!	God doesn't exist, and you waste some time and money.
Don't believe in God	God exists and you go to hell!	God doesn't exist, and you have saved money and time.

Based on this decision matrix, we can see that the expected utility of believing in God is much higher than the expected utility of not believing in God. For the value of going to heaven is of course infinitely positive, whereas the value of going to hell is infinitely negative. Notice that it does not matter how high the probability for God's existence is. Even if one believes that the probability of God's existence is very, very small, Pascal's wager nevertheless suggests that we should believe in God's existence since the potential gain of eternal life in heaven makes the expected utility of believing in God infinitely large as well. What the argument then shows is not that God exists, but that it is rational and prudent to believe in God, since this belief promises a higher expected utility than not believing in God. In day-to-day life, the argument is sometimes presented with the words: "Well, come on and go to church. For if you go, you have nothing to lose and infinitely much to gain!" There can be no doubt that among all the arguments for the existence of God, this one is most persuasive.

Critics of the argument normally point to two main issues. First, our beliefs are not always under our voluntary control. This point can be illustrated with the help of the following example: Suppose I have to take a calculus exam. I am nervous and I know that if I believe that I am going to be successful on this exam, then I will calm down and do as best as I can. In this situation, I have good reasons to believe that I am going to be successful on the calculus test. However, in spite of the fact that it is prudent for me to believe this, it might happen that I simply cannot really make myself believe that I am going to be successful. Without wanting to do it, I start thinking that I will fail this exam because I have always failed math exams. This example shows that what we believe is frequently not a matter of choice. The same might be true for my belief in God. Although Pascal's wager might convince me that it is prudent to believe in God, I might not be able make myself believe it.

FOOD FOR THOUGHT

What do you think? Is your belief in God or your belief in atheism under your voluntary control? Could you decide, at the drop of a hat, that God exists or that he doesn't exist? Or is it perhaps the case that no matter what happens, we would simply continue to believe what we always believed?

The second objection is more serious. Suppose you are convinced by Pascal's wager and want to believe in God. What religion would you join? The interesting thing to notice here is that a version of Pascal's wager can be presented in defense of a Jewish God, a Muslim God, a Christian God, a Hindu God, and so on. The only condition is that the God must promise eternal life to believers and eternal damnation to nonbelievers. To make matters worse, there seem to be potentially infinitely many different descriptions of God that can satisfy that requirement.

This objection—normally referred to as the *Many Gods Objection*—shows that Pascal's wager is not as pragmatically useful as it might seem at first glance. For if there are indeed infinitely many possible descriptions of different Gods available, the expected utility of believing in any one of them becomes rather small.

What Is the Effect of These Arguments?

None of the arguments for God's existence that we have discussed so far seems strong enough to establish the existence of an omnipotent, omniscient, and perfect being beyond all doubt. We have seen that one can raise objections to each of them. Does this mean that belief in God cannot be justified in the light of reason? It is too early to draw such a conclusion. Although none of the arguments alone has been able to prove that God exists, the arguments might have a cumulative effect. Together they might be seen as providing good reasons for belief in classical theism. But even if the arguments together cannot move us to believe in a classical theistic God, it would be premature to conclude that no argument can in principle establish the existence of such a being. From the fact that human thinkers have failed to establish God's existence in the past, it does not follow that it cannot be established in the future. We have seen that some arguments, especially the ontological and the design argument, are continuously developed and refined. It might be possible that a more successful version of one such argument might emerge in the future. We are therefore not justified to announce loudly that it is impossible to prove the existence of God. However, it is not quite clear yet whether we might not be able establish the opposite result. Perhaps we can prove that atheism is true and that God does not exist. Most attempts to establish these conclusions focus on the **problem of evil**. We will therefore discuss this problem in the following sections.

Arguments Against Classical Theism

On Saturday, March 23, 2002 Rodney P. was killed in a car accident with his children—Matthew, 8, Jordan, 9, and Rodney Jr., 10. Their car, rear-ended by another driver, was smashed into the back of a Ford Bronco as they waited at a traffic light. Rodney P. was a popular minister who spent most of his time helping others. The driver who rammed into his car suffered a medical emergency that caused him to lose control of the vehicle. Tragic events like this happen quite frequently in the world in which we live. People die in car accidents, they suffer diseases, they drown in floods, and they starve in famines. How can a good and benevolent God allow all this to happen? It would have been so easy for God to spare the life of Rodney P. and his three young children. All he had to do was to prevent the driver who smashed into them from suffering a heart attack. Why did God not interfere in this situation? This question leads us into the heart of one of the most powerful arguments for atheism: **the problem of evil.** The problem of evil can be presented either as a *logical problem* or as an *evidential problem*. We will start our discussion with the logical problem.

The Logical Problem of Evil

As we have seen in our initial discussion, classical theists do not completely agree on what God is like. However, there can be no doubt that every devout theist must conceive of God as an absolutely good being. If God fails to be good, there seems to be no point in worshipping him. Who, for instance, would worship a being that delights in the suffering of innocent beings? We might fear such a being, and we might try to do anything to make the being well disposed to us. But we would not celebrate its existence, and feel that our lives are better or more meaningful because of such a being. God's goodness is a necessary condition for taking religion seriously.

To call a being good does, however, entail significant logical consequences. Consider the following example. Suppose that Hans, a friend of yours, is a completely good being. One day on his way home, Hans sees a 2-year-old child fall into a pond. There is nobody else around and Hans can see that the child is going to drown if nobody will help. What is Hans going to do? If it is true that Hans is a completely good being, then you know how Hans is going to act. Hans will jump into the pond and try as hard as he can to save the child. There is no other way a good being can act in this situation. Hans might, of course, fail in his efforts to save the child, but he will try as hard as he can to save the child's life. This suggests the following general principle:

1. Every good being tries everything in its power to prevent innocent beings from suffering unnecessary evil.

It is obvious that this principle applies to Hans as well as to all other good beings. So, if we believe that God is good, then the principle implies that God tries everything in his power to prevent innocent beings from suffering unnecessary evil. Notice, however, that God is omnipotent—there are no limits to what he can do. Moreover, God is also omniscient—no innocent being suffers without God being aware of it. This entails (logically) that God must prevent *all* innocent beings from suffering unnecessary evil. This, however, is incompatible with what we can see every day. Every day, children starve to death, or suffer from horrible diseases. Every day, children step on land mines and get maimed or torn to pieces. Every day, children are beaten or sexually abused. God does not seem to take care of them. They are left to die alone. We cannot deny these facts and we are thus confronted with a logical problem: If God exists, and if God is all-good, omniscient, and omnipotent, then innocent beings should not suffer from unnecessary evils (like land mines, diseases, or starvation). But they do suffer from these evils. So God's existence seems logically incompatible with the fact that innocent beings suffer unnecessary evil. If these evils exist (as surely they do), then we are forced to conclude that God doesn't exist. Theism thus appears to be an inconsistent theory. This is a powerful argument in defense of atheism. Most atheists justify their belief in the nonexistence of God with reference to this problem.

FOOD FOR THOUGHT

The suffering of children seems to raise the problem of evil most forcefully. In the following selection from Dostoyevski's novel *The Brothers Karamazov*, one of the main characters, Ivan Karamarzov, explains to his religious brother Alyosha why the suffering of children makes him reject God:

> Listen! I took the case of children only to make my case clearer. Of the other tears of humanity with which the earth is soaked from its crust to its center, I will say nothing. . . . It's beyond all comprehension why the children should suffer, and why they should pay for the harmony. Why should they, too, furnish material to enrich the soil for the harmony of the future? I understand solidarity in sin among men, but there can be no such solidarity with children . . . Some jester will say, perhaps that the child would have grown up and have sinned, but you see he didn't grow up, he was torn to pieces by the dogs at eight years old . . . and so I renounce the higher harmony altogether.

It's not worth the tears of that one tortured child who beat itself on the breast with its little fist and prayed in its stinking outhouse with an unexpiated tear to "dear, kind God"! It's not worth it, because those tears are unatoned for. How are you going to atone for them?

Do you agree that the suffering of children raises the problem of evil most forcefully? If yes, how can a defender of classical theism respond to this?

Is there a way the classical theist can respond to this criticism that God and the existence of evil are incompatible? As long as we conceive of the problem of evil as a logical problem, the theist is in a fairly strong position to respond to this attack. For all the theist needs to show is that it is logically possible that an all-good, omniscient, and omnipotent God allows evil to exist. The philosopher Alvin Plantiga (1932–) developed such a response in detail. The key idea of his **free-will defense** is to argue that even an omnipotent God does not have complete control over his creation as long as the creation contains genuinely free creatures. In short, the free-will defense asserts that it is not within God's power to eliminate all evil since God has given us the power to act freely on our own. Let us illustrate the logic of the free-will defense with reference to the accident of Rodney P. Rodney P. and his three children were killed by another driver. According to the free-will defense, Rodney P., his children, and the other driver are all free creatures. They make decisions and thus determine the character of the world. It is not within God's power to make sure that all their decisions and actions lead to outcomes that are free of suffering. If God were to do that, he would in effect eliminate their free will. It follows therefore that God's existence is logically compatible with the fact that innocent beings suffer horribly.

FOOD FOR THOUGHT

Critics of the free-will defense have pointed out that it seems to restrict God's powers too much. If we understand God's omnipotence as the power to bring about anything that is logically possible, it should be in his power to create a world in which free creatures like us freely always do things that lead to good consequences. In

Continued

such a world there would be no pointless suffering, no vicious murder, and no rape or abuse. Is this a plausible idea? Is it logically possible that free creatures like us always freely do what is right and that God could have created a world in which that is the case? What do you think?

The Evidential Problem of Evil

As we have seen, the logical problem of evil does not provide a watertight case for atheism. It seems logically possible that not even an omnipotent God can eliminate all evil in a world in which human beings have genuine free will. However, there is a more powerful version of the problem of evil available to the atheist: the so-called evidential problem of evil. According to the evidential problem, God's existence is logically compatible with the fact that innocent beings suffer unnecessary evil. However, an advocate of the evidential problem of evil will insist that the existence of unnecessary evil makes God's existence highly implausible. Let us illustrate the basic line of reasoning with the help of an example. Suppose you are a detective and you are investigating the death of a college student, Peter H. Peter has been found shot to death in his car. On the seat next to him, the police found a suicide note. His friends confirm that Peter had been very depressed prior to his death. Two of his best friends report that Peter spoke on more than one occasion about the possibility of committing suicide. In this situation, it seems very reasonable to conclude that Peter in fact committed suicide. All the evidence seems to support this assumption. Notice, however, that this conclusion, although compelling, is not certain. It is certainly logically possible that Peter has been murdered in spite of the fact that all of the evidence points toward a suicide. It is, for instance, logically possible that all his friends are part of the plot to kill him and are therefore lying about his depressed state of mind prior to his death. It is similarly possible that the suicide note was fake, and so on. Although all of this is logically possible, it is extremely improbable and extremely hard to believe. In the absence of further evidence, nobody would seriously believe that Peter's death was murder.

The basic reasoning behind the evidential problem of evil will apply the same kind of thinking to the relationship between God and the existence of evil. Although it is logically possible that the existence of evil is compatible with God's existence, it can be argued that it is highly improbable that God would allow so much evil to take place in his creation. Although God's existence is logically compatible with existence of evil, the amount of suffering in this world makes it irrational to believe that an all-powerful, omnibenevolent God is in fact lurking behind the scenes.

The key issue in the evidential problem of evil is to clarify when and why the existence of evil counts as evidence against the existence of God. Even the most hardened atheist must admit that not all instances of evil count as evidence against God. Consider the following example: Suppose a 6-year-old girl is told by her parents not to ride her bicycle without supervision. She defies the order and injures her knee while riding the bicycle on her own. As a result of her injury she not only experiences pain but she also pays more attention to her parent's commands. Moreover, after her injury, she feels compassion for other children who are injured in accidents. The suffering of the 6-year-old girl clearly cannot count as evidence against God. God clearly had no reason to eliminate this suffering since it ultimately led to higher-order good (compassion and obedience).

To respond to the evidential problem of evil, a theist has to show that all suffering of innocent beings is similar to the suffering of the 6-year-old girl and therefore has purpose. For suffering that has a purpose cannot count as evidence against the existence of God. And if there is no compelling evidence against God, then the evidential case against God collapses. The atheist, on the other hand, will try to show that there are many instances of pointless suffering. For pointless suffering is evil, which we should expect God to eliminate. And the fact that it hasn't been eliminated counts as evidence against the existence of God. If we can find a great amount of pointless suffering in the universe, then it seems irrational to believe in the existence of an all-good God.

FOOD FOR THOUGHT

In order to show that there exist many instances of intense pointless suffering that God could have prevented without thereby losing any greater good, the philosopher Wiliam Rowe writes about a

Continued

fawn trapped in a distant forest that has caught on fire during a lightning storm. The fawn is horribly burned, suffers for days, and finally dies.

Two questions arise in the context of this thought experiment.

1. Can we know that suffering of this kind happens frequently?
2. Can we be sure that there is no hidden purpose to the suffering of the fawn that only God can see?

How would you answer these questions?

It is readily apparent that this debate between the theist and the atheist cannot be resolved in a completely objective way. It depends in part on how we experience and interpret the suffering that takes place in this universe. If we experience the suffering of innocent beings to have purpose, then it seems quite plausible to believe that God exists. If, on the other hand, we see this world as a tragic place in which innocent beings get killed or maimed without purpose, rhyme, or reason, then belief in God must appear foolish and irrational.

In order to make belief in a God more plausible, theologians have developed **theodicies**. A theodicy is an explanation of why God lets innocents suffer on Earth. If we can develop a theodicy that provides a plausible explanation for why God permits all this suffering, then the evidential problem of evil has lost its foundation. Atheists, on the other hand, are normally very quick to point out why no theodicy can explain all instances of suffering. Are there then any plausible theodicies available? This is a question that needs to be answered by each person on an individual basis. The following Food for Thought exercise might help you to decide where you stand on this issue.

FOOD FOR THOUGHT

An attempt to show that an omnipotent, all-good, and omniscient God might have good reasons for letting innocent beings suffer is called a **theodicy**. In the following I describe—very roughly—a number of theodicies. Discuss with others in the class whether these theories are able to show that *all* suffering of innocent beings has a point:

1. *Big-Plan Theodicy:* All suffering of innocent beings is part of a big plan and had to happen. The whole plan, however, is completely good.
2. *Punishment Theodicy:* When we see innocent people suffer terribly, the reason for this is that they have sinned. Their suffering is a punishment for their sins. This solution can be well combined with the idea of Original Sin, that is, all human beings (including children) are sinners since they are descendants of Adam and Eve.
3. *Suffering-Builds-Character Theodicy:* The basic idea is that suffering of innocents will help them to become stronger. All evil offers us the possibility to learn from it and grow into a better human being. This theodicy is sometimes called "Soul-making theodicy."
4. *Limits-of-Human-Knowledge Theodicy:* The basic idea is that we simply are too dumb to understand why God lets innocents suffer. God has his reasons but we humans cannot understand them.
5. *Contrast Theodicy:* This solution asserts that we need evil in the universe to know that there is good. If there were no evil and everything were good, we could not tell that it is good.
6. *Devil Theodicy:* Innocent beings suffer because the devil likes to let innocents suffer.
7. *Test Theodicy:* The basic idea is that this earthly life is just a test. God has thrown us into this world full of evil and pointless suffering in order to find out what kind of beings we are. Without the pointless suffering this test is not complete. If we pass the test, we are going to heaven; if we fail, some more sinister place will wait for us.

Final Remarks on the Problem of God's Existence

Our discussion of arguments for and against the existence of God has shown that the classical theist as well as the atheist have reasons for their positions. Although none of the arguments are entirely successful, they are strong enough to show that neither of the positions is completely without merit. Where does this leave us? A few summarizing observations might be in order. First, we might take the inconclusiveness of our discussion as a reason to embrace an **agnostic** position. By insisting that we cannot know whether God exists, an agnostic seems to keep all his options open. However, an agnostic faces difficulties of his own. A person who holds that God might exist without firmly believing that he does, avoids making any clear decision about God. But our lives become worthwhile not by avoiding decisions but by making them. The American philosopher William James pointed out in his essay *The Will to Believe* that in "real life" we have to choose what seems most reasonable and promising even if we have insufficient evidence. A person who avoids making momentous decisions runs the risk of avoiding life as well. William James illustrates this critique of agnosticism by quoting Fitzjames Stephen:

> In all important transactions of life we have to take a leap in the dark. . . . We stand on a mountain pass in the midst of whirling snow and blinding mist through which we get glimpses now and then of paths which may be deceptive. If we stand still we shall be frozen to death. If we take the wrong road we shall be dashed to pieces. We do not certainly know whether there is any right one. What must we do? "Be strong and of a good courage." Act for the best, hope for the best, and take what comes. . . . If death ends all, we cannot meet death better.[12]

This quotation suggests that we might be better off if we make a clear choice and embrace either theism or atheism. Making a decision, even if it is the wrong one, might be better than remaining in a state of indecision.

We have also seen that the evidential problem of evil makes a pretty strong case for atheism. However, even if one admits that there is no entirely successful theodicy available, one does not have to abandon belief in God. Instead, one might understand the problem of evil as a refutation of a *certain kind of God*, namely the God of classical theism. Some theologians have taken this as a reason to change our traditional understanding of God's nature. Paul Tillich, for example, has suggested that we should not think about God as a being, but rather as Being itself. Whether such alternative conceptions of God are more promising and satisfactory in the light of religious experiences depends in part on how we understand the character of religions experiences. No general, universal answer seems to emerge.

Endnotes

1. I do not want to assert here that our lives become meaningless if God does not exist. It is very well possible to lead a meaningful life without God. It seems nevertheless correct to assert that our lives cannot have any "ultimate meaning" without God, for "ultimate meaning" seems to presuppose the existence of a necessary being.
2. *Glamour,* September 2001, p. 276.
3. Ibid., p. 276.
4. James, William. *The Works of William James: The Varieties of Religious Experience.* Cambridge: Harvard University Press, 1979, p. 47.
5. Ibid., p. 25.
6. This example is inspired by Taylor, Richard. "A Contemporary Version of the Cosmological Argument" in *Philosophy of Religion: Selected Readings.* Edited by Michael Peterson, William Hasker, Bruce Reichenbach, and David Basinger. New York: Oxford University Press, 1996, pp. 167–176.
7. Ibid., p. 192.
8. It is important in this context to realize that the term "necessary being" is not to be understood as logically necessary. For if God were logically necessary then it would be logically impossible that God fails to exist, and that surely is not what we want to assert in this context.
9. This debate between Russell and Copleston can be found in Russell, B. *Why I Am Not a Christian and Other Essays on Religion and Related Subjects.* New York: Simon and Schuster, 1957.
10. For a good discussion of different versions of creationism see Pennock, Robert. *Tower of Babel.* Cambridge: MIT Press, 2000.
11. Darwin, Charles. *On the Origin of Species by Means of Natural Selection, or the Preservation of Favoured Races in the Struggle for Life.* London: Murray, 1859.
12. James, William. *The Will to Believe and Other Essays in Popular Philosophy.* Cambridge: Harvard University Press, 1979.

For Further Reading

Audi, R. and Wainwright, W. (eds.) *Religious Belief and Moral Commitment.* Ithaca, NY: Cornell University Press, 1986.

Kenny, Anthony. *Faith and Reason*. New York: Columbia University Press, 1983.

Mackie, J.L. *The Miracle of Theism*. Oxford: Oxford University Press, 1982.

Penelhum, Terrence (ed.). *Faith*. New York: Macmillan, 1989.

Peterson, M., Hasker, W., Reichenbach, B., and Basinger, D. (eds.). *Philosophy of Religion: Selected Readings*. Oxford: Oxford University Press, 1996.

Peterson, M., Hasker, W., Reichenbach, B., and Basinger, D. *Reason and Religious Belief*. Oxford: Oxford University Press. 1997.

Plantiga, Alvin. *Warranted Christian Belief*. Oxford: Oxford University Press, 2000.

Swinburne, Richard. *Faith and Reason*. Oxford: Clarendon Press, 1981.

CHAPTER SEVEN

WHAT OUGHT WE TO DO?

Moral Intuitions and Moral Principles

On May 24, 2000 Robert Elliot and Kevin Smith were working their usual evening shifts in Ruby's Restaurant. When a fisherman came in and told them that somebody was drowning in the ocean outside, they didn't hesitate. Still wearing their white waiters' uniforms, the men ripped off their boots, jumped into the ocean and kept the man afloat until lifeguards came to the rescue. When we hear this story, it immediately appears to us that Robert Elliot and Kevin Smith performed a morally good action. When actions appear to be morally good or morally wrong, philosophers say that we experience **moral intuitions.** In many circumstances, we have clear intuitions whether we are confronted with a moral wrong or with a moral good. When we hear in the news that a young child has been kidnapped from her bedroom, it immediately appears to us that this action is morally reprehensible. The same is true for stories about theft, arson, or murder. On the other hand, when we hear that somebody has risked her life to save a child from drowning, it immediately appears to us that this action is morally commendable. Unfortunately, our moral intuitions are not always as clear. Consider the following story:

On August 6, 1945 Lt. Col. Paul Tibbets took off from the American Airbase Tinian in a B-29 Super Fortress. On board the airplane were twelve crewmen and one of the first nuclear bombs ever built. The bomb, nicknamed "Little Boy," was 12 feet long and 28 inches in diameter and had an explosive power equal to 20,000 tons of TNT. Seven hours later, Paul Tibbets and his crew dropped "Little Boy" on the Japanese city of Hiroshima. The explosion killed close to 200,000 people and contributed to Japan's decision to accept unconditional surrender a short time later.

When we consider the bombing of Hiroshima, most of us have the following two moral intuitions:

1. Killing thousands of civilians in Hiroshima is morally wrong.

2. Ending the war sooner and saving the lives of many is morally good.

These two intuitions are in conflict with each other. We are torn between different ways to evaluate the same situation. This situation illustrates that if we want to avoid moral confusion, we cannot be satisfied with evaluating situations simply in the light of our initial moral intuitions alone. In addition, we need general **moral principles.** Moral principles are general rules that allow us to classify any action as morally good or morally wrong. Moral principles can help us when we experience conflicting moral intuitions. For example, we might introduce the moral principle that we are always morally required to save as many lives as possible. If we accept this moral principle, we can evaluate the two conflicting intuitions about the bombing of Hiroshima and determine which of them ought to be abandoned.

Discovering and developing general moral principles is the central goal of ethical theory. In this chapter, we will discuss and evaluate some of the most important ethical theories that have been developed. Our task will be to discover what ethical theory is best compatible with most of our basic moral intuitions. A satisfactory moral theory will not only furnish us with moral principles that can explain most of our basic moral intuitions, but it will also help us decide what we are required to do when we are facing moral dilemmas.

FOOD FOR THOUGHT

When we are confronted with complex ethical situations, we frequently experience conflicting moral intuitions. Consider the following case that Paige Mitchell describes in her book *Act of Love: The Killing of George Zygmanik.* Does it appear to you that Lester Zygmanik committed a moral wrong?

On June 17, 1973, George Zygmanik shattered his spine in a motorcycle accident. Formerly an active, athletic individual, he was now a quadriplegic, unable to move any of his limbs. Everything he could feel hurt. His brother, Lester, was at his bedside during most of the next few days. On June 19, George said to Lester, "Hold my hand." After Lester took his hand, he said, "You're my brother. I want you to promise to kill me. I want you to swear to God." On June 20, 1973 Lester Zygmanik walked into the Jersey Shore Medical Center with a sawed-off shotgun under his coat. He entered his brother's room, pointed the gun at his temple, and pulled the trigger. In the ensuing commotion, Lester turned to one of the nurses and said, "I am the one you're looking for. I just shot my brother."

A Fundamental Challenge: Relativism

Although all of us have moral intuitions, many people are very skeptical whether moral intuitions are uniform enough to provide a solid starting point for the construction of objective ethical theories. There can be no doubt that different people differ in their assessment of one and the same moral question. Consider, for instance, the Food for Thought exercise below.

FOOD FOR THOUGHT

Take a look at the following claims and decide whether they appear true or false to you. After you have completed the exercise, compare your responses with the answers of your neighbor.

1. It is morally wrong to lie.
2. It is morally required to take care of one's parents when they are old.
3. Men and women should receive the same pay if they perform the same work.
4. It is better to suffer injustice than to do it.
5. Killing people is morally wrong.
6. All members of a society have the right to receive health care.
7. All members of a society have the right to receive equal educational opportunities.

Continued

8. Eating meat is morally wrong.
9. Homosexuals should have the right to form legal partnerships that offer the same protection and opportunities as heterosexual marriages.
10. People who committed a felony in the past should have the right to vote after they are released from prison.
11. No government has the right to kill any of its citizens.
12. A terminally ill person has the right to insist that his doctor will put him to death.

If you compare your answers to the above exercise to the answers somebody else has given, the chances are high that you will discover significant disagreements. Although most of us probably agree that men and women should receive the same pay if they perform the same work, it is easy to see that people tend to disagree whether it is immoral to eat meat or whether homosexual partners should have the right to marry. These disagreements have led some thinkers to suppose that ethics is a subjective affair. The philosophical position that makes this claim is called **ethical relativism.** An ethical relativist holds that judgments of what we ought to do need to be assessed in relation to the person who is making the judgment. An ethical relativist might say, for example, that the bombing of Hiroshima was good for American soldiers, but bad for Japanese people living there. What the ethical relativist denies is that the bombing of Hiroshima in itself is either morally good or morally bad. Whether ethical relativism is true or false has important consequences for the study of ethics. If ethical relativism is correct, then it is hard to see how there can be moral knowledge. I might believe, for example, that I am morally required to help homeless people, whereas you might believe that helping homeless people is a waste of money and therefore morally wrong. According to relativism, both of these intuitions can be correct. What the relativists will deny is that we can establish, from an objective point of view, whether it is true that helping homeless people is morally required. Relativism supports skepticism about the truth-value of moral claims. Thinkers who believe that we can obtain moral knowledge about ethical questions tend to oppose relativism. The denial of ethical relativism leads to a position called **ethical objectivism.** An ethical objectivist believes that moral judgments are not dependent on our individual wishes, hopes, or aspirations. According to ethical objectivism, there are some universal moral truths that are true for all people at all times. The following chart introduces some key terms in the debate between relativism and objectivism:

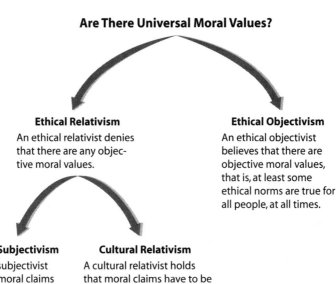

Are There Universal Moral Values?

Ethical Relativism
An ethical relativist denies that there are any objective moral values.

Ethical Objectivism
An ethical objectivist believes that there are objective moral values, that is, at least some ethical norms are true for all people, at all times.

Ethical Subjectivism
An ethical subjectivist holds that moral claims have to be assessed in relation to an individual. Rather than saying "Eating meat is wrong" we should say "Eating meat is wrong for me."

Cultural Relativism
A cultural relativist holds that moral claims have to be assessed in relation to a particular culture. Rather than saying "Female circumcision is morally wrong" we should say "Female circumcision is wrong in the United States."

Before we proceed further with our exploration of ethical theories, it is of obvious interest to determine how plausible ethical relativism is. If we decide that there can be no objective moral values that hold for all people at all times, it will be in principle impossible to find a universally satisfactory moral theory. Let us explore therefore whether there are any compelling arguments in support of this position.

The Case for Subjective Relativism

A subjective relativist believes that ethical judgments depend on the tastes and preferences of each individual person. At first blush, this makes a good deal of sense. If we look around us we can see that each person is unique in his or her preferences and tastes. I might like the music of Johann Sebastian Bach, while you might prefer the songs of Eminem. I like to play soccer, whereas you might like to play baseball. There is no doubt that people differ in what they like and enjoy. It would strike most of us as strange if somebody were to claim that he could establish objectively that playing soccer has no value. If I like to play soccer, then soccer has value for me. Moreover, I am happy to grant you the right to say that playing soccer has no value for you. Whether soccer playing has value depends on the person who plays.

The subjective relativist argues that something very similar is true for moral values. According to ethical relativism, we cannot categorically establish whether eating meat is morally wrong or not. The subjective relativist holds that it all depends on who makes the judgment. Eating meat might be wrong for me and morally right for you. There are two main reasons why people are attracted to subjective relativism. First, subjective relativism is well compatible with our experiences of living in a pluralistic society. When we look around us we see many different people with many different moral beliefs. Some people drink alcohol and smoke; others consider smoking and alcohol to be immoral activities. Some of us think that paying taxes is an important moral duty, whereas others feel perfectly fine when they manipulate their income tax reports. The subjective relativist can respond to this by saying: "To each his own!" He is neither surprised nor annoyed by the fact that people make different moral judgments. It is just what he expects to find. Moreover, subjective relativism also seems very tolerant. A subjective relativist will not try to change your mind about ethical questions. You do what is right for you and I do what is right for me. There is no reason our different opinions cannot coexist.

In light of these considerations, it is no surprise to discover that many people subscribe to subjective relativism. However, there are some serious shortcomings associated with this philosophical position. We will discuss these shortcomings in the next section.

Problems for Subjective Relativism

There are three fundamental problems with subjective relativism. First, subjective relativism is in conflict with some of our most fundamental moral intuitions. Consider, for instance, the events of the Columbine High School shooting on April 20, 1999. Two students, Dylan Klebold and Eric Harris, walked into their high school and went on a shooting spree. Before they committed suicide, they killed 13 students and teachers. If subjective relativism is correct, then we need to accept the following two statements about these shootings.

1. The actions of Dylan Klebold and Eric Harris considered on their own account are neither morally wrong nor morally right.
2. The actions were morally right for Dylan Klebold and for Eric Harris. The shooters felt, after all, that they were merely taking revenge for abuse and insults they had suffered in the past.

The emerging problem is obvious. Most of us would reject both statements as preposterous. They are not compatible with our moral intuitions. It appears to us that the actions of Dylan Klebold and Eric Harris were wrong by themselves and not only in relationship to what anybody thinks. Second, it seems absurd to claim that the shootings were right for Dylan Klebold and Eric Harris. An action does not become right for somebody when the action appears justified to that person. Hitler might have felt justified to kill millions of Jews, but that seems to have no bearing on the issue of whether his actions are morally justified. What these examples show is that we often have clear and strong intuitions that specific actions are simply wrong. The subjective relativist has no way to account for these moral intuitions.

Second, according to subjective relativism, it is impossible to disagree about ethical questions. Let me illustrate this with the help of an example. Suppose you and Tony are ethical subjectivists and Tony has borrowed $20 from you. After Tony has failed to repay the money, you give Tony a call. Tony says, "I have changed my mind; I am not going to give you back that money. I have decided that you have too much money anyway." At this point you will probably respond as follows: "I can't believe what you are saying. You borrowed $20 and you promised to pay it back. If you fail to do so you commit a moral wrong." Given that you and Tony are subjective relativists, he can respond to this objection as follows: "Well, you are mistaken. You think that not paying back the money is morally wrong. This entitles you to say that from your perspective not paying back the money is morally wrong. However, I believe now that not paying back the money is morally right and this entitles me to say that not paying back the money is morally right for me. Both of us are right, but neither of us has the right to impose his opinion on the other."

This conversation shows that subjective relativists cannot have meaningful disagreements and conversations about moral questions. According to subjective relativism, each person has their own opinions about moral matters and these opinions are all compatible with each other. This does not square well with our experiences of moral conversations. When we disagree about moral questions we tend to experience the conflict as a specific disagreement about an objective subject matter. It follows therefore that subjective relativists cannot explain how genuine ethical conversations are possible.

The third weakness of subjective relativism is closely related to the point above. If subjective relativism is true, then our ethical judgments are always correct. If it appears to me that smoking is morally wrong, then I am automatically justified to assert that smoking is wrong for me. According to subjective relativism, I cannot go wrong in my ethical judgments since my ethical judgments are merely the expression of my personal preferences. However, it seems rather strange to assert that we are ethically infallible. In many situations it makes perfect sense to assert that somebody has a false moral belief. Consider the case of John, who sincerely believes that people who commit adultery should be stoned to death. It appears to most of us that John is mistaken on this point. Stoning does not appear to be an appropriate punishment for any wrongdoing. But if we accept subjective relativism, the belief that adulterers should be stoned to death is morally right for John as long as he sincerely believes it. If we want to maintain that it is possible for John (or anybody else, for that matter) to have false moral beliefs, it seems necessary to embrace some form of ethical objectivism.

The last three arguments show why very few thinkers take subjective relativism seriously. Although subjective relativism has some initial plausibility, it is not a theory that is compatible with our moral intuitions and our experiences of having meaningful moral conversations. If we want a plausible moral theory, we need to look somewhere else.

The Case for Cultural Relativism

Although subjective relativism fails, it is possible to present a more promising version of relativism. **Cultural relativists** admit that individual persons can be mistaken about their moral judgments. However, cultural relativists do not conclude from this that ethical objectivism is correct. They assert instead that moral judgments need to be understood in the context of a given culture. According to cultural relativism, a given action is morally wrong if one's culture does not approve of the action, and an action is morally right if one's culture approves of the action. The culture in the United States, for example, does not approve of stealing. In the United States, it is therefore morally wrong to steal cars, horses, or any other property that belongs to somebody else. In Saudi Arabia, the culture expects men to have beards. It is therefore morally right for Saudi men to have beards. The overall motto of cultural relativism is: When in Rome, do as the Romans do! The idea that actions need to be morally evaluated in the context of the culture in which they occur is intuitively plausible. There are several arguments that support cultural relativism.

First, there can be little doubt that the culture in which we grow up has an impact on our moral intuitions. The fact that certain actions find our approval while others strike us as reprehensible has a lot to do with our childhood and education. We grow up hearing from our parents that taking the toys of our friends without permission is wrong, but that sharing our lunch with them is morally good. Later on, teachers in school reinforce the same lessons. It is therefore plausible to suppose that our moral intuitions and feelings are not the result of objective, rational thinking, but rather the product of the culture in which we have been raised.

Second, different cultures endorse different moral and legal practices. In the United States, it is perfectly fine for women and men go to the beach in a small bikini or tight bathing suit. In Scandinavian countries, it is acceptable to bathe naked, while most Muslim countries require women to cover most of their bodies in public. A cultural relativist is not surprised by this. This is just what she expects to find. Different countries have different customs, and each country determines what is morally right in that country. Cultural relativism is therefore well compatible with the great variety of differing moral rules that are practiced in different countries.

FOOD FOR THOUGHT

1. List five activities that are perfectly acceptable in the United States, but completely unacceptable in another culture.
2. List five activities that are immoral in the United States, but perfectly acceptable in other cultures.

Third, cultural relativism appears to be a very tolerant and peaceful position. Suppose, for instance, that moral objectivism is true and that there is only one set of moral rules for all humanity. Suppose further that we discover two different cultures that embrace radically opposed sets of moral values. If moral objectivism is correct, we must conclude that one of these cultures is wrong and that one culture is morally superior to the other. Many people may feel very uncomfortable drawing such a conclusion. What right do we have to elevate one culture over another? Cultural relativism can solve this dilemma. A cultural relativist can say that both cultures are correct as long as they stay within their own sphere. This is a very attractive solution to an otherwise thorny problem. These three arguments show that cultural relativism is not only an intuitive, but also a well-supported philosophical position. Let us now explore whether there are any major difficulties with this way of thinking about ethics.

Problems for Cultural Relativism

Cultural relativism is open to several major objections. First, we have seen that many cultural relativists are proud of the fact that cultural relativism seems to further cooperation and respect between different cultures. According to cultural relativism, no culture has the right to assert that their cultural practices are superior to those of any other. Closer analysis reveals, however, that cultural relativism does not necessarily advance cooperation between cultures. Consider the case of the Vikings. The Vikings supported themselves for the most part by raiding, burning, and looting monasteries, cities, and farms all over Northern Europe. If cultural relativism is correct, we cannot condemn the Vikings. They are simply following their own cultural practices according to which raiding and plundering other cities is morally praiseworthy. What this example shows is that cultural relativism does not necessarily lead to a peaceful cooperation between cultures. It all depends on the cultures that inter-act. If one of the cultures is very aggressive, cultural relativism sanctions war and oppression. Notice also that the losing culture in such a conflict has no right to complain toward the winning, aggressive culture. The losing culture has to accept that the more aggressive culture simply fol-lows a different set of moral rules. Many people find this result unset-tling; they believe that peaceful cooperation between diverse cultures is an important value. However, it appears that the best way to promote this value is to admit that peaceful cooperation between cultures is a moral value that applies to all cultures at all times. This is tantamount to embracing a version of moral objectivism since it entails that we reject full-blown cultural relativism and accept at least one universal moral value.

Second, cultural relativism cannot explain the influence of moral critics. Consider the example of Martin Luther King, Jr. Martin Luther King, Jr. grew up in a culture that practiced segregation. The over-whelming majority of his contemporaries believed that it is a good thing to keep the lives of black and white Americans separated. Martin Luther King, Jr. became an outspoken and influential critic of this practice. Now, we praise him for his courage. We declare with a sense of pride that Martin Luther King, Jr. performed morally good actions when he opposed his own culture and fought for the equality of black and white Americans. Notice, however, that cultural relativists cannot explain this phenomenon easily. If cultural relativism were correct, we would have to conclude that Martin Luther King's actions were morally wrong. He re-fused, after all, to accept what his culture told him was morally neces-sary. Cultural relativism fails therefore to provide an adequate explana-tion for why the actions of moral critics are worthy of moral praise. Notice that an ethical objectivist does not face this problem. She can simply adopt the position that segregation is morally wrong in any cul-ture at any time and that Martin Luther King's perspective on race rela-tions was therefore morally superior to the perspective of most of his contemporaries.

Third, we have seen that cultural relativists support their position by pointing to the great variety of moral codes that can be found across dif-ferent cultures. They argue that cultural relativism provides the best ex-planation of why different cultures embrace such different moral norms. Let us call the argument that follows these lines the anthropological argument in defense of cultural relativism. It is helpful to put the anthropological argument for cultural relativism in normal form. The argument then looks as follows:

1. Different cultures live according to very different moral standards.
2. If there were a universal moral standard that holds for all cultures, then different cultures would live according to similar moral standards.

Therefore: There are no universal moral standards (i.e., ethical objectivism is false).

Although this argument initially appears to be persuasive, closer examination reveals some serious flaws. For instance, is the second premise plausible? Suppose there are universal moral standards. Why would we expect every culture to accept these standards? It could very well be the case that some cultures fail to recognize universal moral truths. What the cultural relativist overlooks is the possibility that cultures can undergo moral development. There was a time when the majority of Americans accepted slavery as a profitable institution. But as time passed, the country realized that it was embracing and supporting a moral evil. Nowadays, it is very rare to find defenders of slavery. The country therefore has moved on and changed its moral perspective for the better. If we accept this idea that moral progress is possible, then we can see how moral diversity among different cultures is compatible with the existence of objective moral norms. It is plausible to suppose that different cultures recognize and discover objective moral norms in different ways. Eventually, if the development goes on long enough, all cultures might embrace a very similar set of moral norms. This is, however, a very slow process and until it is completed, we should not be surprised to find great cultural and moral diversity among different cultures.

FOOD FOR THOUGHT

Most people agree that it is a sign of moral progress that slavery was abandoned in the United States. Can you think of other developments in American society that might be considered moral progress? Moreover, what are some current cultural practices that future generations might consider barbaric and immoral?

The second weakness of the anthropological argument for cultural relativism is related to premise 1. Most cultural relativists take it for granted that there are great differences between the moral norms of different cultures. Closer examination seems to reveal, however, that different cultures might be much more similar with respect to their ethical values than the cultural relativist would like us to believe. First, it is quite plausible to suppose that all cultures share a certain basic set of core values. All cultures, for example, promote truth-telling and caring for children. The reason for this is obvious. No culture can survive for long if it does not cherish certain practices. A whole culture full of liars is bound to sink into chaos, and a culture that does not care for its children is bound to dissappear. Something similar can be said for many core values: they are essential to the survival of any culture. This suggests that there must be a core set of ethical beliefs that is shared across all cultures. Second, certain moral differences between different cultures are caused by nonmoral background beliefs and not by differences in moral values. Consider the example of an Inuit tribe that encourages older members to walk away from camp and subsequently freeze to death in the open.[1] At first glance, we might suppose that this culture lives according to very different values from our own society. It appears as if the Inuit culture does not care for their elders. We might think that this culture is cruel and mean to its older members. However, suppose you find out that the Inuit believe that you need to die with a healthy body in order to have fun in the afterlife. The fact that they encourage older members to die early is therefore an act of kindness. They care about their older parents very much and that is the reason they encourage them to die when they still have healthy bodies. What this example shows is that cultural differences are often caused not by differences in moral values, but rather by differences in nonmoral beliefs about the world and the afterlife. Cultural relativists are too quick to conclude that different cultures embrace radically different value systems.

FOOD FOR THOUGHT

Can you think of other examples where moral differences are not caused by a difference in moral values but rather by a difference in factual beliefs about the world?

Our discussion shows therefore that both premises of the anthropological argument for cultural relativism are open to serious objections. The anthropological argument for cultural relativism is therefore much weaker and less persuasive than it appears at first glance.

Final Remarks on Cultural Relativism

Although full-blown cultural relativism does not lead to a satisfactory ethical position, it would be unwise to dismiss cultural relativism as completely misguided. In some respects, cultural relativism is quite correct. Our upbringing and our cultural training have a lasting effect on our moral intuitions. It is dangerous to assume that our thinking about moral questions is free of cultural biases. Cultural relativism draws our attention to the fact that our moral intuitions are sometimes the result of cultural prejudice. It is therefore necessary that we scrutinize our own intuitions carefully and eliminate possible biases. Our moral intuitions are trustworthy only if they are in harmony with sound ethical principles.

FOOD FOR THOUGHT

Can you think of some cultural practices that make most of us in the United States feel morally uncomfortable, but which might be morally completely acceptable when we ignore our cultural prejudices?

Moreover, when we study and learn about other cultures, it is very often helpful to ignore our own moral perspective and to accept other cultures as they are. As long as we are too closely tied to our own cultural and moral perspectives, we tend to be biased observers. A dose of cultural relativism is often a necessary element in becoming a successful cultural anthropologist or sociologist. We can, however, embrace these positive aspects of cultural relativism without accepting that there are no universal and objective moral values.

Our discussion so far has shown that there are no conclusive reasons to abandon the belief in the existence of universal moral values. But our defense of universal moral values is shallow unless we can specify in greater detail what these universal moral values are supposed to be like. In our subsequent discussion, we will try to clarify these universal values by investigating whether any of the mainstream normative ethical theories that have been developed in the past can explain all (or at least most) of our moral intuitions.

Some Important Ethical Theories

The goal of a successful ethical theory is to provide a set of fundamental moral principles that is in harmony with our moral intuitions and helps us to clarify what we should do when we face difficult moral decisions. It is quite challenging (if not impossible) to evaluate the merits of a given ethical theory from a completely objective point of view. Whether we find a given normative ethical theory cogent and compelling depends in part on the specific character of our moral intuitions. This does not mean that we have to embrace relativism, but it entails that each person has to determine for himself or herself whether a given moral theory fits better with their moral intuitions than another one. The following discussion is designed to give readers the chance to explore some of the main ethical theories that have been developed in the past. Let us start our exploration of normative ethical theories with a summary of the various positions that we are going to discuss.

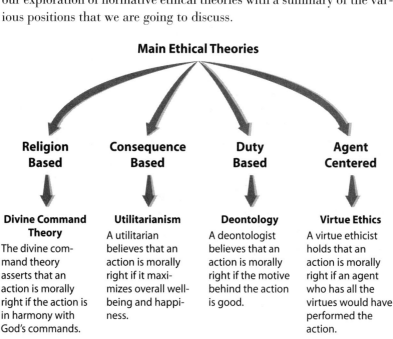

Main Ethical Theories

Religion Based	Consequence Based	Duty Based	Agent Centered
Divine Command Theory The divine command theory asserts that an action is morally right if the action is in harmony with God's commands.	**Utilitarianism** A utilitarian believes that an action is morally right if it maximizes overall well-being and happiness.	**Deontology** A deontologist believes that an action is morally right if the motive behind the action is good.	**Virtue Ethics** A virtue ethicist holds that an action is morally right if an agent who has all the virtues would have performed the action.

Divine Command Theory

To many people, it seems obvious that morality and religion are closely related. One can understand God not only as the creator of the universe, but also as the source of rules that guide humans and the universe as a whole. Just as God is often portrayed as the creator of the laws of nature, so God can be seen as the author of the rules of morality. Ivan Karamazov, a character in Dostoevsky's novel *The Brothers Karamazov*, articulates this idea well when he argues that if there is no God, everything is permitted. For those who see such a close relationship between God and morality, it is natural to adopt a position that philosophers tend to refer to as **divine command theory.**

The Case for the Divine Command Theory   The basic idea of divine command theories is that an action is morally right if the action is in accordance with God's commands, and an action is morally wrong if the action is in conflict with the commands of God. Let us illustrate the effect of the divine command theory with the help of an example. Suppose Hajo is a professional bank robber who has evaded the authorities and who now lives pleasantly in villa at the Cote D'Azure. He asks us what we think of his life and his accomplishments. If we accept the divine command theory, we will probably tell him that his past actions were morally wrong. If he wants to know why, we can reply that he has failed to follow God's commands. God, we might add, commands us not to steal. Moreover, God also commands us to give to the poor. So instead of spending all his money on luxuries he should, at the very minimum, share it with the poor.

Our words might have little impact on Hajo, but the situation shows why the divine command theory is attractive. The divine command theory can explain clearly why there are objective and universal moral values. There are universal moral values because a divine being has uttered universal commands that hold for every human being. Moral rules are therefore independent of subjective preferences and cultural norms. No matter what Hajo might think about his actions, his actions are wrong. Second, the divine command theory provides a compelling motivation to be moral. Bank robber Hajo might think that his life of crime paid off handsomely, but he has no chance to escape his just deserts. For God is an omniscient and infallible enforcer of moral rules. Third, the divine command theory gives us a certain sense of security. It is often difficult to decide on one's own whether a specific action is morally acceptable or not. Religious traditions have been around for a long time, and embedded within them are clear prescriptions of how we should live our lives. These prescriptions make it easier for us to recognize what is morally required.

Problems for the Divine Command Theory   Although the divine command theory has its appeal, it also leads to some grave difficulties. First, according to the divine command theory, universal moral values require that there be universal divine commands. But how can we determine what these universal divine commands are? If God were to speak to us directly we would have no difficultly understanding his commands. But most of us are not in this position. We have to rely on the testimony of established religions. Unfortunately, different religions disagree about what God wants us to do. Jews, for example, think that God doesn't want us to eat pork and that he requires us to keep the Sabbath holy. Muslims also eat no pork, but they believe that God requires us to pray five times a day. Hindus consider the cow to be sacred and refuse to eat beef, whereas the Christian God is indifferent to the eating of pork and beef. Is there any plausible way to decide what religion has the correct understanding of God's commands? If there is none, then the divine command theory faces a serious epistemic problem. Although the theory tells us that morality requires us to follow God's commands, the theory fails to provide a method that enables us to determine what God's commands actually are.

FOOD FOR THOUGHT

Different religions have a very different understanding of what God commands us to do. Give a list of ten actions that are demanded of us according to one religion but not demanded of us according to a different religion.

Second, for the sake of argument, let us assume that we could establish clearly what God has commanded. In order that these commands turn out to be useful guides for our life, we have to interpret them.

Suppose, for example, that we could establish with absolute certainty that God commands us not to kill. What does this command require us to do? Should we conclude, for instance, that it is morally wrong to become a soldier or to defend oneself? Does the command entail that the killing of animals is wrong? If the command is to offer us any help in guiding our life, we need a precise interpretation and explanation of what the command entails. But such an interpretation can only be given by somebody who already has substantial moral knowledge. And this moral knowledge cannot, if we are to avoid circular reasoning, be derived from God's commands.

Third, it seems clear that God's commands cannot be arbitrary. Few people would think that torturing babies would become morally right if God were to command it. God cannot command whatever strikes his fancy, but he will command us to perform those actions that are intrinsically right. If we agree with this conclusion, and it is hard to see how one could disagree, then we admit automatically that moral norms are prior and more fundamental than God's pronouncements. It follows therefore that God's commands are insufficient to provide a complete explanation why actions are morally right or wrong.

FOOD FOR THOUGHT

A good illustration of this difficulty for the divine command theory is given by the biblical story of Abraham and Isaac. According to the Bible, God commands Abraham to kill his son Isaac. Although God eventually interferes and prevents Abraham from killing his son, the question arises whether killing a child can become morally right when God commands it to be done. What do you think? How would you have responded if you were in Abraham's situation?

There are further weaknesses of the divine command theory. However, our discussion so far suffices to show that the divine command theory does not offer a satisfactory account of what moral norms there are. Let us investigate whether other moral theories fare any better.

Utilitarianism

The Basic Idea The term "utilitarianism" does not refer to one single and uniform ethical theory, but rather to a group of ethical theories. Two key ideas are at the center of any utilitarian account of morality:

1. Human happiness is the ultimate moral good.
2. Actions should be evaluated in the light of their consequences.

Both principles are intuitively plausible. Let us start with the first principle. Why should we think that happiness is the most important good? At first glance, it might seem as if different people disagree about what kind of things are good. One of us desires fame, another money, and a third person might desire a quiet farm life in North Dakota. John Stuart Mill (1806–1873), one of the best known advocates of utilitarianism, pointed out that in spite of the apparent variety of desires among different people, all of us ultimately only seek one thing: namely, happiness. The person who desires a quiet farm life in North Dakota does so because he expects this kind of life to make him happy. The same is true for the person who desires money. She expects money to make her happy. Happiness is the common ultimate goal. If somebody asks me why I want to be happy, it is reasonable to reply that the question makes no sense. Although I can desire money or fame for the sake of happiness, happiness cannot be desired for the sake of anything else. Happiness is an ultimate good that is desired for its own sake.

FOOD FOR THOUGHT

Is it possible to desire something although we do not think that it makes us happy? If yes, give an example. If no, does this establish that happiness is the most important good in life?

These considerations make it plausible that happiness is indeed the ultimate good in our lives. Once this point has been established, it makes sense to argue that all other goods have value only insofar as they contribute to general happiness. When I say, for example, that George has a good job, I mean to assert that George has a job that makes him happy. A job that leads to misery cannot be good. This general idea that things have value insofar as they contribute to happiness can be applied to our thinking about morality as well. This is where the second principle of utilitarianism originates. Utilitarian thinkers argue that an action is morally right insofar as the action contributes to general happiness. John Stuart Mill explains this central point of utilitarianism as follows:

> The creed which accepts as the foundation of morals "utility" or the "greatest happiness principle" holds that actions are right in proportion as they tend to promote happiness; wrong as they tend to produce the reverse of happiness.[2]

Let us illustrate this central principle of utilitarianism with respect to the story of Robin Hood. You might recall that Robin Hood is an outlaw who lives in Sherwood Forest and who fights against the Sheriff of Nottingham. Robin and his men steal from the rich and give to the poor. Are Robin's actions morally right? Some people might condemn Robin Hood because he breaks laws, but a utilitarian would not agree with such an analysis. From a utilitarian perspective, it is not important to know whether Robin Hood follows laws or not. What counts is whether his actions contribute to general happiness. And in this respect, Robin Hood fares well. Although he steals, he shares the proceeds with the poor. He contributes thereby to the happiness of the people around him. A utilitarian would conclude therefore that Robin Hood's actions are morally right.

The example of Robin Hood also raises a crucial question. Although Robin and his men contribute to the happiness of the poor, they make the rich quite miserable. There can be no doubt that the Sheriff of Nottingham and other noble men would be much happier if Robin were to stop stealing. Is Robin Hood morally justified to make some people happy but others miserable? In order to answer this question, utilitarian thinkers introduce strict egalitarianism. When we calculate the consequences of our actions, we need to take into account the happiness of everybody affected. In these calculations everybody counts as one, and nobody as more than one. This means that we cannot pay special attention to our own happiness or to the happiness of the people we like. Even if Robin dislikes the Sheriff of Nottingham he needs to keep in mind that his actions make him unhappy. Stealing from the rich and giving to the poor is therefore morally justified only if it produces more net happiness. The "net" happiness of an action is the happiness it causes minus the unhappiness it causes. Since more poor people than rich people are affected by Robin Hood's actions, it is plausible to suppose that Robin Hood's robbery produces a positive amount of net happiness. Robin's actions are therefore morally justified. Notice, however, that a utilitarian might change his assessment of the situation if Robin Hood were to steal from many different rich people and distribute the money only among his few best friends. The moral status of Robin's actions depends on how many people's lives are happier as a result of his stealing.

Utilitarianism looks out for the well-being and happiness of the majority. However, utilitarian thinking does not always go hand in hand with majority rule. There are situations in which a utilitarian would advocate to make the majority of people slightly unhappy in order to save a few people from great misery. Can you think of some policies that affect most people negatively but which nevertheless maximize overall net happiness?

The Robin Hood example not only shows us that utilitarianism takes into account the well-being and happiness of everybody, but it also shows us that we need to be able to measure and compare the degree to which our actions make people happy. To do that, we need to know more about what happiness is.

Pleasure and Happiness   Traditionally, utilitarian thinkers explain happiness in terms of pleasure and pain. This is not unreasonable. If I come across a person who experiences intense pain, it seems natural to describe the person as unhappy. On the other hand, if I come across a person who experiences many pleasant sensations, it is plausible to call the person happy. Philosophers who believe that happiness is a result of how much pleasure and pain we experience are called **hedonists.** It is important not to misunderstand the basic message of hedonism. When we talk about pleasures and pains we are not only talking about physical pleasures like having sex or eating a good steak. Many other activities are pleasant as well, and might offer longer lasting and more fulfilling pleasurable experiences. Raising a child, writing a book, or going on vacation are all activities that can lead to long-term pleasures. The first philosophers who advocated hedonism, the Epicureans, argued, for example, that the greatest pleasures in life are friendship and peace of mind.

FOOD FOR THOUGHT

A person who believes that happiness is a result of how much pleasure and pain we experience in our lives is called a hedonist. Are you a hedonist or do you believe that there is more to happiness than maximizing pleasure and minimizing pain? If yes, what is the hedonist missing? Can you give a description of a happy life that is not also a very pleasant life?

The two main advocates of utilitarianism, Jeremy Bentham (1748–1832) and John Stuart Mill, were both hedonists. However, they advocated different forms of hedonism. Bentham advocated a strict quantitative version of hedonism. According to Bentham, we can measure all pleasures and pains according to one scale. For example, watching your favorite TV show might produce 3 units of pleasure, but spending an evening with a good friend might produce 20 units of pleasure. So if you have to choose between watching TV and going out with your friend, you should choose the evening with your friend. Bentham called these kinds of calculations **hedonistic calculus.**

John Stuart Mill agreed with Bentham that we need to calculate happiness in terms of pleasure and pain, but Mill insisted that there are qualitative differences between different pleasures. In order to understand the difference between Bentham's and Mill's thinking about happiness, it is useful to consider a specific example. Suppose that you are a very lonely person who has no friends. That means, of course, that you will never spend a pleasant evening with a good friend. So you can never get those 20 units of pleasure that a nice evening with a good friend produces. However, according to Bentham's theory, the lonely person can still lead a very happy life. Since watching your favorite TV show produces 3 units of pleasure, you can simply watch seven episodes of your favorite TV show instead of going out with a good friend. Watching seven good TV shows will produce 21 units of pleasure, and your life will therefore be as happy as the life of the person who spends an evening with a good friend.

John Stuart Mill disagrees on this point. According to Mill, not all pleasures are commensurable with each other. Mill thinks that a life full of simple pleasures will not amount to a happy human life. He writes in this context: "Few human creatures would consent to be changed into any of the lower animals for a promise of fullest allowance of a beast's pleasures."[3] Mill's point seems plausible. It is difficult to imagine that any human would be satisfied and happy with a life that only permits us to eat and sleep, even if the food is excellent and the bed very comfortable. To account for this, Mill introduced the idea that pleasures do not only differ in quantity, but also in quality. Some activities, like playing a musical instrument, will lead to such a high qualitative pleasure that no amount of lower pleasures can easily make up for it.

Although Mill's position appears initially more plausible than Bentham's view, Mill's approach to hedonism raises some serious questions. If we agree with him that there are important qualitative differences between pleasures, the question arises how we can measure these qualitative distinctions? Mill thought that people with sufficient life experience would ultimately all agree about what kind of pleasures are qualitatively higher and which ones are lower. But this seems overly optimistic. Even very refined and well-educated people might disagree whether reading a good book is a qualitative higher pleasure than watching your favorite football team win the Super Bowl.

FOOD FOR THOUGHT

Do you agree with John Stuart Mill that some activities are of such high qualitative character that they are essential to a happy human life? Take a look at the following activities. Which of these activities, if any, do you think are most essential for leading a happy human life? If possible, produce a qualitative ranking.

1. Exercising regularly.
2. Working in a job that pays well.

Continued

3. Eating in good restaurants.
4. Owning a big house.
5. Having friends.
6. Helping people in need.
7. Having children.
8. Writing letters or a diary.
9. Watching TV.
10. Being politically active in one's community.
11. Watching movies.
12. Having a lover.
13. Having a good sense of humor.
14. Listening to good music.
15. Talking about philosophical problems.

Moreover, Mill's qualitative ranking of pleasures seems to imply that pleasure and pain are not the only values there are. This, however, seems incompatible with the hedonistic tenets of utilitarianism.

Although there is no general consensus among utilitarian thinkers about how pleasure and happiness are related, utilitarianism is nevertheless an attractive moral theory. In most circumstances, it is pretty clear what kinds of actions promote or diminish general welfare. Utilitarianism is, therefore, a moral theory that produces clear and direct suggestions of what is morally required of us. This is especially helpful when we are confronted with difficult ethical dilemmas. Moreover, utilitarianism also explains well why moral thinking must be impartial. Utilitarian calculations take into account the well-being of everybody to an equal degree. This explains well why any form of egoism is incompatible with a moral point of view. Utilitarianism also has a good answer to the question why we should be moral. According to utilitarianism, we care about morality because we are interested in making people happy. Increasing general well-being and happiness is a natural human endeavor, and utilitarianism can therefore demonstrate why the demands of morality are not something abstract and alien, but rather something that is a natural part of our existence.

Problems for Utilitarianism   Although utilitarianism is an attractive moral theory, it also faces a number of well-known problems. First, it seems as if maximizing general happiness requires us in certain situations to perform immoral actions. Consider the following example. Suppose you are a doctor in a remote hospital in the Andes. One day three very important people of the village get seriously sick (the priest, the only teacher, and the mayor). The teacher has lung cancer, the priest has kidney failure, and the mayor needs a new liver. If all three die, the village will be in serious trouble. As an experienced surgeon, you know that you could save the three lives if you had the necessary organs. Suddenly you realize that Freddie, a friendless but very healthy young man who is disliked by everybody in the village, happens to be in the hospital to have his tonsils removed; he could provide the necessary organs. Since Freddie is an antisocial loner, he would never volunteer his organs to save the three important people. However, you realize that you could simply take Freddie's organs during his tonsil surgery without his permission and save the mayor, the teacher, and the priest. What should you do?

This is of course a very artificial example, but it illustrates that utilitarianism can get us into trouble. Removing Freddie's organs without his permission seems to be morally wrong, but the action nevertheless seems to maximize general happiness. It follows therefore that utilitarianism will not always go hand in hand with our intuitions about what is morally required. A good utilitarian might respond to this objection that our moral intuitions are not always reliable and should be revised in light of utilitarian consideration. But many draw different conclusions from these types of situations. The philosopher A. C. Ewing writes, for example, that "utilitarian principles, logically carried out, would result in far more cheating, lying and unfair action than any good man would tolerate."[4]

FOOD FOR THOUGHT

Can you think of other situations in which maximizing general welfare requires us to perform actions that according to common-sense morality are immoral?

A closely related objection to utilitarianism charges that utilitarian thinking cannot explain why we should respect people's rights. The philosopher James Rachels gives the example of a Peeping Tom who secretly takes pictures of his undressed neighbor Ms. York.[5] Rachels writes: "Suppose that he does this without ever being detected and that he uses the photographs entirely for his own amusement, without showing them to anyone. In these circumstances it is clear that the only consequence of his actions is an increase in his own happiness. No one else, including Ms. York, is caused any unhappiness at all. How, then, could utilitarianism deny that the Peeping Tom's actions are right?" This example shows nicely that utilitarian thinking is not easily compatible with our thinking about moral rights. Most of us would agree that everybody has the right to privacy, and that the Peeping Tom has violated Ms. York's rights to privacy. Thus, for those who take moral rights to be a central element in their moral thinking, utilitarianism seems unacceptable.

The third major objection against utilitarianism has to do with promise making. Suppose that I have promised to pick Susan up from the airport. On the way to the airport, I stop at a convenience store and run into a homeless man who is walking to a hospital with severe stomach pains. If I offer him a ride to the hospital, I will not be able to meet Susan at the airport. What should I do? From a utilitarian perspective, it seems clear that bringing the homeless man to the hospital has priority. It is, after all, possible that the homeless man will experience severe health problems if he is not treated soon, while Susan's well-being will not be as seriously affected by my failure to show up at the airport.

These examples show that utilitarianism only requires us to keep promises if doing so will maximize general happiness. In all other cases, it is not only morally permissible but actually morally required to break the promise instead. Many philosophers find this result problematic. The philosopher John Rawls, for example, writes in this context: "What would one say of someone who, when asked why he broke a promise, replied simply that breaking it was best on the whole? Assuming that his reply is sincere . . . one would question whether or not he knew what it means to say 'I promise.'"[6]

FOOD FOR THOUGHT

Many objections against utilitarianism have to do with promise making. William Shaw describes a nice version of a deathbed promise. In a passage from his book *Contemporary Ethics: Taking Account of Utilitarianism*, he writes:

> An elderly woman living alone in poor circumstances with few friends or relatives is dying, and you are at her bedside. She draws your attention to a small case under her bed, which contains some mementos along with the money she has managed to save over the years, despite her apparent poverty. She asks you to take the case and to promise to deliver its contents, after she dies, to her nephew living in another state. Moved by her plight and by your affection for her, you promise to do as she bids. After a tearful good-bye, you take the case and leave. A few weeks later the old woman dies, and when you open her case you discover that it contains $50,000. No one else knows about the money or the promise that you made. . . . Now suppose further that the nephew is a compulsive gambler and heavy drinker and that you know that, if you were to give him the $50,000 as promised, he would rapidly squander the money.

What would a utilitarian do in this situation? What would you do? What is morally required?

Utilitarianism also seems to be too demanding. Keep in mind that utilitarianism requires us to maximize general happiness constantly. Suppose now that you are spending a lazy Sunday in bed. It seems clear that this action does not maximize general happiness. Instead of lying in bed, you could visit a nursing home and play cards with its elderly residents, or you could at least call your mother, or write a letter to your uncle. All of these activities would contribute more to general happiness than lying in bed. It seems to follow therefore that spending a lazy Sunday in bed is an immoral action. But that is a very curious conclusion. Most of us would reject the idea that spending a lazy Sunday is morally wrong. Commonsense morality draws the distinctions between **obligatory actions,** that is, actions that are morally required, and **supererogatory actions,** that is, actions that are praiseworthy but not strictly required. Going to a nursing home on your free Sunday to play cards with the elderly residents appears to be a supererogatory action but not an obligatory one. Utilitarianism makes it difficult, if not impossible, to distinguish clearly between obligatory actions and supererogatory actions.

FOOD FOR THOUGHT

Practice your understanding of the difference between obligatory actions and supererogatory actions. Which of the following actions are morally obligatory and which ones are supererogatory?

1. Not parking in a handicap parking spot.
2. Studying as hard as you can for your final exams.
3. Being honest on your income tax report.
4. Giving at least some money to charity.
5. Spending time with your parents.
6. Making sure that your children receive the best possible education.
7. Supporting your own country in times of war.

FOOD FOR THOUGHT

Utilitarianism also has problems incorporating our special obligations as parents, siblings, or relatives into our moral thinking. The following example illustrates this problem:

> Suppose you are the parent of a beautiful 3-year-old son. This summer you are cruising the Atlantic on an expensive cruise ship. Disaster strikes. The ship sinks. You somehow manage to get on a lifeboat with a motor. All around you, people are drowning and crying for help. Suddenly you see your son 100 yards away. He is frantically trying to stay afloat. In order to save your son you must drive the life boat to him. However, just as you are about to do that, you see that two children are about to drown 10 yards away in the opposite direction.

What would you do? What would utilitarianism require you to do? What do you think is the morally right thing to do?

The last four arguments show that a utilitarian account of morality faces some serious challenges. Some philosophers have tried to overcome these challenges by refining utilitarian thinking. It is, however, tempting to investigate whether nonconsequentialist moral theories might not produce a more acceptable moral position. We will explore this question in the next two sections.

Duty-Based Theories

The Importance of a Good Will   The German philosopher Immanuel Kant (1724–1804) developed one of the main alternatives to consequence-based moral thinking. Kant's moral theory is often referred to as **deontology,** since the concept of duty plays an important role in it. Two key ideas are at the center of Kant's thinking about morality.

1. Only a good will has ultimate moral value.

2. Moral rules must be universal and binding for all rational beings.

Let us start with the first idea. We have seen that utilitarian thinkers take happiness as their starting point for thinking about values. Why does Kant not follow suit? Kant agrees that being happy is a good thing, but points out that there is no necessary connection between being happy and being moral. It seems obvious that many immoral people can manage to be quite happy. Happiness thus is only contingently related to being moral. The same is true for many other qualities as well. We can be beautiful, successful, talented, industrious, rich, and smart, but none of these qualities is necessarily connected to being moral. What then is a sure sign of being moral?

FOOD FOR THOUGHT

Do you agree with Kant that morally corrupt people can be happy? Some philosophers, for example, Plato, have argued that happiness and moral conduct always go hand in hand and that immoral people are bound to be unhappy. Can you think of some famous immoral people who were genuinely happy?

To clarify Kant's thinking on this point, it will be helpful to consider an example. Consider the case of two fathers, Abdullah and Leon. Each is a single dad with one son. Abdullah is a dedicated father. Every day, he comes home from work early to spend more time with his son. He is interested in his progress, plays with him, and takes an active role in his education. Leon, on the other hand, is indifferent to his son. He is mostly interested in his own life, and cares about his son only if it does not require him to make any sacrifices. He drops him off at day care whenever he has the opportunity, and complains to his friends that having a child was the worst mistake in his life. Unfortunately, things turn out differently than most would expect. Abdullah's son grows up to be a selfish and sadistic drug dealer, while Leon's son grows up to be a wonderful and considerate doctor.

Although Abdullah's efforts to be a good father fail to have good results, Kant would argue that Abdullah is nevertheless the better father. We are good, not because we succeed in our efforts, but rather because we try as hard as we can. This is the key idea in Kant's analysis of moral goodness. We are morally good because we have a **good will.** Kant writes in this context:

> There is no possibility of thinking of anything at all in the world, or even out of it, which can be regarded as good without qualification, except a good will.[7]

Kant's idea that a good will is the central component in leading a morally good life is plausible. It makes sense to say that we should not be judged on the basis of what we achieve, but rather on the basis of what we try to achieve. However, Kant's concept of a good will also raises a crucial question. When exactly can we be sure that our will is good?

According to Kant, all our actions are explicitly or implicitly connected to motives. Take the example of going to college. The decision to go to college might have been prompted by several different motives. Perhaps you go to college because you want to get a good job, or because you want to learn, or because you want to meet nice people. Everybody who makes the decision to go to college has a reason for why she has taken this step. Once we realize that our actions are connected to motives, we can understand what makes our will a good will. Kant argues that our will is good if the motives behind our actions are morally good motives.

This is, of course, not yet a satisfactory explanation. We still do not know when motives are morally good motives. This is where the second main element of Kant's ethical theory comes into play. Suppose that the U.S. government passes a law that requires all Americans with black hair to pay a special tax. Kant would argue that we could know right away (i.e., a priori) that this law cannot be a moral law. According to Kant, a law or a principle can only be moral if it applies to *all* people equally. This might look like a minor point, but Kant suggests that this idea that moral principles must necessarily be universal principles furnishes us with a formal criterion that lets us test whether we are dealing with moral principles or not. Whenever one comes across a principle, we can ask whether it is applicable to all human beings and in all possible situations. If it is not, then the principle cannot be a moral principle.

Let us now return to the issue of motives. We have seen that Kant argues that a will is a good will if the motives that prompt it to act are morally good. We have also seen that Kant argues that principles are morally good only if they are applicable to all human beings in all situations. These two points together put Kant into a position to develop his central moral idea: a will is good if it acts on motives that are applicable to all human beings. Kant himself puts the point as follows:

> Act only according to that maxim whereby you can at the same time will that it should become a universal law.[8]

The Categorical Imperative   Kant calls this principle the **Categorical Imperative.** The Categorical Imperative is well known and often mentioned, but it is frequently not well understood. Let us therefore illustrate the implications of accepting the Categorical Imperative with the help of some examples.

Suppose you are employed at a fast food restaurant called "Quick Hunger." You do not like the job very much and you use your late-night shift to give free food to your friends, against company rules. Your practice is not discovered, but one day, as you look at your paycheck, you realize that the owner of "Quick Hunger" has never paid you the full weekend shift differential he has promised you. Suppose you go to the owner and throw a fit. You say: "You have no right to cheat me. I deserve to be paid what I was promised." There is something strange about this. Kant would argue that your will is involved in a contradiction. On the one hand, you think it is okay to give free food to your friends and thus steal from the owner of "Quick Hunger," but on the other hand you expect the owner to be honest and keep his promises. This is what happens when one acts on motives that are not compatible with the

Categorical Imperative. One ends up contradicting oneself. It is therefore paramount to act on principles that are universalizable and thus compatible with the Categorical Imperative. This is the only way in which we can act on a will that does not contradict itself.

Let us look at another example. Suppose you are on your daily morning jog and you hear somebody yelling for help. It sounds as if somebody is being assaulted. You cannot yet see anything because the screams come from an area that is hidden from your view. You are very afraid and feel a strong desire to run away and call the police from a safe place. What should you do? According to Kant, we need to take a good look at our motives. If you run away because you are afraid that you will endanger yourself, then you probably act on the following motive: If I am very afraid and I hear somebody crying for help then it is OK to run away. We now need to see whether this motive is compatible with the Categorical Imperative. Can one wish that everybody adopted this motive so that it would become a universal law? If you answer "yes," then imagine what would happen if during your next morning jog, you are assaulted and you cry for help. In this situation, it is obvious that you want somebody to help you even if they are afraid to do so. But this wish is not compatible with the prior principle. It follows therefore that your will is involved in a contradiction. On the one hand, you wish it to be the case that everybody runs away when they are afraid, but on the other hand you wish that people would help you when you are assaulted even if they should happen to be afraid. This shows that the principle in question is not acceptable. It cannot be wished to be a universal law, because such a wish involves us in a contradiction.

FOOD FOR THOUGHT

Test you understanding of the Categorical Imperative by deciding whether the following motives can be wished to be universal laws of nature:

1. I never give money to people in need because poor people are lazy losers who should help themselves.
2. The only reason I want to go to college is because I think this is the best place to have wild sex.
3. I want to go to medical school because I want to make tons of money.

4. I go to college because I want to develop my talents so that I can make the world a better place.
5. I never kill anybody because killing people is always wrong.
6. I give ten percent of my income to charity so that others who are less fortunate can have better lives.
7. If people yell at me I never yell back because I think that yelling at people is silly and wrong.

Kant's insistence that we should only act on those motives that we can wish to be universally adopted entails that we have a number of important moral duties, including:

1. Do not lie.
2. Do not kill yourself.
3. Give to charity.
4. Develop your talents.

If you do not clearly see why the Categorical Imperative entails that we have these duties, ask yourself whether you can wish it to be the case that people would not accept these duties and try to determine whether this involves your will in a contradiction.

FOOD FOR THOUGHT

A well-known ethical rule of thumb is the so-called **Golden Rule,** which says: "Do unto others as you would have them do unto you!" The Golden Rule is similar to the Categorical Imperative, but they also differ from each other. Can you think of examples where the Golden Rule and the Categorical Imperative make different recommendations?

Kant's Categorical Imperative also explains why we always have to treat other people with respect. Suppose that you own the only factory in a small town. Your factory produces batteries and is the only employer in town. You know that during the production process your workers are exposed to lead. There are strict limits on how much lead is acceptable.

Testing the level of lead exposure of your workers is required, but also very expensive. Since you are good friends with the government inspector, you have been able to get by without any lead inspections. Is your behavior morally acceptable? It is easy to see that this action is not compatible with the Categorical Imperative. We cannot wish it to be the case that we carelessly harm others in order to reap economic profits. This example also illustrates that the Categorical Imperative does not permit us to treat others (in this case, the workers) simply as a means to an end. Kant saw this implication and suggested therefore that the Categorical Imperative can also be formulated in the following way:

> Act in such a way that you treat humanity, whether in your own person or in the person of another, always at the same time as an end and never simply as a means.[9]

This so-called second formulation of the Categorical Imperative stresses that we can never use people as mere puppets in our plans. We always have to respect that others are rational agents who have the right to determine their own course of action. Respecting this means that we respect their **autonomy.**

FOOD FOR THOUGHT

The second formulation of the Categorical Imperative stresses that we should never treat others as a means to an end only. Give some examples of situations where people are treated as a means to an end only.

Kant's moral philosophy has a number of advantages. First, Kant derives moral principles simply on the basis of rational and a priori reasoning. This demonstrates that moral principles are independent of time and place, and are binding for all human beings. Second, deontological ethics tells us that we have a number of strict duties. We must try to fulfill these duties under all circumstances. There are no exceptions. This categorical and rigorous advocacy of duties helps us when we face difficult moral decisions. Third, Kant's theory of ethics shows us that human beings have infinite worth. Most of us probably always suspected that there is something morally wrong with putting a price on a human life. Is a human life worth one million dollars or perhaps ten million dollars? Deontological thinking demonstrates that each of us is worth an infinite amount, for each of us has to be seen as an ultimate end and not just as the means to some purpose. Finally, deontological ethics is well compatible with the idea that we have fundamental moral rights. We have seen that according to Kant we have to respect the autonomy of others in all situations. This lends itself to the idea that we are born with fundamental rights (like the right to life and the pursuit of happiness) that nobody can take away from us. Such rights-based moral thinking is familiar to most of us, and Kant's ethics provides a good foundation for it.

FOOD FOR THOUGHT

Utilitarianism and deontological thinking frequently lead to conflicting recommendations of what we should do in difficult moral situations. In the following situation, a convinced utilitarian will act differently than a full-blown deontologist. What would you do?

> Suppose you are a famous anthropologist. One day you find a remote tribe in the middle of the Amazon rain forest. The tribe is really surprised by your visit. After all, you are the first stranger they have ever seen. The tribe is just in the middle of a religious ritual. They are preparing to execute 20 prisoners from a neighboring tribe as a gift to the sun god. However, since they also want to honor you, they offer you the honor of strangling one of the prisoners with your own hands. If you do that they will let the others go back to their tribe. If you refuse to accept the honor, they will sacrifice all 20 people. You try to tell them that your god does not allow you to strangle people, but the tribe leader is unwilling to make any deals. He is very clear: either you strangle one of the prisoners or else all 20 will be killed.

Problems for Kant's Ethics   The biggest weakness of deontological thinking is that it does not allow the consequences of our actions to be of ethical significance. We have seen that Kant makes the will the central element in his ethical value system. Our will is good if we try to act according to principles that are compatible with the Categorical Imperative. It does not matter what consequences our good will actually brings about. This neglect of consequences leads to paradoxical results.

Suppose that your best friend Susan has an argument with her husband Felix. Susan is very upset and decides that it is better to spend the night at your house away from her husband. Two hours later, Felix stands at your door and is carrying an axe. He breathes heavily and seems very angry. He asks you whether Susan is staying with you. What do you do? It seems extremely likely that most of us would choose to tell Felix a lie. We might say, for example: "Felix, I am surprised to see that Susan is not with you. I have no idea where she might be. Can I help you look for her?" The reason for this blatant lie is clear: If you do not lie, the consequences will be terrible. A deontologist would insist, however, that we have to tell the truth. We have, after all, a perfect duty never to tell a lie, and consequences do not matter. That recommendation seems crazy! In some situations consequences do matter a great deal, and they should therefore influence our decisions. This shows that deontological thinking is too restricted. Kant's insistence that a good will is sufficient for moral goodness seems misguided.

FOOD FOR THOUGHT

Can you think of other situations in which telling a lie is not only morally permitted, but even morally required of us?

A closely related problem with Kant's ethics is caused by situations in which duties conflict with each other. It is not far fetched to assume that in certain situations our duty to respect the autonomy of others can be in conflict with the duty to save as many lives as possible. Kant's ethics gives us no recipe of how to prioritize duties when they conflict. This lack of clarity makes it difficult to apply a deontological thinking in challenging ethical situations.

FOOD FOR THOUGHT

Describe a number of situations in which important and central duties are in conflict with each other.

There are further weaknesses of deontological ethical theories, but the two discussed problems make it clear that deontology faces some serious challenges. Some deontological thinkers, for example, W. D. Ross, have tried to respond to these difficulties by refining deontological ethical thinking. It is, however, interesting to see whether a completely different approach to ethics might not fare better. Such an alternative approach is provided by virtue ethics. We will explore it in the next and last section of this chapter.

Virtue-Based Theories

The Importance of Moral Character   Although utilitarianism and deontology are often presented as opposing ethical theories, they have something in common: both try to develop general and universal criteria that allow us to classify actions as either morally good or bad. Utilitarianism and deontology are therefore action- and rule-centered ethical theories. Virtue ethics takes a different approach. Virtue ethics highlights the role of the agent in moral deliberations. Let us illustrate this difference with the help of an example. Suppose you have to explain to a child why stealing is morally wrong. According to a rule- or duty-oriented ethical theory, one might say the following: Stealing is wrong because it violates our duty to respect the property rights of other people. A virtue ethical thinker will prefer a different type of explanation. She might say: Stealing is wrong because stealing corrupts our character. From a virtue ethical perspective, judgments about character are more fundamental than judgments about rules, duties, and obligations. Virtue ethics replaces the question "What ought I to do?" with the question "What sort of person ought I to be?" We therefore should focus our energies on improving our moral character rather than finding abstract moral rules that allow us to classify actions.

This introduces a new direction into our thinking about ethical theory. We can forgo our search for universal moral rules, and focus instead on clarifying what type of moral character is praiseworthy. An agent's character is good insofar as the agent possesses virtues and lacks vice. Virtues are character traits that allow agents to act habitually well. Honesty, for example, is a virtue. People who are honest are people who have a strong disposition to speak the truth in all situations. Many people lack this virtue. Some people have the character that tempts them to exaggerate constantly. Having such a character is a vice. Compassion is another virtue. Persons with compassion can relate well to people who suffer and thus are motivated to help people in need. In addition to honesty and compassion, there are many other positive and praiseworthy character traits that are considered to be virtues. The ancient Greek philosopher Aristotle (384–322 BCE) was the first to provide a systematic account of the virtues. In the *Nichomachean Ethics*, he argues that moral virtues are character traits that are a mean between two vices. Courage, for example, is a mean between cowardice and rashness. The coward has the type of character that causes him to feel fear too strongly (a state of excess). The rash person feels fear not sufficiently (state of deficiency). Only the courageous person has the kind of character that allows him to feel fear to the right degree and at the right time. The courageous person, therefore, has a tendency to act appropriately when she faces dangerous situations. The nature of other moral virtues like temperance, generosity, magnificence, high-mindedness, controlled anger, friendliness, and modesty, can also be analyzed as states of characters that lie in between two vices. Generosity, for example, is a mean between stinginess and wastefulness. Modesty is a mean between shamelessness and bashfulness. This is Aristotle's doctrine of the mean. Aristotle draws attention to the fact that finding the mean cannot be accomplished by theoretical reflection alone. Developing a virtues character requires life experience and practical wisdom.

Over time, Aristotle's virtue theory became the dominant account of the virtues. In medieval discussions, the particular virtues described by Aristotle and the ancient Greeks became known as the cardinal virtues. Medieval thinkers added the Christian virtues of humility, chastity, obedience, faith, and love to the list. In the 18th century, it was common to add frugality, industry, cleanliness, and tranquillity to the list of important moral virtues. These various lists of virtues highlight one peculiar feature of virtue ethics. There is no general agreement of how many virtues there are. At different times, different thinkers have developed very different lists of virtues. Any attempt to develop a definite list must be somewhat arbitrary and subject to cultural influences.

FOOD FOR THOUGHT

Although it is relatively easy to list various virtues and vices, it is much more difficult to describe in detail what these virtues or vices actually are. Take a look at each of the following virtues and explain to your neighbor what you think these virtues entail. Give some concrete examples and check whether both of you understand the virtues and vices in a similar fashion.

Virtues: civility, courage, compassion, courteousness, dependability, fairness, friendliness, generosity, good temper, honesty, justice, loyalty, and moderation.

Vices: envy, lust, gluttony, anger, covetousness, sloth, greed, and selfishness.

The absence of a definite list of virtues can actually be seen as an advantage of virtue ethics. We have seen that Aristotle stresses the importance of practical wisdom in the acquisition of moral virtues. Practical wisdom is by its nature concerned with particular, situation-specific "know-how" rather than with abstract and general rules. This means that it is perfectly fine if different agents focus on different virtues if they happen to live in different societies. It is appropriate that a person in ancient Athens aims to develop a different character than a person who lives in present-day New York City. Moreover, a person's occupation must also be taken into account. A good nurse has to develop a different character than a banker or a university professor. In order to provide guidance, virtue ethical thinkers stress the importance of role models. A role model is a person of excellent moral character who habitually acts well and who feels pleasure when exercising her virtues. Once we have found a virtuous role model, we have found a list of important virtues and a goal that we can strive to achieve. Moreover, role models also help us to decide what we should do in difficult situations. If the role model is close by we can ask them for advice, or, when that is not possible, we can simply imagine what our virtuous role model would do.

FOOD FOR THOUGHT

Role models play an important role in virtue ethical thinking. From the list of the following persons, decide which of these is in your opinion the best role model. Which of them is the worst?

1. Socrates
2. Buddha
3. Oprah Winfrey
4. Jesus Christ
5. Abraham Lincoln
6. Mahatma Gandhi
7. Martin Luther King, Jr.
8. Mohammed
9. Mother Teresa
10. Alan Greenspan
11. Tom Hanks

Advantages of Virtue Ethics   Virtue ethics has a number of attractive features. By concentrating on moral character rather than on abstract rules, virtue ethics stresses that becoming a moral person is mostly a matter of receiving the right education and upbringing. Utilitarianism and deontology make it appear as if becoming morally good is simply a matter of applying the right moral principles. This produces the misleading impression that being moral is a theoretical matter rather than a practical affair. By stressing the importance of role models, practical wisdom, and moral education, virtue ethical thinking provides us with a practical moral framework that squares well with common sense.

Second, virtue ethics seems to provide the correct account of moral motivation. To illustrate this, it will be useful to consider an example. Suppose three adult sisters call their mother on her birthday. The oldest daughter is a deontologist. She calls her mother because it is the right thing to do. The second daughter is utilitarian, and she calls her mother because it maximizes general welfare. Both of these motives for calling one's mother on her birthday seem artificial and even a bit callous. Let us compare these motivations to what moves the third daughter. The third daughter is a virtue ethical thinker who calls her mother because she has developed the kind of character that makes it pleasant to call one's mother on her birthday. She does not ask herself whether it is her duty to do this or what the consequences of her actions are; she simply acts out of a feeling of affection for her mother. This example shows that a virtue ethical theory provides a much more realistic and plausible account of what motivates people to perform morally good actions.

Third, virtue ethics makes it possible to give weight to special relationships within our ethical deliberations. Classical ethical theories like utilitarianism and deontology require us to adopt a position of strict impartiality. According to these theories, morality requires that we care as much for the well-being of strangers as we care about the well-being of our children. In many situations, this absolute impartiality seems forced and inhumane. Virtue ethics allows us to pay attention to the special moral obligations that arise in the context of being a lover, a parent, and a good friend.

FOOD FOR THOUGHT

Can you describe situations in which we might be morally required to violate a strict sense of impartiality? For example, is it morally acceptable to prefer the well-being of one's own country over that of other countries? Is it morally permitted to give more weight to the well-being of one's own children than to the well-being of other children?

Finally, virtue ethics provides a more flexible moral framework than competing ethical theories. We have seen in our prior discussion that utilitarian thinking as well as deontological thinking are confronted with counterexamples. This is because both theories demand that we apply one theoretical principle in all situations. Virtue ethics does not face such a problem. According to virtue ethics, we should perform those actions that a completely virtuous person would perform as well. But this opens up the possibility that our role model will sometimes think in terms of consequences and sometimes in terms of strict duty. We thus are able to incorporate the best recommendations of the two main competitors within a virtue ethical framework.

Problems for Virtue Ethics   We have seen that virtue ethics moves away from the question "What ought we to do?" and focuses instead on the analysis of moral character traits. However, it is clear that we study and develop moral theories in order to find answers to specific moral questions. We want to know whether it is morally right to execute dangerous criminals or whether it is morally required of us to help a terminally sick patient to die. It is difficult to see how virtue ethics can provide much help in answering these questions.

We have seen that virtue ethics recommends that we do what a completely virtuous person would do. But this recommendation raises two crucial epistemic questions.

1. How can we identify a completely virtuous person?

2. How does the role model know what to do in difficult ethical situations?

The first of these questions might be answered in a pragmatic way. We might simply accept somebody as a role model if the society around us accepts the person as a role model as well. Aristotle, for example, tells us that Pericles and men like him have practical wisdom.[10] But this recommendation only makes sense in the context of the Athenian community. If we adopt this method, virtue ethics seems to require that we accept the moral judgments of our society and thus seems to embrace a form of cultural relativism. On the other hand, if we reject this pragmatic answer we need to develop some objective and timeless criteria how to recognize and identify completely virtuous persons. This, however, might not only be difficult but actually impossible.

Let us now turn to the second issue. How does the virtuous person know what to do in difficult ethical situations? In many situations different virtues are in conflict with each other. The honest thing to do is not always the most prudent or the most courageous. How are we to weigh the different virtues against each other? The most plausible answer to this question is that the role model must appeal to some general moral rules that are provided by classical ethical theories. This suggests, however, that virtue ethics cannot stand completely on its own. It might be best to regard virtue ethics as a part of an overall theory of ethics rather than as a complete theory itself.

Final Remarks on the Problem of Morality

We started our discussion of ethics by criticizing moral relativism. There are good reasons to think that there are at least some universal moral norms that apply to all people, in all cultures, at all times. However, our discussion of famous moral theories did not produce a unanimous winner. Divine command theories, utilitarianism, deontology, and virtue ethics offer different accounts of morality and we were not able to identify one theory as superior to all the others. This is puzzling. If moral objectivism is correct and there truly exists an objective moral reality that is independent of our moral judgments, shouldn't we be in a position to recognize that one ethical theory provides a better description of moral reality than all the other theories? A moral relativist will count this result as evidence against moral objectivism. He will argue that our inability to identify one moral theory as superior to all the others is best compatible with moral relativism. However, we do not have to draw such a conclusion. We can agree with Plato and argue that moral values are the most difficult entities to be clearly grasped by human intellect. We thus can hope that in the future, philosophers who are a bit smarter than us will find an ultimate unified moral theory. The second option to avoid moral relativism entails that we embrace a form of moral pluralism. Moral pluralism holds that moral reality consists in multiple and competing moral values. If we accept this view, we can understand each internally consistent moral theory as explaining a part of moral reality. According to this picture, every consistent moral theory contributes something to our moral understanding, but no theory can claim that it is entirely accurate.

Endnotes

1. This story is probably factually false. If I am informed correctly, Inuits probably never treated elders in this way. However, it does not matter whether the story is historically accurate or not; it illustrates well why certain drastic behavioral differences between different cultures can be caused by nonmoral background beliefs and not by differences in moral values.
2. Mill, John Stuart. *Utilitarianism.* Indianapolis: Hackett, 1979.
3. Ibid., p. 9.

4. Ewing, A.C. *Ethics*. London: English Universities Press, 1953, p. 40.
5. Rachels, James. *The Elements of Moral Philosophy*, 4th ed. New York: McGraw-Hill, 2003, pp. 112–113.
6. Rawls, John. "Two Concepts of Rules." *Philosophical Review* (January 1955), 64(1):3–32, p. 17.
7. Kant, Immanuel. *Grounding for a Metaphysics of Morals*. Indianapolis: Hackett, 1981, p. 7.
8. Ibid., p. 30.
9. Ibid., p. 36.
10. Aristotle. *Nicomachean Ethics*, 1140b8-10. Indianapolis: Hackett, 1999.

For Further Reading

Anscombe, Elisabeth. *Collected Papers*. Minneapolis: University of Minnesota Press, 1981.

Ellin, Joseph. *Morality and the Meaning of Life: An Introduction to Ethical Theory*. Orlando: Hartcourt, 1995.

Frankena, William. *Ethics*. Englewood: Prentice-Hall, 1973.

Rachels, James. *The Elements of Moral Philosophy*, 4th ed. New York: McGraw-Hill, 2003.

Shaw, William. *Contemporary Ethics: Taking Account of Utilitarianism*. Oxford: Blackwell, 1998.

Singer, Peter (ed.). *A Companion to Ethics*. Oxford: Blackwell, 1993.

Smart, J.J.C. and Williams, Bernard. *Utilitarianism: For and Against*. Cambridge: Cambridge University Press, 1973.

Index

Announcing . . .
The Longman Publishers and Penguin Books Partnership in Philosophy

Note to Instructors: Bundle any of the titles listed below with *Ultimate Questions: Thinking About Philosophy* and your students will receive up to 60% off the price of the Penguin book! Contact your local Allyn & Bacon/Longman sales representative for details on how to create a Penguin-Longman Value Package.

Early Socratic Dialogues
Plato
Edited by Trevor J. Saunders
Penguin Classic

Meditations and Other Metaphysical Writings
René Descartes
Translated and Introduced by Desmond M. Clarke
Penguin Classic

The Penguin Dictionary of Philosophy
Edited by Thomas Mautner
Penguin

The Last Days of Socrates: Euthyphro, The Apology, Crito, Phaedo
Plato
Translated by Hugh Tredennick
Introduction and Notes by Harold Tarrant
Penguin Classic

Ten Great Works of Philosophy
Edited by Robert Paul Wolff
Signet Classic

The Varieties of Religious Experience: A Study in Human Nature
William James
Edited and Introduced by Martin E. Marty
Penguin Classic